Lecture Notes in Computer Scie

T0238084

Commenced Publication in 1973
Founding and Former Series Editors:
Gerhard Goos, Juris Hartmanis, and Jan van Leeuwen

François Fages   Sylvain Soliman (Eds.)

Principles and Practice of Semantic Web Reasoning

Third International Workshop, PPSWR 2005
Dagstuhl Castle, Germany, September 11-16, 2005
Proceedings

 Springer

Volume Editors

François Fages
Sylvain Soliman
INRIA Rocquencourt - Projet CONTRAINTES, Domaine de Voluceau
Rocquencourt, BP 105, 78153 Le Chesnay Cedex, France
E-mail: {francois.fages, sylvain.soliman}@inria.fr

Library of Congress Control Number: 2005931600

CR Subject Classification (1998): H.4, H.3, I.2, F.4.1, D.2

ISSN   0302-9743
ISBN-10   3-540-28793-0 Springer Berlin Heidelberg New York
ISBN-13   978-3-540-28793-3 Springer Berlin Heidelberg New York

Springer is a part of Springer Science+Business Media

springeronline.com

© Springer-Verlag Berlin Heidelberg 2005
Printed in Germany

Typesetting: Camera-ready by author, data conversion by Scientific Publishing Services, Chennai, India
Printed on acid-free paper   SPIN: 11552222   06/3142   5 4 3 2 1 0

Preface

The promise of the Semantic Web is to move from a Web of data to a Web of meaning and distributed services. This vision of the Web has attracted researchers from different horizons with the aims of defining new architectures and languages necessary to make it possible, and of developing the first applications of these concepts.

This book contains the articles selected for publication and presentation at the workshop "Principles and Practice of Semantic Web Reasoning" PPSWR 2005, together with three invited talks. Three major aspects of Semantic Web research are represented in this selection: architecture issues, language issues, and reasoning methods. These advances are investigated in the context of new design principles and challenging applications.

The PPSWR 2005 workshop was part of the Dagstuhl seminar on the Semantic Web organized by F. Bry (Univ. München, Germany), F. Fages (INRIA Rocquencourt, France), M. Marchiori (MIT, Cambridge, USA) and H.-J. Ohlbach (Univ. München, Germany), held in Dagstuhl, Germany, 11–16 September 2005. It was supported by the European Network of Excellence REWERSE (Reasoning on the Web with Rules and Semantics, http://rewerse.net). This four-year project includes 27 European research and development organizations, and is intended to bolster Europe's expertise in Web reasoning systems and applications. It consists of eight main working groups: "Rule Markup Language", "Policy Language, Enforcement, Composition", "Composition and Typing", "Reasoning-Aware Querying", "Evolution", "Time and Location", "Adding Semantics to the Bioinformatics Web", and "Personalized Information Systems". The papers in this volume reflect most of the topics investigated in REWERSE; one third of them come from outside REWERSE.

July 2005   François Fages and Sylvain Soliman

Organization

Organizers

François Bry, University of Munich, Germany
François Fages, INRIA Rocquencourt, France
Massimo Marchiori, MIT Cambridge, USA
Hans-Jürgen Ohlbach, University of Munich, Germany

Program Committee

Slim Abdennadher, German University in Cairo, Egypt
François Bry, University of Munich, Germany
François Fages, INRIA Rocquencourt, France (Program Chair)
Enrico Franconi, Free University of Bozen-Bolzano, Italy
Anna Goy, University of Turin, Italy
Nicola Henze, IFIS Hannover, Germany
Manuel Hermenegildo, Universidad Politécnica de Madrid, Spain
Valérie Issarny, INRIA Rocquēncourt, France
François Laburthe, Bouygues, Saint-Quentin-en-Yvelines, France
Jan Maluszynski, Linköping University, Sweden
Massimo Marchiori, MIT Cambridge, USA
Hans-Jürgen Ohlbach, University of Munich, Germany
Marie-Christine Rousset, LRI Orsay, François
Peter Pater-Schneider, Bell Labs, Murray Hill, USA
Uta Schwertel, University of Munich, Germany
Sylvain Soliman, INRIA Rocquencourt, France (Proceedings Chair)
Gerd Wagner, Eindhoven University of Technology, Netherlands
Howard Williams, Heriot-Watt University, Edinburgh, UK
Guizhen Yang, SRI Menlo Park, USA

Table of Contents

Architectures

Languages

Reasoning

SomeWhere in the Semantic Web

P. Adjiman, P. Chatalic, F. Goasdoué, M.-C. Rousset, and L. Simon

PCRI: Université Paris-Sud XI & CNRS (LRI), INRIA (UR Futurs),
Bâtiment 490, Université Paris-Sud XI,
91405 Orsay cedex, France
{adjiman, chatalic, fg, mcr, simon}@lri.fr

Abstract. In this paper, we describe the SomeWhere semantic peer-to-peer data management system that promotes a "small is beautiful" vision of the Semantic Web based on simple personalized ontologies (e.g., taxonomies of classes) but which are distributed at a large scale. In this vision of the Semantic Web, no user imposes to others his own ontology. Logical mappings between ontologies make possible the creation of a web of people in which personalized semantic marking up of data cohabits nicely with a collaborative exchange of data. In this view, the Web is a huge peer-to-peer data management system based on simple distributed ontologies and mappings.

1 Introduction

The Semantic Web [1] envisions a world wide distributed architecture where data and computational resources will easily inter-operate based on semantic marking up of web resources using *ontologies*. Ontologies are a formalization of the semantics of application domains (e.g., tourism, biology, medecine) through the definition of classes and relations modeling the domain objects and properties that are considered as meaningful for the application. Most of the concepts, tools and techniques deployed so far by the Semantic Web community correspond to the "big is beautiful" idea that high expressivity is needed for describing domain ontologies. As a result, when they are applied, the current Semantic Web technologies are mostly used for building thematic portals but do not scale up to the web. In contrast, SomeWhere promotes a "small is beautiful" vision of the Semantic Web [2] based on simple personalized ontologies (e.g., taxonomies of atomic classes) but which are distributed at a large scale. In this vision of the Semantic Web introduced in [3], no user imposes to others his own ontology but logical mappings between ontologies make possible the creation of a web of people in which personalized semantic marking up of data cohabits nicely with a collaborative exchange of data. In this view, the web is a huge peer-to-peer data management system based on simple distributed ontologies and mappings.

Peer-to-peer data management systems have been proposed recently [4,5,6,7] to generalize the centralized approach of information integration systems based on single mediators. In a peer-to-peer data management system, there is no central mediator: each peer has its own ontology and data or services, and can

F. Fages and S. Soliman (Eds.): PPSWR 2005, LNCS 3703, pp. 1–16, 2005.

mediate with some other peers to ask and answer queries. The existing systems vary according to (a) the expressive power of their underlying data model and (b) the way the different peers are semantically connected. Both characteristics have impact on the allowed queries and their distributed processing.

In Edutella [8], each peer stores locally data (educational resources) that are described in RDF relatively to some reference ontologies (e.g., http://dmoz.org). For instance, a peer can declare that it has data related to the concept of the dmoz taxonomy corresponding to the path *Computers/Programming/Languages/Java*, and that for such data it can export the *author* and the *date* properties. The overlay network underlying Edutella is a hypercube of super-peers to which peers are directly connected. Each super-peer is a mediator over the data of the peers connected to it. When it is queried, its first task is to check if the query matches with its schema: if that is the case, it transmits the query to the peers connected to it, which are likely to store the data answering the query; otherwise, it routes the query to some of its neighbour super-peers according to a strategy exploiting the hypercube topology for guaranteeing a worst-case logarithmic time for reaching the relevant super-peer.

In contrast with Edutella, Piazza [4,9] does not consider that the data distributed over the different peers must be described relatively to some existing reference schemas. Each peer has its own data and schema and can mediate with some other peers by declaring *mappings* between its schema and the schemas of those peers. The topology of the network is not fixed (as in Edutella) but accounts for the existence of mappings between peers: two peers are logically connected if there exists a mapping between their two schemas. The underlying data model of the first version of Piazza [4] is relational and the mappings between relational peer schemas are inclusion or equivalence statements between conjunctive queries. Such a mapping formalism encompasses the *Local-as-View* and the *Global-as-View* [10] formalisms used in information integration systems based on single mediators. The price to pay is that query answering is undecidable except if some restrictions are imposed on the mappings or on the topology of the network [4]. The currently implemented version of Piazza [9] relies on a tree-based data model: the data is in XML and the mappings are equivalence and inclusion statements between XML queries. Query answering is implemented based on practical (but not complete) algorithms for XML query containment and rewriting. The scalability of Piazza so far does not go up to more than about 80 peers in the published experiments and relies on a wide range of optimizations (mappings composition [11], paths pruning [12]), made possible by the centralized storage of all the schemas and mappings in a global server.

In SomeWhere, we have made the choice of being fully distributed: there are neither super-peers nor a central server having the global view of the overlay network. In addition, we aim at scaling up to thousands of peers. To make it possible, we have chosen a simple class-based data model in which the data is a set of resource identifiers (e.g., URIs), the schemas are (simple) definitions of classes possibly constrained by inclusion, disjunction or equivalence statements, and mappings are inclusion, disjunction or equivalence statements between classes of different peer schemas. That data model is in accordance with the W3C recommendations since it is captured by the propositional fragment of the OWL ontology language (http://www.w3.org/TR/owl-semantics).

The paper is organized as follows. Section 2 defines the SomeWhere data model. In Section 3, we show how the corresponding query rewriting problem can be reduced by a propositional encoding to distributed reasoning in propositional logic. In Section 4, we describe the properties of the message based distributed reasoning algorithm that is implemented in SomeWhere, and we report experiments on networks of 1000 peers. Section 5 surveys some recent related work on peer-to-peer data management systems. We conclude and present our forthcoming work in Section 6.

2 SomeWhere Data Model

In SomeWhere a new peer joins the network through some peers that it knows (its acquaintances) by declaring mappings between its own ontology and the ontologies of its acquaintances. Queries are posed to a given peer using its local ontology. The answers that are expected are not only instances of local classes but possibly instances of classes of peers distant from the queried peer if it can be infered from the peer ontologies and the mappings that those instances are answers of the query. Local ontologies, storage descriptions and mappings are defined using a fragment of OWL DL which is the description logic fragment of the Ontology Web Language recommended by W3C. We call OWL PL the fragment of OWL DL that we consider in SomeWhere, where PL stands for propositional logic. OWL PL is the fragment of OWL DL reduced to the disjunction, conjunction and negation constructors for building class descriptions.

2.1 Peer Ontologies

Each peer ontology is made of a set of class definitions and possibly a set of equivalence, inclusion or disjointness axioms between class descriptions. A class description is either the universal class ($\top$), the empty class ($\bot$), an atomic class or the union ($\sqcup$), intersection ($\sqcap$) or complement ($\neg$) of class descriptions.

The name of atomic classes are unique to each peer: we use the notation $P{:}A$ for identifying an atomic class A of the ontology of a peer P. The *vocabulary* of a peer P is the set of names of its atomic classes.

Class descriptions

	Logical notation	OWL notation
universal class	$\top$	*Thing*
empty class	$\bot$	*Nothing*
atomic class	$P{:}A$	*classID*
conjunction	$D1 \sqcap D2$	*intersectionOf(D1 D2)*
disjunction	$D1 \sqcup D2$	*unionOf(D1 D2)*
negation	$\neg D$	*complementOf(D)*

Axioms of class definitions

	Logical notation	OWL notation
Complete	$P{:}A \equiv D$	$Class(P{:}A\ complete\ D)$
Partial	$P{:}A \sqsubseteq D$	$Class(P{:}A\ partial\ D)$

Axioms on class descriptions

	Logical notation	OWL notation
equivalence	$D1 \equiv D2$	$EquivalentClasses(D1\ D2)$
inclusion	$D1 \sqsubseteq D2$	$SubClassOf(D1\ D2)$
disjointness	$D1 \sqcap D2 \equiv \bot$	$DisjointClasses(D1\ D2)$

2.2 Peer Storage Descriptions

The specification of the data that is stored locally in a peer P is done through the declaration of atomic *extensional classes* defined in terms of atomic classes of the peer ontology, and assertional statements relating data identifiers (e.g., URIs) to those extensional classes. We restrict the axioms defining the extensional classes to be inclusion statements between an atomic extensional class and a description combining atomic classes of the ontology. We impose that restriction in order to fit with a *Local-as-View* approach and an open-world assumption within the information integration setting [10]. We will use the notation $P{:}ViewA$ to denote an extensional class $ViewA$ of the peer P.

Storage description
declaration of extensional classes:

Logical notation	OWL notation
$P{:}ViewA \sqsubseteq C$	$SubClassOf(P{:}ViewA\ \ C)$

assertional statements:

Logical notation	OWL notation
$P{:}ViewA(a)$	$individual(a\ type(P{:}ViewA))$

2.3 Mappings

Mappings are disjointness, equivalence or inclusion statements involving atomic classes of different peers. They express the semantic correspondence that may exist between the ontologies of different peers.

The *acquaintance graph* accounts for the connection induced by the mappings between the different peers within a given SomeWhere peer-to-peer network.

Definition 1 (Acquaintance graph). *Let* $\mathcal{P} = \{P_i\}_{i \in [1..n]}$ *a collection of peers with their respective vocabularies* Voc_{P_i}. *Let* $Voc = \bigcup_{i=1}^{n} Voc_{P_i}$ *be the vocabulary of* $\mathcal{P}$. *Its* acquaintance graph *is a graph* $\Gamma = (\mathcal{P}, \text{ACQ})$ *where* $\mathcal{P}$ *is the set of vertices and* $\text{ACQ} \subseteq Voc \times \mathcal{P} \times \mathcal{P}$ *is a set of labelled edges such that for every* $(c, P_i, P_j) \in \text{ACQ}$, $i \neq j$ *and* $c \in Voc_{P_i} \cap Voc_{P_j}$.

A labelled edge (c, P_i, P_j) expresses that peers P_i and P_j know each other to be sharing the class c. This means that c belongs to the intentional classes of P_i (or P_j) and is involved in a mapping with intentional classes of P_j (or P_i).

2.4   Schema of a SomeWhere Network

In a SomeWhere network, the schema is not centralized but distributed through the union of the different peer ontologies and the mappings. The important point is that each peer has a partial knowledge of the schema: it just knows its own local ontology and the mappings with its acquaintances.

Let $\mathcal{P}$ be a SomeWhere peer-to-peer network made of a collection of peers $\{P_i\}_{i\in[1..n]}$. For each peer P_i, let O_i, V_i and M_i be the sets of axioms defining respectively the local ontology of P_i, the declaration of its extensional classes and the set of mappings stated at P_i between classes of O_i and classes of the ontologies of the acquaintances of P_i. The schema $\mathcal{S}$ of $\mathcal{P}$ is the union $\bigcup_{i\in[1..n]} O_i \cup V_i \cup M_i$ of the ontologies, the declaration on extensional classes and of the sets of mappings of all the peers of $\mathcal{P}$.

2.5   Semantics

The semantics is a standard logical formal semantics defined in terms of *interpretations*. An interpretation I is a pair $(\Delta^I, .^I)$ where Δ is a non-empty set, called the domain of interpretation, and $.^I$ is an interpretation function which assigns a subset of Δ^I to every class identifier and an element of Δ^I to every data identifier.

An interpretation I is a *model* of the distributed schema of a SomeWhere peer-to-peer network $\mathcal{P} = \{P_i\}_{i\in[1..n]}$ iff each axiom in $\bigcup_{i\in[1..n]} O_i \cup V_i \cup M_i$ is satisfied by I.

Interpretations of axioms rely on interpretations of class descriptions which are inductively defined as follows:

- $\top^I = \Delta^I$, $\bot^I = \emptyset$
- $(\neg C)^I = \Delta^I \backslash C^I$
- $(C_1 \sqcup C_2)^I = C_1^I \cup C_2^I$, $(C_1 \sqcap C_2)^I = C_1^I \cap C_2^I$

Axioms are satisfied if the following holds:

- $C \sqsubseteq D$ is satisfied in I iff $C^I \subseteq D^I$
- $C \equiv D$ is satisfied in I iff $C^I = D^I$
- $C \sqcap D \equiv \bot$ is satisfied in I iff $C^I \cap D^I = \emptyset$

A SomeWhere peer-to-peer network is *satisfiable* iff its schema has a model.

Given a SomeWhere peer-to-peer network $\mathcal{P} = \{P_i\}_{i\in[1..n]}$, a class description C *subsumes* a class description D iff in each model I of the schema of $\mathcal{P}$, $D^I \subseteq C^I$.

2.6   Illustrative Example

We illustrate the SomeWhere data model on a small example of four peers modeling four persons Ann, Bob, Chris and Dora, each of them bookmarking URLs about restaurants they know or like, according to their own taxonomy for categorizing restaurants.

Ann, who is working as a restaurant critics, organizes its restaurant URLs according to the following classes:

- the class $Ann{:}G$ of restaurants considered as offering a "good" cooking, among which she distinguishes the subclass $Ann{:}R$ of those which are rated: $Ann{:}R \sqsubseteq Ann{:}G$
- the class $Ann{:}R$ is the union of three disjoint classes $Ann{:}S1$, $Ann{:}S2$, $Ann{:}S3$ corresponding respectively to the restaurants rated with $1, 2$ or 3 stars:
$Ann{:}R \equiv Ann{:}S1 \sqcup Ann{:}S2 \sqcup Ann{:}S3$
$Ann{:}S1 \sqcap Ann{:}S2 \equiv \bot \quad Ann{:}S1 \sqcap Ann{:}S3 \equiv \bot$
$Ann{:}S2 \sqcap Ann{:}S3 \equiv \bot$
- the classes $Ann{:}I$ and $Ann{:}O$, respectively corresponding to Indian and Oriental restaurants
- the classes $Ann{:}C$, $Ann{:}T$ and $Ann{:}V$ which are subclasses of $Ann{:}O$ denoting Chinese, Taï and Vietnamese restaurants respectively: $Ann{:}C \sqsubseteq Ann{:}O$, $Ann{:}T \sqsubseteq Ann{:}O$, $Ann{:}V \sqsubseteq Ann{:}O$

Suppose that the data stored by Ann that she accepts to make available deals with restaurants of various specialties, and only with those rated with 2 stars among the rated restaurants. The extensional classes declared by Ann are then:
$Ann{:}ViewS2 \sqsubseteq Ann{:}S2$, $Ann{:}ViewC \sqsubseteq Ann{:}C$,
$Ann{:}ViewV \sqsubseteq Ann{:}V$, $Ann{:}ViewT \sqsubseteq Ann{:}T$,
$Ann{:}ViewI \sqsubseteq Ann{:}I$

Bob, who is found of Asian cooking and likes high quality, organizes his restaurant URLs according to the following classes:
- the class $Bob{:}A$ of Asian restaurants
- the class $Bob{:}Q$ of high quality restaurants that he knows

Suppose that he wants to make available every data that he has stored. The extensional classes that he declares are $Bob{:}ViewA$ and $Bob{:}ViewQ$ (as subclasses of $Bob{:}A$ and $Bob{:}Q$): $Bob{:}ViewA \sqsubseteq Bob{:}A$, $Bob{:}ViewQ \sqsubseteq Bob{:}Q$

Chris is more found of fish restaurants but recently discovered some places serving a very nice cantonese cuisine. He organizes its data with respect to the following classes:
- the class $Chris{:}F$ of fish restaurants,
- the class $Chris{:}CA$ of Cantonese restaurants

Suppose that he declares the extensional classes $Chris{:}ViewF$ and $Chris{:}ViewCA$ as subclasses of $Chris{:}F$ and $Chris{:}CA$ respectively: $Chris{:}ViewF \sqsubseteq Chris{:}F$, $Chris{:}ViewCA \sqsubseteq Chris{:}CA$

Dora organizes her restaurants URLs around the class $Dora{:}DP$ of her preferred restaurants, among which she distinguishes the subclass $Dora{:}P$ of pizzerias and the subclass $Dora{:}SF$ of seafood restaurants.
Suppose that the only URLs that she stores concerns pizzerias: the only extensional class that she has to declare is $Dora{:}ViewP$ as a subclass of $Dora{:}P$:
$Dora{:}ViewP \sqsubseteq Dora{:}P$

Ann, **Bob**, **Chris** and **Dora** express what they know about each other using mappings stating properties of class inclusion or equivalence.

Ann is very confident in Bob's taste and agrees to include Bob' selection as good restaurants by stating $Bob{:}Q \sqsubseteq Ann{:}G$. Finally, she thinks that Bob's Asian restaurants encompass her Oriental restaurant concept: $Ann{:}O \sqsubseteq Bob{:}A$

Bob knows that what he calls Asian cooking corresponds exactly to what Ann classifies as Oriental cooking. This may be expressed using the equivalence statement : $Bob{:}A \equiv Ann{:}O$ (note the difference of perception of Bob and Ann regarding the mappings between $Bob{:}A$ and $Ann{:}O$)

Chris considers that what he calls fish specialties is a particular case of Dora seafood specialties: $Chris{:}F \sqsubseteq Dora{:}SF$

Dora counts on both Ann and Bob to obtain good Asian restaurants : $Bob{:}A \sqcap Ann{:}G \sqsubseteq Dora{:}DP$

Figure 1 describes the resulting acquaintance graph. In order to alleviate the notations, we omit the local peer name prefix except for the mappings. Edges are labeled with the class identifiers that are shared through the mappings.

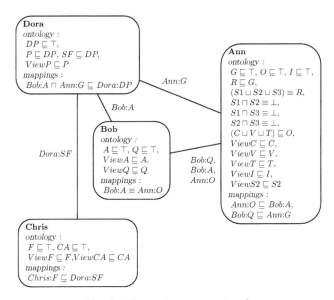

Fig. 1. The restaurants network

3   Query Rewriting

In SomeWhere, each user interrogates the peer-to-peer network through one peer of his choice, and uses the vocabulary of this peer to express his query. Therefore, queries are logical combinations of classes of a given peer ontology.

The corresponding answer sets are expressed in intention in terms of the combinations of extensional classes that are *rewritings* of the query. The point is that extensional classes of several distant peers can participate to the rewritings, and thus to the answer of a query posed to a given peer.

Given a SomeWhere peer-to-peer network $\mathcal{P} = \{P_i\}_{i\in[1..n]}$, a logical combination Q_e of extensional classes is a *rewriting* of a query Q iff Q subsumes Q_e. Q_e is a *maximal rewriting* if there does not exist another rewriting Q'_e of Q (strictly) subsuming Q_e.

In the SomeWhere setting, query rewriting can be equivalently reduced to distributed reasoning over logical propositional theories by a straighforward propositional encoding of the distributed schema of a SomeWhere network.

Before presenting the propositional encoding in Section 3.2 and the distributed consequence finding algorithm in Section 4, we illustrate the corresponding query processing on the example of Section 2.6.

3.1 Illustrative Example (Continued)

Consider that a user queries the restaurants network through the **Dora** peer by asking the query $Dora{:}DP$, meaning that he is interested in getting as answers the set of favourite restaurants of Dora:

- Using $Dora{:}P{\sqsubseteq}Dora{:}DP$ and $Dora{:}ViewP{\sqsubseteq}Dora{:}P$, we obtain $Dora{:}ViewP$ as a local rewriting corresponding to the extensional class of pizzeria URLs stored by Dora.
- Using $Dora{:}SF{\sqsubseteq}Dora{:}DP$, the fact that $Dora{:}SF$ is shared with $Chris$ by the mapping $Chris{:}F{\sqsubseteq}Dora{:}SF$, and $Chris{:}ViewF{\sqsubseteq}Chris{:}F$, we obtain $Chris{:}ViewF$ as a new rewriting meaning that another way to get restaurants liked by Dora is to obtain the Fish restaurants stored by Chris.
- Finally, using the mapping $Bob{:}A{\sqcap}Ann{:}G{\sqsubseteq}Dora{:}DP$, the query leads to look for rewritings of $Bob{:}A{\sqcap}Ann{:}G$, where both $Bob{:}A$ and $Ann{:}G$ are shared with neighbor peers. In such cases our algorithm uses a split/recombination approach. Each shared component (here $Bob{:}A$ and $Ann{:}G$) is then processed independently as a subquery, transmitted to its appropriate neighbors and associated with some queue data structure, where its returned rewritings are accumulated. As soon as at least one rewriting has been obtained for each component, the respective queued rewritings of each component are recombined to produce rewritings of the initial query. This recombination process continues incrementally, as new rewritings for a component are produced. Note that since each subcomponent is processed asynchronously, the order in which recombined rewritings are produced is unpredictable. For the sake of simplicity, in the following we consider sequentially the results obtained for the two subqueries $Bob{:}A$ and $Ann{:}G$:

– On the Bob peer, because of $Bob{:}ViewA{\sqsubseteq}Bob{:}A$, $Bob{:}ViewA$ is a local rewriting of $Bob{:}A$, which is transmitted back to the Dora peer, where it is queued for a future combination with rewritings of the other subquery $Ann{:}G$.

In addition, guided by the mapping $Ann{:}O{\equiv}Bob{:}A$, the Bob peer transmits to the Ann peer the query $Ann{:}O$. The Ann peer processes that query locally and transmits back to the Bob peer the rewriting $Ann{:}ViewC \sqcup Ann{:}ViewT \sqcup Ann{:}ViewV$, which in turn is transmitted back to the Dora peer as an additional rewriting for the subquery $Bob{:}A$ and queued there.

– On the Ann peer, using $Ann{:}R \sqsubseteq Ann{:}G$, $(Ann{:}S1 \sqcup Ann{:}S2 \sqcup Ann{:}S3) \equiv Ann{:}R$ and $Ann{:}ViewS2 \sqsubseteq Ann{:}S2$, $Ann{:}ViewS2$ is obtained as a local rewriting of $Ann{:}G$. It is transmitted back to the Dora peer where it is queued for re-combination. Let us suppose that the two rewritings of $Bob{:}A$ ($Bob{:}ViewA$ and $Ann{:}ViewC \sqcup Ann{:}ViewT \sqcup Ann{:}ViewV$) have aleady been produced at that time. Their combination with $Ann{:}ViewS2$ gives two rewritings which are sent back to the user:

  * $Ann{:}ViewS2 \sqcap Bob{:}ViewA$, meaning that a way to obtain restaurants liked by Dora is to find restautants that are both stored by Ann as rated with 2 stars and by Bob as Asian restaurants,

  * $Ann{:}ViewS2 \sqcap (Ann{:}ViewC \sqcup Ann{:}ViewT \sqcup Ann{:}ViewV)$ meaning that another way to obtain restaurants liked by Dora is to find restautants stored by Ann as restaurants rated with 2 stars and also as Chinese, Thai or Vietnamese restaurants. Note that this rewriting, although obtained via different peers after splitting/recombination, turns out to be composed only of extensional classes of the same peer: Ann.

Still on the Ann peer, because of the mapping $Bob{:}Q \sqsubseteq Ann{:}G$, Ann transmits the query $Bob{:}Q$ to Bob, which transmits back to Ann $Bob{:}ViewQ$ as a rewriting of $Bob{:}Q$ (and thus of $Ann{:}G$). Ann then transmits $Bob{:}ViewQ$ back to Dora as a rewriting of $Ann{:}G$, where it is queued for combination. On Dora's side, $Bob{:}ViewQ$ is now combined with the queued rewritings of $Bob{:}A$ ($Bob{:}ViewA$ and $Ann{:}ViewC \sqcup Ann{:}ViewT \sqcup Ann{:}ViewV$). As a result, two new rewritings are sent back to the user:

  * $Bob{:}ViewQ \sqcap Bob{:}ViewA$ meaning that to obtain restaurants liked by Dora one can take the restaurants that Bob stores as high quality restaurants and as Asian restaurants,

  * $Bob{:}ViewQ \sqcap (Ann{:}ViewC \sqcup Ann{:}ViewT \sqcup Ann{:}ViewV)$ providing a new way of getting restaurants liked by Dora: those that are both stored as high quality restaurants by Bob and as Chinese, Thai or Vietnamese restaurants by Ann.

3.2   Propositional Encoding of Query Rewriting in SomeWhere

The propositional encoding concerns the schema of a SomeWhere network and the queries. It consists in transforming each query and schema statement into a propositional formula using class identifiers as propositional variables.

The propositional encoding of a class description D, and thus of a query, is the propositional formula $Prop(D)$ obtained inductively as follows:

  • $Prop(\top) = true$, $Prop(\bot) = false$
  • $Prop(A) = A$, if A is an atomic class
  • $Prop(D_1 \sqcap D_2) = Prop(D_1) \land Prop(D_2)$
  • $Prop(D_1 \sqcup D_2) = Prop(D_1) \lor Prop(D_2)$
  • $Prop(\neg D) = \neg(Prop(D))$

The propositional encoding of the schema $\mathcal{S}$ of a SomeWhere peer-to-peer network $\mathcal{P}$ is the distributed propositional theory $Prop(\mathcal{S})$ made of the formulas obtained inductively from the axioms in $\mathcal{S}$ as follows:

- $Prop(C \sqsubseteq D) = Prop(C) \Rightarrow Prop(D)$
- $Prop(C \equiv D) = Prop(C) \Leftrightarrow Prop(D)$
- $Prop(C \sqcap D \equiv \bot) = \neg Prop(C) \vee \neg Prop(D)$

From now on, for simplicity purpose, we use the propositional clausal form notation for the queries and SomeWhere peer-to-peer network schemas.

As an illustration, let us consider the propositional encoding of the example presented in Section 2.6. Once in clausal form and after the removal of tautologies, we obtain (Figure 2) the acquaintance graph where each peer schema is described as a propositional theory.

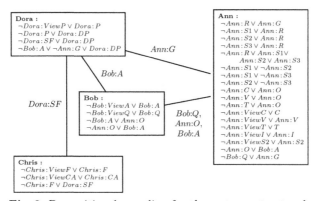

Fig. 2. Propositional encoding for the restaurant network

Proposition 1 states that the propositional encoding transfers satisfiability and establishes the connection between (maximal) conjunctive rewritings and clausal proper (prime) implicates.

Definition 2 (Proper prime implicate wrt a theory). *Let T be a clausal theory and q be a clause. A clause m is said to be:*

- *a prime implicate of q wrt T iff $T \cup \{q\} \models m$ and for any other clause m', if $T \cup \{q\} \models m'$ and $m' \models m$ then $m' \equiv m$.*
- *a proper prime implicate of q wrt T iff it is a prime implicate of q wrt T and $T \not\models m$.*

Proposition 1 (Propositional transfer). *Let $\mathcal{P}$ be a SomeWhere peer-to-peer network and let $Prop(S(\mathcal{P}))$ be the propositional encoding of its schema. Let V_e be the set of all the extensional classes.*

- *$S(\mathcal{P})$ is satisfiable iff $Prop(S(\mathcal{P}))$ is satisfiable.*
- *q_e is a maximal conjunctive rewriting of a query q iff $\neg Prop(q_e)$ is a proper prime implicate of $\neg Prop(q)$ wrt $Prop(S(\mathcal{P}))$ such that all its variables are extensional classes.*

Proposition 1 gives us a way to compute *all* the answers of a query. The maximal conjunctive rewritings of a query q within a peer-to-peer network $\mathcal{P}$ correspond to the negation of the proper prime implicates of $\neg q$ wrt the propositional encoding of the schema of $S(\mathcal{P})$. Since the number of proper prime implicates of a clause wrt a clausal theory is finite, every query in SomeWhere has a finite number of maximal conjunctive rewritings. Therefore, according to [13], the set of *all* of its answers is exactly the union of the answer sets of its rewritings and is obtained in PTIME data complexity.

In the following section, we present a distributed consequence finding algorithm which computes the set of proper prime implicates of a literal wrt a distributed propositional clausal theory. According to Proposition 1, if this algorithm is applied to a distributed theory resulting from the propositional encoding of the schema of a SomeWhere network, with the extensional classes symbols as *target variables*, and triggered with a literal $\neg q$, it computes in fact the negation of the maximal conjunctive rewritings of the *atomic* query q. Since in our setting the maximal rewritings of an arbitrary query can be obtained by combining the maximal rewritings of its atomic components, we focus on the computation of the rewritings of atomic queries.

4   Algorithmic Machinery and Experiments

The SomeWhere peer-to-peer data management system relies on a distributed algorithm presented in [14]. For this paper to be self-contained, we describe the three message passing procedures of the algorithm which are implemented locally at each peer. They are triggered by the reception of a *query* (resp. *answer, final*) message, sent by a Sender peer to a receiver peer, denoted by Self, which executes the procedure. Procedures handle an history initialized to the empty sequence. An history *hist* is a sequence of triples (l, P, c) (where l is a literal, P a peer, and c a clause). An history $[(l_n, P_n, c_n), \ldots, (l_1, P_1, c_1), (l_0, P_0, c_0)]$ represents a branch of reasoning initiated by the propagation of the literal l_0 within the peer P_0, and the splitting of the clause c_0: for every $i \in [0..n - 1]$, c_i is a consequence of l_i and P_i, and l_{i+1} is a literal of c_i, which is propagated in P_{i+1}.

RECEIVEQUERYMESSAGE is triggered by the reception of a *query* message $m(Sender, Receiver, query, hist, l)$ sent by the peer *Sender* to the peer *Receiver* which executes the procedure: on the demand of *Sender*, with which it shares the variable of l, it processes the literal l.

RECEIVEANSWERMESSAGE is triggered by the reception of an *answer* message $m(Sender, Receiver, answer, hist, r)$ sent by the peer *Sender* to the peer *Receiver* which executes the procedure: it processes the answer r (which is a clause the variables of which are target variables) sent back by *Sender* for the literal l (last added in the history) ; it may have to combine it with other answers for literals being in the same clause as l.

RECEIVEFINALMESSAGE is triggered by the reception of a *final* message $m(Sender, Receiver, final, hist, true)$: the peer *Sender* notifies the peer *Receiver* that computation for the literal l (last added in the history) is completed.

Those procedures handle two local data structures:

ANSWER($l, hist$) caches answers resulting from the propagation of l within the reasoning branch corresponding to $hist$;

FINAL($q, hist$) is set to true when the propagation of q within the reasoning branch of the history $hist$ is completed. The reasoning is initiated by the user (denoted by a particular peer $User$) sending to a given peer P a message $m(User, P, query, \emptyset, q)$, which triggers the procedure RECEIVEQUERYMESSAGE($m(User, P, query, \emptyset, q)$) that is locally executed by P.

In the following procedures, since they are locally executed by the peer which receives the message, we denote by $Self$ the receiver peer. We also assume that:

• for a literal q, $Resolvent(q, P)$ denotes the set of clauses obtained by resolution between q and a clause of P,

• for a literal q, $\bar{q}$ denotes its complementary literal,

• for a clause c of a peer P, $S(c)$ (resp. $L(c)$) denotes the disjonction of literals of c whose variables are shared (resp. not shared) with any acquaintance of P. $S(c) = \square$ thus expresses that c does not contain any shared variable,

• $Target(P)$ is the language of clauses (including $\square$) involving only variables that are extensonial classes of P.

• $\oslash$ is the distribution operator on sets of clauses: $S_1 \oslash \cdots \oslash S_n = \{c_1 \vee \cdots \vee c_n \mid c_1 \in S_1, \ldots, c_n \in S_n\}$. If $L = \{l_1, \ldots, l_p\}$, $\oslash_{l \in L} S_l$ denotes $S_{l_1} \oslash \cdots \oslash S_{l_p}$.

The following theorems summarize the main properties of this distributed message passing algorithm and thus of the SomeWhere peer-to-peer data management system. Theorem 1 states the termination and the soundness of the algorithm. Theorem 2 states its completeness under the condition that each peer theory is saturated by resolution. Theorem 3 states that the user is notified of the termination when it occurs, which is crucial for an anytime algorithm. Full proofs are given in [15]. In the following theorems, let $\mathcal{T}$ be the propositional encoding of the schema $S(\mathcal{P})$ of a peer-to-peer SomeWhere network, let $\neg q$ the negation of an atomic query q, let T be the propositional encoding of the local schema and mappings of the asked peer.

Theorem 1 (Soundness). *If T receives from the user the message $m(User, T, query, \emptyset, \neg q)$, then:*

• *a finite number of answer messages will be produced ;*

• *each produced answer message $m(T, User, answer, [(\neg q,\ T, \_)], r)$ is such that r is an implicate of $\neg q$ wrt $S(\mathcal{P})$ which belong to $Target(\mathcal{P})$.*

Theorem 2 (Completeness). *If each local theory is saturated by resolution and if T receives from the user the message $m(User, T, query, \emptyset, \neg q)$, then for each proper prime implicate r of $\neg q$ wrt $S(\mathcal{P})$ belonging to $Target(\mathcal{P})$, an answer message $m(T, User, answer, [(\neg q, T, \_)], r)$ will be produced.*

Theorem 3 (Termination notification). *If r is the last result returned in an answer message $m(T, User, answer,\ [(\neg q, T, \_)], r)$ then the user will be notified of the termination by a message $m(T, User, final, [(\neg q, T, true)], true)$.*

It is important to notice that $\square$ can be returned by our algorithm as a proper prime implicate because of the lines (1) to (3) and (8) to (10) in RECEIVE-QUERYMESSAGE. In that case, as a corollary of the above theorems, the union the propositional encoding of the schema of the SomeWhere network and the query is detected unsatisfiable. Therefore, our algorithm can be exploited for checking the satisfiability of the global schema at each join of a new peer.

Algorithm 1: Message passing procedure for processing queries

RECEIVEQUERYMESSAGE($m(Sender, Self, query, hist, q)$)

(1) **if** $(\bar{q}, \_, \_) \in hist$
(2)   **send** $m(Self, Sender, answer, [(q, Self, \square)|hist], \square)$
(3)   **send** $m(Self, Sender, final, [(q, Self, true)|hist], true)$
(4)**else if** $q \in Self$ or $(q, Self, \_) \in hist$
(5)   **send** $m(Self, Sender, final, [(q, Self, true)|hist], true)$
(6)**else**
(7)   LOCAL($Self$) $\leftarrow \{q\} \cup Resolvent(q, Self)$
(8)   **if** $\square \in$ LOCAL($Self$)
(9)   **send** $m(Self, Sender, answer, [(q, Self, \square)|hist], \square)$
(10)   **send** $m(Self, Sender, final, [(q, Self, true)|hist], true)$
(11) **else**
(12)   LOCAL($Self$) $\leftarrow \{c \in$ LOCAL($Self$)$| L(c) \in Target(Self)\}$
(13)   **if** for every $c \in$ LOCAL($Self$), $S(c) = \square$
(14)   **foreach** $c \in$ LOCAL($Self$)
(15)   **send** $m(Self, Sender, answer, [(q, Self, c)|hist], c)$
(16)   **send** $m(Self, Sender, final, [(q, Self, true)|hist], true)$
(17)   **else**
(18)   **foreach** $c \in$ LOCAL($Self$)
(19)   **if** $S(c) = \square$
(20)   **send** $m(Self, Sender, answer, [(q, Self, c)|hist], c)$
(21)   **else**
(22)   **foreach** literal $l \in S(c)$
(23)   **if** $l \in Target(Self)$
(24)   ANSWER($l, [(q, Self, c)|hist]$) $\leftarrow \{l\}$
(25)   **else**
(26)   ANSWER($l, [(q, Self, c)|hist]$) $\leftarrow \emptyset$
(27)   FINAL($l, [(q, Self, c)|hist]$) $\leftarrow false$
(28)   **foreach** $RP \in$ ACQ($l, Self$)
(29)   **send** $m(Self, RP, query, [(q, Self, c)|hist], l)$

Algorithm 2: Message passing procedure for processing answers

RECEIVEANSWERMESSAGE($m(Sender, Self, answer, hist, r)$)

(1)$hist$ is of the form $[(l', Sender, c'), (q, Self, c)|hist']$
(2)ANSWER($l', hist$) $\leftarrow$ ANSWER $(l', hist) \cup \{r\}$
(3)RESULT$\leftarrow \oslash_{l \in S(c)\backslash\{l'\}}$ANSWER($l, hist$) $\oslash \{L(c) \lor r\}$
(4)**if** $hist' = \emptyset$, $U \leftarrow User$ **else** $U \leftarrow$ the first peer P' of $hist'$
(5)**foreach** $cs \in$ RESULT
(6) **send** $m(Self, U, answer, [(q, Self, c)|hist'], cs)$

Algorithm 3: Message passing procedure for notifying termination
RECEIVEFINALMESSAGE($m(Sender, Self, final, hist, true)$)
(1)$hist$ is of the form $[(l', Sender, true), (q, Self, c)|hist']$
(2)FINAL($l', hist$) $\leftarrow true$
(3)**if** for every $l \in S(c)$, FINAL($l, hist$) $= true$
(4)   **if** $hist' = \emptyset$ $U \leftarrow User$ **else** $U \leftarrow$ the first peer P' of $hist'$
(5)   **send** $m(Self, U, final, [(q, Self, true)|hist'], true)$
(6)   **foreach** $l \in S(c)$
(7)   ANSWER($l, [(l, Sender, \_), (q, Self, c)|hist']$) $\leftarrow \emptyset$

5   Related Work

As we have pointed it out in the introduction, the SomeWhere peer data management system distinguishes from Edutella [8] by the fact that there is no need of super-peers. It does not require either a central server having the global view of the overlay network, as in Piazza [4,9] or in [16].

The recent work around the coDB peer data management system [17] supports dynamic networks but the first step of the distributed algorithm is to let each node know the network topology. In contrast, in SomeWhere no node does not have to know the topology of the network.

The Kadop system [18] is an infastructure based on distributed hash tables for constructing and querying peer-to-peer warehouses of XML resources semantically enriched by taxonomies and mappings. The mappings that are considered are simple inclusion statement between atomic classes. Compared to KadoP (and also to DRAGO [19]), the mapping language that is dealt with in SomeWhere is more expressive than simple inclusion statements between atomic classes. It is an important difference which makes SomeWhere able to *combine* elements of answers coming from different sources for answering a query, which KadoP or DRAGO cannot do.

SomeWhere implements in a simpler setting the vision of peer-to-peer data management systems proposed in [20] for relational databases.

6   Conclusion and Future Work

We have presented the SomeWhere semantic peer-to-peer data management system. Its data model is based on the propositional fragment of the Ontology Web Language recommended by W3C. SomeWhere implements a fully peer-to-peer approach. We have conducted a significant experimentation on networks of 1000 peers. It is presented in [21]. To the best of our knowledge, this is the first experimental study on such large peer-to-peer data management systems. The motivations of this experimentation was twofold. First, to study how deep and how wide reasoning spreads on the network. Second, to evaluate the time needed to obtain answers and to check to what extent SomeWhere is able to support the traffic load.

SomeWhere is the basis of the MediaD project with France Télécom, which aims at enriching peer-to-peer web applications (e.g., Someone [3]) with reasoning services.

We plan to extend SomeWhere in three directions.

We first plan to tackle the problem of possible inconsistency of the distributed schema which can occur because of the mappings, even if the local theories are all consistent. In principle, our algorithm is able to check whether adding a new theory and set of mappings to a consistent SomeWhere network of theories leads to an inconsistency. Therefore, we could forbid a new peer to join the network if it makes the global schema inconsistent, and thus guarantee by contruction that query processing applies on consistent SomeWhere networks. However, this solution is probably too rigid and restrictive to be accepted in practice by users who want to join a SomeWhere network. At least, a new peer whose join leads to an inconsistency would like to know with which other peer(s) its ontology is inconsistent. The problem of detecting the causes of an inconsistency is not trivial and has been extensively studied for centralized theories or knowledge bases. We need to investigate that issue in the SomeWhere distributed setting. We could also decide not to correct the inconsistency but to confine it and answer queries within consistent sub-networks.

Second, we want to extend the SomeWhere data model with binary relations. We are currently exhibiting another propositional transfert for peers relying on the RDF/RDFS data model and accepting conjunctive queries.

Finally, we plan to plug SomeWhere onto a Chord infrastructure [22] in order to make SomeWhere more robust to frequent changes in the network due to peers joins and leaves. In addition, the look-up service offered by Chord could be exploited for optimization purposes of the current SomeWhere query processing.

References

1. Berners-Lee, T., Hendler, J., Lassila, O.: The semantic web. Scientific American **284** (2001) 35–43 Essay about the possibilities of the semantic web.
2. Rousset, M.C.: Small can be beautiful in the semantic web. In: ISWC 2004, International Semantic Web Conference. (2004)
3. Plu, M., Bellec, P., Agosto, L., van de Velde, W.: The web of people: A dual view on the WWW. In: Int. World Wide Web Conf. (2003)
4. Halevy, A., Ives, Z., Suciu, D., Tatarinov, I.: Schema mediation in peer data management systems. In: ICDE'03. (2003)
5. Ooi, B., Shu, Y., Tan, K.L.: Relational data sharing in peer data management systems. **23** (2003)
6. Arenas, M., Kantere, V., Kementsietsidis, A., Kiringa, I., Miller, R., Mylopoulos, J. In: The Hyperion project: From data integration to data coordination. (2003)
7. Bernstein, P., Giunchiglia, F., Kementsietsidis, A., Mylopoulos, J., Serafini, L., Zaihraheu, I.: Data management for p2p computing: A vision. In: WebDB. (2002)
8. Nedjl, W., Wolf, B., Qu, C., Decker, S., Sintek, M., al.: Edutella: a p2p networking infrastructure based on rdf. In: WWW'02. (2002)
9. Halevy, A., Ives, Z., Tatarinov, I., Mork, P.: Piazza: data management infrastructure for semantic web applications. In: WWW'03. (2003)

10. Halevy, A.Y. In: Logic-based techniques in data integration. Kluwer Academic Publishers (2000) 575–595
11. Madhavan, J., Halevy, A.: Composing mappings among data sources. In: VLDB 03. (2003)
12. Tatarinov, I., Halevy, A.: Efficient query reformulation in peer data management systems. In: SIGMOD 04. (2004)
13. Goasdoué, F., Rousset, M.C.: Answering queries using views. ACM Journal - Transactions on Internet Technology (TOIT) **4** (2004)
14. Adjiman, P., Chatalic, P., Goasdoué, F., Rousset, M.C., Simon, L.: Distributed reasoning in a p2p setting, short paper. In: ECAI. (2004) 945–946
15. Adjiman, P., Chatalic, P., Goasdoué, F., Rousset, M.C., Simon, L.: Distributed reasoning in a p2p setting. Technical report, http://www.lri.fr/~goasdoue/bib/ACGRS-TR-1385.pdf (2004)
16. Calvanese, D., Giacomo, G.D., Lenzerini, M., Rosati, R.: Logical fondation of p2p data integration. In: PODS, Paris, France (2004)
17. Franconi, E., Kuper, G., Lopatenko, A., Zaihrayeu, I.: Queries and updates in the codb p2p database system. In: VLDB 2004. (2004)
18. Abiteboul, S., Manolescu, I., Preda, N.: Constructing and querying p2p warehouses of xml resources. In: Workshop on Semantic Web and Databases. (2004)
19. Serafini, L., Tamilin, A.: Drago: Distributed reasoning architecture for the semantic web. Technical report, ITC-IRST (2004)
20. Bernstein, P., Giunchiglia, F., Kementsietsidis, A., Mylopoulos, J., Serafini, L., Zaihrayeu, I.: Data management for p2p computing: a vision. In: Proceedings of WebDB 2002. (2002)
21. Adjiman, P., Chatalic, P., Goasdoué, F., Rousset, M.C., Simon, L.: Scalability study of p2p consequence finding. In: IJCAI, IJCAI (2005)
22. Stoica, I., Morris, R., Karger, D., Kaasshoek, M., Balakrishnan, H.: Chord: a scalable p2p lookup service for internet applications. In: Conference on applications, technologies, archtecture and protocols for computer communications. (2001)

A Framework for Aligning Ontologies

Patrick Lambrix and He Tan

Department of Computer and Information Science,
Linköpings universitet, Sweden
{patla, hetan}@ida.liu.se

Abstract. Ontologies are an important technology for the Semantic Web. In different areas ontologies have already been developed and many of these ontologies contain overlapping information. Often we would therefore want to be able to use multiple ontologies and thus the ontologies need to be aligned. Currently, there exist a number of systems that support users in aligning ontologies, but not many comparative evaluations have been performed.

In this paper we present a general framework for aligning ontologies where different alignment strategies can be combined. Further, we exemplify the use of the framework by describing a system (SAMBO) that is developed according to this framework. Within this system we have implemented some already existing alignment algorithms as well as some new algorithms. We also show how the framework can be used to experiment with combinations of strategies. This is a first step towards defining a framework that can be used for comparative evaluations of alignment strategies. For our tests we used several well-known bio-ontologies.

1 Introduction

Intuitively, ontologies (e.g. [10,6]) can be seen as defining the basic terms and relations of a domain of interest, as well as the rules for combining these terms and relations. They are considered to be an important technology for the Semantic Web. Ontologies are used for communication between people and organizations by providing a common terminology over a domain. They provide the basis for interoperability between systems. They can be used for making the content in information sources explicit and serve as an index to a repository of information. Further, they can be used as a basis for integration of information sources and as a query model for information sources. They also support clearly separating domain knowledge from application-based knowledge as well as validation of data sources. The benefits of using ontologies include reuse, sharing and portability of knowledge across platforms, and improved maintainability, documentation, maintenance, and reliability. Overall, ontologies lead to a better understanding of a field and to more effective and efficient handling of information in that field. In the field of bioinformatics, for instance, the work on ontologies is recognized as essential in some of the grand challenges of genomics research [1] and there is much international research cooperation for the development of ontologies (e.g. the Gene Ontology (GO) [5] and Open Biomedical Ontologies (OBO) [19]

F. Fages and S. Soliman (Eds.): PPSWR 2005, LNCS 3703, pp. 17–31, 2005.
© Springer-Verlag Berlin Heidelberg 2005

efforts) and the use of ontologies for the Semantic Web (e.g. the EU Network of Excellence REWERSE [23,24]).

Many ontologies have already been developed and many of these ontologies contain overlapping information. Often we would therefore want to be able to use multiple ontologies. For instance, companies may want to use community standard ontologies and use them together with company-specific ontologies. Applications may need to use ontologies from different areas or from different views on one area. Ontology builders may want to use already existing ontologies as the basis for the creation of new ontologies by extending the existing ontologies or by combining knowledge from different smaller ontologies. In each of these cases it is important to know the relationships between the terms in the different ontologies. We say that we align two ontologies when we define the relations between terms in the different ontologies. We merge two ontologies when we, based on the alignment relations between the ontologies, create a new ontology containing the knowledge included in the source ontologies.

Ontology alignment and merging is recognized as an important step in ontology engineering that needs more extensive research (e.g. [20]). Currently, there exist a number of systems that support users in merging or aligning ontologies in the same domain. These systems use different techniques, but it is not clear how well these techniques perform for different types of ontologies. Few comparative evaluations on ontology merging and alignment have been performed [12,13,20] and no tools for supporting these kinds of evaluations exist yet [8].

In this paper we propose a framework for aligning ontologies. We identify different types of strategies (section 3.1) and show how these strategies can be integrated in one framework (section 3.2). Further, we exemplify the use of the framework by describing a system (SAMBO) that is developed according to this framework (section 4). Within this system we have implemented some already existing alignment algorithms as well as some new algorithms. We also show how the framework can be used to combine different strategies and to experiment with these combinations. This is a first step towards defining a framework that can be used for comparative evaluations of alignment and merging strategies. We tested different combinations of alignment algorithms on several bio-ontologies and discuss the results in section 5. In the next section we provide some background on (bio-)ontologies and ontology alignment systems.

2   Background

2.1   Ontologies

Ontologies differ regarding the kind of information they can represent. From a knowledge representation point of view ontologies can have the following components (e.g. [10,26]). Concepts represent sets or classes of entities in a domain. Instances represent the actual entities. They are, however, often not represented in ontologies. Further, there are many types of relations. Finally, axioms represent facts that are always true in the topic area of the ontology. These can be such things as domain restrictions, cardinality restrictions or disjointness restrictions. Depending on which of the components are represented and the kind of information that can be represented, we can distinguish between different kinds of ontologies such as controlled vocabularies, taxonomies, thesauri, data models, frame-based ontologies and knowledge-based ontologies. These different types of ontologies can be represented in a spectrum of representation formalisms ranging from very informal to strictly formal. For instance, some of the most expressive representation formalisms in use for ontologies are description logic-based languages such as DAML+OIL and OWL.

2.2 Bio-ontologies

In this paper we have chosen to use test cases based on bio-ontologies (e.g. [10]). There are several reasons for this. Research in bio-ontologies is recognized as essential in some of the grand challenges of genomics research [1]. The field has also matured enough to develop standardization efforts. An example of this is the organization of the first conference on Standards and Ontologies for Functional Genomics (SOFG) in 2002 and the development of the SOFG resource on ontologies. Further, there exist ontologies that have reached the status of de facto standard and are being used extensively for annotation of databases. Also, OBO was started as an umbrella web address for ontologies for use within the genomics and proteomics domains. Many bio-ontologies are already available via OBO. There are also many overlapping ontologies available in the field.

The ontologies that we use in this paper are GO ontologies, Signal-Ontology (SigO), Medical Subject Headings (MeSH) and the Anatomical Dictionary for the Adult Mouse (MA). The GO Consortium is a joint project which goal is to produce a structured, precisely defined, common and dynamic controlled vocabulary that describes the roles of genes and proteins in all organisms. Currently, there are three independent ontologies publicly available over the Internet: biological process, molecular function and cellular component. The GO ontologies are a de facto standard and many different bio-databases are today annotated with GO terms. The terms in GO are arranged as nodes in a directed acyclic graph, where multiple inheritance is allowed. The purpose of the SigO project is to extract common features of cell signaling in the model organisms, try to understand what cell signaling is and how cell signaling systems can be modeled. SigO is a publicly available controlled vocabulary of the cell signaling system. It is based on the knowledge of the Cell Signaling Networks data source [30] and treats complex knowledge of living cells such as pathways, networks and causal relationships among molecules. The ontology consists of a flow diagram of signal transduction and a conceptual hierarchy of biochemical attributes of signaling molecules. MeSH is a controlled vocabulary produced by the American National Library of Medicine and used for indexing, cataloguing, and searching for biomedical and health-related information and documents. It consists of sets of terms naming descriptors in a hierarchical structure. These descriptors are organized in 15 categories, such as the category for anatomic terms, which is the category we use in the evaluation. MA is cooperating with the Anatomical Dictionary for Mouse Development

(EMAP) to generate an anatomy ontology (controlled vocabulary) covering the entire lifespan of the laboratory mouse. It organizes anatomical structures spatially and functionally, using is-a and part-of relationships.

2.3   Ontology Alignment and Merging Systems

There exist a number of ontology alignment systems that support the user to find inter-ontology relationships. Some of these systems are also ontology merging systems. However, up to date only two comparative evaluations of ontology merge systems have been performed. The EU OntoWeb project [20] evaluated the systems PROMPT [16] based on Protégé (with extension Anchor-PROMPT [17]), Chimaera [14] (described, not evaluated), FCA-Merge [28] and ODEMerge. This evaluation focused on such things as functionality, interoperability and visualization, but did not include tests on the quality of the alignment. In [12,13] PROMPT, Chimaera and a previous version of SAMBO were evaluated in terms of the quality of the alignment as well as the time it takes to align ontologies with these tools. There are other tools such as ArtGen [15], ASCO [11], GLUE [2], HCONE [9], IF-Map [33], iMapper [27], ITTalks [29], QOM [3], and S-Match [7], but these have not appeared in comparative evaluation studies. For the sake of brevity, we do not describe the different systems in detail, but we show a summary of the strategies that are used by the systems in table 1 in the next section.

3   Framework for Ontology Alignment

In this section we introduce a framework for ontology alignment. We describe different strategies for alignment and show they can be integrated in a general framework. Although we focus on alignment, we also briefly show how the framework can be extended to also cover ontology merging.

3.1   Strategies

Different strategies are based on different kinds of knowledge that can be exploited during the alignment process to enhance the effectiveness and efficiency. Some of the approaches use information inherent in the ontologies. Other approaches require the use of external sources. We describe currently used strategies and in table 1 we give an overview of the used strategies per system.

- *Strategies based on linguistic matching.* These approaches make use of textual descriptions of the concepts and relations such as names, synonyms and definitions. The similarity measure between concepts is based on comparisons of the textual descriptions. Simple string matching approaches and information retrieval approaches (e.g. based on frequency counting) may be used. Most systems use this kind of strategies.
- *Structure-based strategies.* These approaches use the structure of the ontologies to provide suggestions. Typically, a graph structure over the concepts is provided through is-a, part-of or other relations. The similarity of concepts

Table 1. Strategies used by alignment systems

	linguistic	structure	constraints	instances	auxiliary
ArtGen	name	parents, children		domain-specific documents	WordNet
ASCO	name, label description	parents, children, siblings, path from root			WordNet
Chimaera	name	parents, children			
FCA-Merge	name			domain-specific documents	
GLUE	name	neighborhood		instances	
HCONE	name	parents, children			WordNet
IF-Map				instances	a reference ontology
iMapper		leaf, non-leaf, children, related node	domain, range	documents	WordNet
ITTalks		parents, children		documents	
(Anchor-) PROMPT	name	direct graphs			
QOM	name label	parents, children	equivalence		
SAMBO	name, synonym	is-a and part-of, descendants and ancestors		documents	WordNet, UMLS
S-Match	label	path from root	semantic relations codified in labels		WordNet

is based on their environment. An environment can be defined in different ways. For instance, using the is-a relation (e.g. [13]) an environment could be defined using the parents (or ancestors) and the children (or descendants) of a concept. Some approaches also use other relations (e.g. [17]).

— *Constraint-based approaches.* In this case the axioms are used to provide suggestions. For instance, knowing that the range and domain of two relations are the same, may be an indication that there is a relationship between the relations. Similarly, when two concepts are both disjoint with a third concept, we may have a similarity between the first two concepts. On their own these approaches may not be sufficient to provide high quality suggestions, but they may complement other approaches to reduce the number of irrelevant suggestions. Constraint-based approaches are currently used by only a few systems.

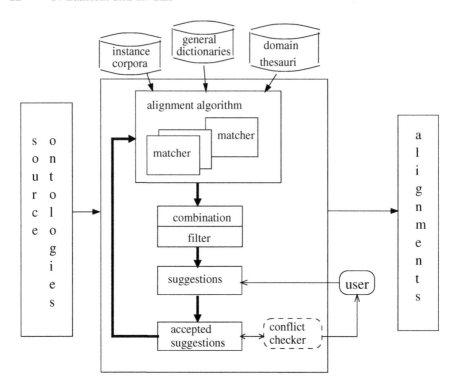

Fig. 1. A general alignment strategy

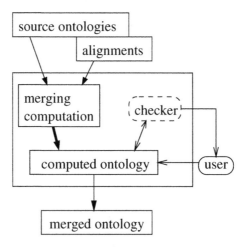

Fig. 2. A general merging algorithm

– *Instance-based strategies.* In some cases instances are available directly or can be obtained. For instance, the entries in biological databases that are annotated with GO terms, can be seen as instances for these GO terms. When instances are available, they may be used in defining similarities between concepts.

- *Use of auxiliary information.* Dictionaries and thesauri representing general or domain knowledge, or intermediate ontologies may be used to enhance the alignment process. They provide external resources to interpret the intended meaning of the concepts and relations in an ontology (e.g. [15]). Also information about previously merged ontologies may be used. Many systems use auxiliary information.
- *Combining different approaches.* The different approaches use different strategies to compute similarity between concepts. Therefore, a combined approach may give better results. Although most systems combine different approaches, not much research is done on the applicability and performance of these combinations.

3.2   Framework

In figure 1 we propose a general alignment framework. An alignment algorithm receives as input two source ontologies. The algorithm can include several matchers. Each matcher utilizes knowledge from one or multiple sources. For instance, a linguistic matcher uses textual descriptions and may use auxiliary information in the form of a general dictionary. The matchers calculate similarities between the concepts and relations from the different source ontologies. Alignment suggestions are then determined by combining and filtering the results generated by one or more matchers. For instance, similarity results from a linguistic matcher and a learning matcher may be combined and the pairs of concepts and relations with a similarity value above a certain threshold are retained as alignment suggestions. By using different matchers and combining them and filtering in different ways we obtain different alignment strategies. The suggestions are presented to the user who accepts or rejects the suggestions. The acceptance and rejection of a suggestion may influence further suggestions. Also, some matchers (e.g. some structural matchers as in [17,13]) require as input already accepted suggestions. Further, a conflict checker is used to avoid conflicts introduced by alignment relationships. The output of the alignment algorithm is a set of alignment relations between concepts and relations from the source ontologies.

Figure 2 shows a simple merging algorithm. A new ontology is computed from the source ontologies and their identified alignment. The checker is used to avoid conflicts as well as to detect unsatisfiable concepts and, if so desired by the user, to remove redundancy.

4   SAMBO

In this section we describe a prototype of SAMBO, an ontology alignment and merging tool implemented according to the framework described in section 3.

4.1   System

The current implementation of SAMBO is a web-based system that helps a user to merge two ontologies into a new ontology with unique names for terms. In this implementation the system supports ontologies in OWL and DAML+OIL formats. After loading the source ontologies, the user can start the alignment process. The system separates the process into two steps: aligning relations and aligning concepts. The second step can be started after the first step is finished. In each step, the user can choose to manually merge terms (i.e. equivalent terms) or introduce is-a relationships in the ontologies, or to have the system propose suggestions. The user can choose to accept or reject the suggestions. Upon an action of the user, the suggestion list is updated. If the user rejects a suggestion where two different terms have the same name, she is required to rename one of the terms. At each point in time the user can view the ontologies represented in trees with the information on which actions have been performed, and she can check how many suggestions there are left for the step. After the user accomplishes the alignment process, the system receives the final alignment list and can be asked to create the new ontology. The system merges the terms in the alignment list, computes the consequences, makes the additional changes that follow from the operations, and finally copies the other terms to the new ontology. Furthermore, SAMBO uses a DIG description logic reasoner (e.g. Racer [25], FaCT [4]) to provide a number of reasoning services. The user can ask the system whether the new ontology is consistent and can ask for information about unsatisfiable concepts and cycles in the ontology.

4.2 Alignment Algorithm

For this implementation of SAMBO we experimented with the combination of already existing strategies as well as some newly implemented strategies.

The *terminological matcher* contains matching algorithms based on the textual descriptions (names and synonyms) of concepts and relations. In the current implementation, the matcher includes two approximate string matching algorithms, n-gram and edit distance, and a linguistic algorithm. A n-gram is a set of n consecutive characters extracted from a string. Similar strings will have a high proportion of n-grams in common. Edit distance is defined as the number of deletions, insertions, or substitutions required to transforming one string into the other. The greater the edit distance, the more different the strings are. The linguistic algorithm computes the similarity of the terms by comparing the lists of words of which the terms are composed. Similar terms have high proportion of words in common in the lists. A porter stemming algorithm is employed to each word. Further, a general thesaurus, WordNet [32], is used to enhance the similarity measure by looking up the hypernym relationships of the pairs of words in WordNet. All these matchers were evaluated in [13]. The terminological matcher outputs similarity values by combining the results from these three algorithms using weights. The similarity between a concept C_1 from the first source ontology and a concept C_2 from the second source ontology is defined as $tsim(C_1, C_2) = \sum_{k=1}^{3} w_k * tsim_k(C_1, C_2)$ where w_k are the weights assigned to the algorithms. If the weights are chosen carefully, this combination can overcome the weaknesses of the individual algorithms. In our experiments we used the weights 0.3, 0.3 and 0.21 for the linguistic algorithm, edit distance and n-gram, respectively.

The *structural matcher* is an iterative algorithm based on the *is-a* and *part-of* hierarchies of the ontologies (table 2). The algorithm requires as input a list of alignment relations and can therefore not be used in isolation. The intuition behind the algorithm is that if two concepts lie in similar positions in the two hierarchies, then probably they are similar. The propagation coefficients indicate how well the similarity of a given alignment propagates to its neighbors, and ranges from 0 to 1. Similarity of identified alignments propagates to their ancestors and descendants, but the effect diminishes with respect to distance, and therefore a maximal distance can be set optionally.

Table 2. The structure-based algorithm

$//MatchSet(O_1, O_2)$ is the set of identified alignment relations.
for each element (c_{1i}, c_{2j}) **in** $MatchSet(O_1, O_2)$
　　for all ancestors c_{1m} **of** c_{1i}
　　　for all ancestors c_{2n} **of** c_{2j}
　　　$//c_p$ is the propagation coefficient for the *is-a/part-whole* relation
　　　$//l(c_{1i}, c_{1m})$ is the length of the path between c_{1i} and c_{1m}
　　　$ssim(c_{1m}, c_{2n}) = \frac{c_p}{l(c_{1i}, c_{1m})} * \frac{c_p}{l(c_{2j}, c_{2n})}$
　　for all descendants c_{1p} **of** c_{1i}
　　　for all descendants c_{2q} **of** c_{2j}
　　　$//c_c$ is the propagation coefficient for the *inverse-is-a/whole-part* relation
　　　$ssim(c_{1p}, c_{2q}) = \frac{c_c}{l(c_{1i}, c_{1p})} * \frac{c_c}{l(c_{2j}, c_{2q})}$

Another strategy is to use *domain knowledge*. We utilize the domain lexicon Unified Medical Language System (UMLS) [31], a repository of biomedical vocabularies. The similarity of two terms in the source ontologies is determined by how they are mapped to terms in UMLS.

We also included a *learning matcher*. We created a corpus containing documents extracted from PubMed [21]. To each term in the source ontologies we assign at most 100 documents, which are the abstracts of the articles retrieved from PubMed using the name of the term as the search term. The similarity value between a concept C_1 in the first source ontology and concept C_2 in the second source ontology is computed as $lsim(C_1, C_2) = [P(C_1|C_2) + P(C_2|C_1)]/2$, where the probability $P(C_1|C_2)$ is estimated to be the fraction of the total number of documents associated with C_2 that are also classified to be associated with C_1, and similarly for $P(C_2|C_1)$. A naive Bayes classifier is applied to classify documents.

The matchers compute similarity values in [0..1], where 1 indicates an expected similarity. The suggestions proposed to the user are those whose similarity values are higher than a threshold (filter in figure 1). The user is given the choice to employ one or several matchers during the alignment process. The suggestions can be determined based on the similarity value from one matcher, or the combination of the similarity values measured by several matchers using weights, $sim(C_1, C_2) = (\sum_{k=1}^{n} w_k * sim_k(C_1, C_2))/n$, where n is the number of combined matchers and sim_k and w_k represent the similarity values and weights, respectively, for the different matchers (combination in figure 1).

5   Evaluation

In the evaluation we compare the quality of the alignment suggestions that are generated by our different matchers and their combinations.

5.1   Test Cases

We created five test cases based on two groups of bio-ontologies. For the first two cases we use a part of a GO ontology together with a part of SigO. Each case was chosen in such a way that there was an overlap between the GO part and the SigO part. The first case, *behavior* (B), contains 57 terms from GO and approximately 10 terms from SigO. The second case, *immune defense* (ID), contains 73 terms from GO and 15 terms from SigO. We used more terms from GO than from SigO because the granularity of GO is higher than the granularity of SigO for these topics.

The other cases are taken from two bio-ontologies that are available from OBO: MeSH (anatomy category) and MA. The two ontologies cover a similar subject domain, anatomy, and are developed independently. The three cases used in our test are: *nose* (containing 15 terms from MeSH and 18 terms from MA), *ear* (containing 39 terms from MeSH and 77 terms from MA), and *eye* (containing 45 terms from MeSH and 112 terms from MA). We translated the ontologies from the GO flat file format to OWL retaining identifiers, names, synonyms, definitions and is-a and part-of relationships.

5.2   Comparison of Matchers

We compare the quality of the suggestions that are generated by the different matchers and their combinations.

In table 3 we present information about the suggestions generated by the individual matchers: terminological, terminological using WordNet, algorithm using domain knowledge (UMLS), and learning. The cases are given in the first column. The second column represents the number of expected suggestions. For instance, in the 'ear' case, there are 29 alignments that are specified by domain experts. This is the minimal set of suggestions that matchers are expected to generate for a perfect recall. This set does not include the inferred suggestions. Inferred suggestions will be inferred by the merging algorithm and we therefore consider them neither as correct nor as wrong suggestions. An example of an inferred suggestion is that incus is a kind of ear ossicle. In this case we know that auditory bone (MA) is the same as ear ossicle (MeSH), and incus is a kind of auditory bone in MA. Then the system should derive that incus is a kind of ear ossicle. The learning matcher (last column) generates 14 suggestions of which

Table 3. Comparison of algorithms

Case	E.Sugs	Terminological	T.+ WordNet	Domain	Learning
B	4	4/4/0	4/4/0	4/4/0	4/4/0
ID	8	6/4/2	6/4/2	4/4/0	5/5/0
nose	7	6/6/0	6/6/0	7/7/0	5/5/0
ear	29	26/26/0	27/27/0	25/25/0	14/14/0
eye	28	21/21/0	22/21/1	21/21/0	19/16/3

14 suggestions are correct and no suggestion is wrong. The structural matcher requires a set of already identified alignments as input, and thus there are no results for the structural matcher in table 3.

The test ontologies provide a lot of synonyms and therefore the quality of the suggestions from the terminological matcher is good. The matcher finds suggestions where the names of terms are completely different, e.g. (inner ear, labyrinth), where inner ear has labyrinth as synonym. The matcher also gives suggestions where the names of terms are slightly different, e.g. (stapes, stape). By using a general dictionary (WordNet), it finds suggestions such as (perilymphatic channel, cochlear aqueduct) where cochlear aqueduct has perilymphatic duct as synonym, and duct is a synonym of channel in WordNet. On the other hand, since endothelium is a kind of epithelium in WordNet, it generates a wrong suggestion (corneal endothelium, corneal epithelium). The quality of the suggestions from the domain matcher is also good. The matcher finds suggestions of which the terms have completely different names and synonyms, or have no synonyms at all, e.g. (external acoustic meatus, ear canal). The matcher works for some terms with slightly different names, e.g. (optic disc, optic disk), which are mapped to the concept optic disc in UMLS, but does not work on others, e.g. (stapes, stape), which are mapped to different concepts in UMLS. The quality of the suggestions from the learning matcher varies in the different ontologies in this evaluation. In the 'ID' case it produces the best result among the matchers. It avoids the wrong suggestions with slightly different names, such as (B cell activation, T Cell Activation). It also finds the suggestion (natural killer cell activation, Natural Killer Cell Response), which is not found by other matchers. However, in the 'eye' case it produces the worst result. In this case all its correct suggestions are also found by the other matchers. The quality of the suggestions from the learning matcher depends on the associated documents retrieved from PubMed. One factor that plays a role in this is that the terms are used as search strings and thus may appear anywhere in the documents. Another factor is that for some concepts only few documents are retrieved.

Table 4 shows the quality of the *extra* suggestions generated by the structural matcher based on the alignment results given by the other matchers, where (1) indicates the terminological algorithm plus WordNet, (2) indicates the domain matcher, (3) is the learning matcher, and (4) indicates the structural matcher. For example, in the 'ID' case and the terminological matcher, the structural matcher generates 17 new suggestions of which no suggestion is correct, one suggestion is wrong, and 16 are inferred suggestions. In this evaluation the structural

Table 4. Structural matcher

Case	(1)+(4)	(2)+(4)	(3)+(4)
B	0/0/0/0	0/0/0/0	0/0/0/0
ID	17/0/1/16	17/0/1/16	0/0/0/0
nose	0/0/0/0	0/0/0/0	0/0/0/0
ear	19/0/2/17	21/0/2/19	2/0/0/2
eye	16/0/0/16	16/0/0/16	20/0/0/16

Table 5. Combination of algorithms

Case	E.Sugs	(1)+(2)	(1)+(3)	(2)+(3)	(1)+(2)+(3)
B	4	4/4/0	4/4/0	4/4/0	4/4/0
ID	8	4/4/0	6/6/0	5/5/0	6/6/0
nose	7	7/7/0	7/7/0	7/7/0	7/7/0
ear	29	28/28/0	28/28/0	28/28/0	29/29/0
eye	30	22/22/0	21/21/0	21/21/0	22/22/0

matcher is actually not needed in the 'B' case as the other algorithms already performed perfectly. In the other cases the structural matcher only returned inferred suggestions and some wrong suggestions. The fact that no more correct suggestions are found may be explained by the fact that the missing suggestions concern concepts in completely different positions in the two hierarchies. For other missing suggestions the concepts have a common ancestor or common descendants, but the ancestor or descendants are too distant for the similarity values to be influenced.

Table 5 presents the quality of the suggestions considering the combination of the different matchers. In table 5 we do not include the structural matcher because of its poor quality. In the evaluation we observe that if we carefully assign the weights for the matchers, the combination can always eliminate the wrong suggestions but still keep all the correct suggestions generated by the respective matchers. In the 'ID' case the combination also contributes a new correct suggestion. For instance, when combining the three matchers we obtain the best results in our experiments for all cases when we assign the weights 1.2, 2.0 and 1.6. Lower weights lead to the loss of correct suggestions and higher weights generate a number of wrong suggestions.

An advantage of using a system like SAMBO is that one can experiment with different (combinations of) strategies and different (combinations of) types of ontologies. For instance, our evaluation gives an indication about what (combinations of) strategies may work well for aligning ontologies with similar properties as our test ontologies. For instance, in our tests the terminological matcher gives good results while the best results are obtained by combining all (1, 2 and 3) matchers. However, when choosing a strategy other factors may also play a role. For instance, the combination strategy is more time consuming than the strategy using only the terminological matcher.

6   Conclusions

In this paper we have shown that different kinds of strategies are used by current alignment systems. We presented a framework for aligning ontologies where these different strategies can be combined. The framework can be used as a basis for building ontology alignment systems. We exemplified this by describing SAMBO, a system that is developed according to the framework and that implements different strategies.

Further, the framework can be used to experiment with combinations of strategies. This is a first step towards a general framework that can be used for comparative evaluations of alignment strategies. In this paper we experimented with different strategies and their combinations and showed results for well-known bio-ontologies.

In the future we will use the framework as a basis for implementing new strategies and test these strategies and their combinations using different types of ontologies. This will result in recommendations on which (combinations of) strategies are well suited for aligning which kinds of ontologies.

Acknowledgements

We thank Vaida Jakonienė and Bo Servenius for comments on the system. We also acknowledge the financial support of the Center for Industrial Information Technology and of the EU Network of Excellence REWERSE (Sixth Framework Programme project 506779).

References

1. Collins F, Green E, Guttmacher A, Guyer M (2003) A vision for the future of genomics research. *Nature* 422:835-847.
2. Doan A, Madhavan J, Domingos P, Halevy A (2003) Ontology matching: A machine learning approach. Staab, Studer (eds) *Handbook on Ontologies in Information Systems*, pp 397-416, Springer.
3. Ehrig M, Staab S (2004) QOM - quick ontology mapping. *Proceedings of 3rd International Semantic Web Conference*, LNCS 3298, pp 683-697.
4. FaCT. http://www.cs.man.ac.uk/~horrocks/FaCT/
5. The Gene Ontology Consortium (2000) Gene Ontology: tool for the unification of biology. *Nature Genetics*, 25(1):25-29. http://www.geneontology.org/.
6. Gómez-Pérez A (1999) Ontological Engineering: A state of the Art. *Expert Update* 2(3):33-43.
7. Giunchiglia. F, Shvaiko P, Yatskevich M (2004) S-Match: an algorithm and an implementation of semantic matching. *Proceedings of the European Semantic Web Symposium*, LNCS 3053, pp 61-75.
8. KnowledgeWeb Consortium (2004) Deliverable 2.2.4 (Specification of a methodology, general criteria, and benchmark suites for benchmarking ontology tools). http://knowledgeweb.semanticweb.org/

9. Kotis K, Vouros GA (2004) The HCONE Approach to Ontology Merging. *The Semantic Web: Research and Applications, First European Semantic Web Symposium*, LNCS 3053, pp 137 - 151.

10. Lambrix P (2004) Ontologies in Bioinformatics and Systems Biology. Chapter 8 in Dubitzky W, Azuaje F (eds.) *Artificial Intelligence Methods and Tools for Systems Biology*, pp 129-146, Springer. ISBN: 1-4020-2859-8.

11. Le BT, Kuntz RD, Gandon F (2004) On ontology matching problem (for building a corporate semantic web in a multi-communities organization). *Proceedings of 6th International Conference on Enterprise Information Systems*.

12. Lambrix P, Edberg A (2003) Evaluation of ontology merging tools in bioinformatics. *Proceedings of the Pacific Symposium on Biocomputing*, pp 589-600.

13. Lambrix P, Tan H (2005) Merging DAML+OIL Ontologies. Barzdins, Caplinskas (eds) *Databases and Information Systems - Selected Papers from the Sixth International Baltic Conference on Databases and Information Systems*, pp 249-258, IOS Press.

14. McGuinness D, Fikes R, Rice J, Wilder S (2000) An Environment for Merging and Testing Large Ontologies. *Proceedings of the Seventh International Conference on Principles of Knowledge Representation and Reasoning*, pp 483-493.

15. Mitra P, Wiederhold G (2002) Resolving terminological heterogeneity in ontologies. *Proceedings of the ECAI Workshop on Ontologies and Semantic Interoperability*.

16. Noy NF, Musen M (2000) PROMPT: Algorithm and Tool for Automated Ontology Merging and Alignment. *Proceedings of Seventeenth National Conference on Artificial Intelligence*, pp 450-455.

17. Noy NF, Musen M (2001) Anchor-PROMPT: Using Non-Local Context for Semantic Matching. *Proceedings of the IJCAI Workshop on Ontologies and Information Sharing*, pp 63-70.

18. Noy NF, Musen M (2002) Evaluating Ontology-Mapping Tools: Requirements and Experience. *Proceedings of the EKAW Workshop on Evaluation of Ontology Tools*.

19. Open Biomedical Ontologies. http://obo.sourceforge.net/

20. OntoWeb Consortium (2002) Deliverables 1.3 (A survey on ontology tools) and 1.4 (A survey on methodologies for developing, maintaining, evaluating and reengineering ontologies). http://www.ontoweb.org

21. PubMed. http://www.ncbi.nlm.nih.gov/entrez/query.fcgi

22. Pinto HS, Gómez-Pérez A, Martins JP (1999) Some Issues on Ontology Integration. *Proceedings of the IJCAI Workshop on Ontologies and Problem-Solving Methods*.

23. REWERSE. Backofen R, Badea M, Burger A, Fages F, Lambrix P, Nutt W, Schroeder M, Soliman S, Will S (2004) State-of-the-art in Bioinformatics. REWERSE Deliverable A2-D1.

24. REWERSE. Backofen R, Badea M, Barahona P, Burger A, Dawelbait G, Doms A, Fages F, Hotaran A, Jakonienė V, Krippahl L, Lambrix P, McLeod K, Möller S, Nutt W, Olsson B, Schroeder M, Soliman S, Tan H, Tilivea D, Will S (2005) Usage of bioinformatics tools and identification of information sources. REWERSE Deliverable A2-D2.

25. Racer. http://www.cs.concordia.ca/~haarslev/racer/

26. Stevens R, Goble C, Bechhofer S (2000) Ontology-based knowledge representation for bioinformatics. *Briefings in Bioinformatics* 1(4):398-414.

27. Su XM, Hakkarainen S, Brasethvik T (2004) Semantic enrichment for improving systems interoperability. *Proceedings of the 2004 ACM Symposium on Applied Computing*, pp 1634-1641.

28. Stumme G, Mädche A (2001) FCA-Merge: Bottom-up merging of ontologies. *Proceedings of the 17th International Joint Conference on Artificial Intelligence*, pp 225-230.
29. Sushama P, Yun P, Timothy F (2002) Using Explicit Information To Map Between Two Ontologies, *Proceedings of the AAMAS 2002 Workshop on Ontologies in Agent Systems*.
30. Takai-Igarashi T, Nadaoka Y, Kaminuma T (1998) A Database for Cell Signaling Networks. *Journal of Computational Biology* 5(4):747-754.
31. UMLS. http://www.nlm.nih.gov/research/umls/about_umls.html
32. WordNet. http://wordnet.princeton.edu/
33. Kalfoglou Y, Schorlemmer M (2003) IF-Map: an ontology mapping method based on information flow theory. *Journal of data semantics*, 1:98-127.

A Revised Architecture for Semantic Web Reasoning

Peter F. Patel-Schneider

Bell Labs Research, Lucent Technologies
pfps@research.bell-labs.com

Abstract. The current architecture for the Semantic Web, with its emphasis on
RDF syntactic and semantic compatability, has severe problems when expressive
Semantic Web languages are incorporated. An architecture less tied to RDF is
proposed. In this architecture different Semantic Web languages can have different syntaxes but must use the same models. This revised architecture provides
significant advantages over the currrent Semantic Web architecture while still remaining true to the vision of the Semantic Web.

1   Introduction

Because the aim of the Semantic Web is to make information on the Web more process-
able by computers, reasoning must be a vital part of the Semantic Web. Initial accounts of
the Semantic Web, in particular, the initial versions of The Resource Description Framework (RDF) [Ora Lassila and Ralph R. Swick, 1999] and its schema extension, the RDF
Schema Specification (RDFS) [Dan Brinkley and R. V. Guha, 2000], were without a
formal semantic account, and thus did not support reasoning.

The current RDF recommendations include both a formal syntax
[Dave Beckett, 2004] and semantics [Hayes, 2004] for RDF and RDFS
[Dan Brinkley and R. V. Guha, 2004]. The W3C Web Ontology Language (OWL)
[Dean *et al.*, 2004] has been given a semantics [Patel-Schneider *et al.*, 2004] that fits
well on top of RDF. This thus appears to put the Semantic Web on a firm semantic
foundation.

However, making OWL an extension of RDF was not without problems. This shows
up in two versions of OWL: OWL DL, which has a different, mostly-compatible semantics from RDF and only extends part of RDF; and OWL Full, which has full compatability with RDF, but does not enjoy the computational benefits of OWL DL.

Extensions beyond OWL to first-order logic are even more problematic. In fact,
an extension of RDF to incorporate all of first-order logic gives rise to paradoxes
[Patel-Schneider, 2005], because a truth predicate is needed to encode first-order logic
in the RDF syntax.

The problem is that RDF is not suitable as a basis for both the syntax *and* semantics
of the Semantic Web. Some way of escaping from the RDF-provided meaning of the
RDF syntax is needed for expressive Semantic Web languages.

2   The Current Semantic Web Architecture

The current architecture of the Semantic Web is based on the well-known Semantic Web
stack described by Tim Berners-Lee in 2000. (See the left-hand side of Figure 1.) This

F. Fages and S. Soliman (Eds.): PPSWR 2005, LNCS 3703, pp. 32–36, 2005.

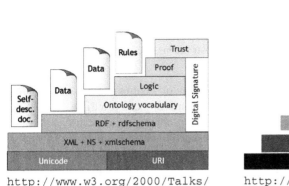
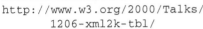
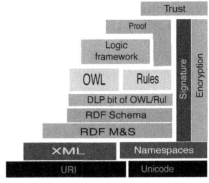

http://www.w3.org/2000/Talks/
1206-xml2k-tbl/

http://www.w3.org/2005/Talks/
0511-keynote-tbl/

Fig. 1. Initial and New Semantic Web architecture

is only a high-level picture of the Semantic Web, and thus leaves out a lot of details. The general impact of this picture, particularly as it has been interpreted during the development of RDF, RDFS, and OWL, is that RDF forms the basis of the Semantic Web, both for syntax and semantics.

All Semantic Web documents thus should have the syntax of RDF, and this syntax should be read as encoding RDF triples [Graham Klyne and Jeremy Carroll, 2004], which form the abstract syntax of RDF. Further, the meaning of these triples should include their RDF model-theoretic meaning [Hayes, 2004], that is, all triples can be thought of a atomic facts.

There are other aspects of the Semantic Web Architecture. These include the use of URI references as identifiers, XML Schema datatypes as datatypes, and the use of model-theoretic entailment as the primary semantic relationship. As well, the Semantic Web was envisioned as a stack of languages, each building directly and completely on the lower languages. Thus the ontology layer built on the RDF layer, and the logic layer built on the ontology layer.

Recent accounts of the Semantic Web architecture (the right-hand side of Figure 1) have split the single stack into two side-by-side extensions of RDF for ontologies and rules. However, this does not change the fundamental role of RDF in the Semantic Web architecture.

3   Problems with the Current Architecture

Unfortunately, RDF is just not adequate for this fundamental place in the Semantic Web architecture. The problems are two-fold, both syntactic and semantic.

On the syntactic side, all RDF has to offer for syntax is triples. It is true that triples are indeed adequate for encoding all sorts of ground information, and thus appear form an adequate syntactic basis. However, encoding complex syntactic information in triples is painful, as shown by the difficult official OWL syntax. For example, the triple encoding of the simple Description Logic construct $(\forall r.C) \sqcap (\geqslant 3\, r)$ is

_:c rdf:type owl:Class . _:c owl:intersectionOf _:l1 . _:l1 rdf:type rdf:List . _:l1 rdf:first _:c1 . _:l1 rdf:rest _:l2 . _:l2 rdf:type rdf:List . _:l2 rdf:first _:c2 . _:l2 rdf:rest rdf:nil . _:c1 rdf:type owl:Restriction . _:c1 owl:onProperty r . _:c1 owl:allValuesFrom C . _:c2 rdf:type owl:Restriction . _:c2 owl:onProperty r . _:c2 owl:minCardinality 3 .

Not only is this ugly and verbose, there is the problem of what to do with various sorts of malformed bits of syntax, such as constructs with missing or extra triples.

The semantic side is even more problematic. The problem arises because each triple in RDF is a fact. This means that all the triples needed to encode syntax are facts, and these facts must be true before they can be inferred, independent of any other meaning that these syntactic facts encode. This requires complex machinery to require that the these facts are true when necessary, and this complex machinery can cause semantic paradoxes.

The semantic paradoxes were avoided in OWL by not requiring that self-referential syntactic structures must be inferrrable. This means that certain kinds of inferences that one might want are not inferrable in OWL, but does mean that OWL has a non-paradoxical semantics. However, this kind of solution is not available for first-order logic with equality, as equality can be used as a substitute for self-reference [Patel-Schneider, 2005].

4   A Revised Architecture for the Semantic Web

The problem is the use of triples as facts that encode syntax. So retaining the use of triples to encode syntax but making them not be facts will indeed eliminate the problem. However, this doesn't make triples any nicer for encoding syntax. As well, the syntax-encoding triples don't mean what they mean in RDF, so treating them as RDF doesn't make sense. This means that RDF tools will not perform correctly on these triples.

A different way to go is to allow different syntaxes for different Semantic Web languages. To fit into the Semantic Web vision, these syntaxes should use IRI references as identifiers and XML Schema datatypes. To fit into the World Wide Web these syntaxes should be XML dialects.

What then unifies the Semantic Web is a common semantic framework. Separate syntaxes for OWL, rule languages like SWRL [Horrocks *et al.*, 2005], and first-order logic including variants like Simple Common Logic (http://www.w3.org/2004/12/rules-ws/paper/103/) can be specified and their semantics given as extra conditions added to the RDF model theory. The new syntaxes can be made full partners in the Semantic Web by giving them MIME types. This does require the use of multiple parsers, but writing parsers is quite easy. To keep the single stack view of the Semantic Web only requires that systems for the higher levels also parse the syntax for the lower levels.

This revised architecture does not really require extra work in writing non-parsing tools, as one might expect. User-interface, reasoning, and other tools for the Semantic Web are of necessity already tailored for each level of the Semantic Web stack. For example, a tool for building RDF knowledge bases is not useful for ontology building in OWL, even though OWL can be written as RDF triples. Separate ontology-building tools like Protege or OilEd are needed for this purpose. Such tools are likely to be easier to write in the revised architecture, as they will not have to worry about the kinds of malformed syntax that are possible when encoding complex syntactical constructs in RDF triples.

Certain reasoning tasks can also be easier in this revised syntax. It has recently (private communication, but should be public shortly) been shown that a source of undecidability in OWL Full is the RDF ability to manipulate the RDF properties that encode OWL syntax.

This multi-syntax architecture has other potential benefits. It is possible to use content negotiation to allow less-capable systems to access approximations of complex information. For example, if an RDFS-only system asks for an OWL ontology it can be given the classification taxonomy of that ontology, as computed by an OWL reasoner, in RDFS form. This gives the RDFS system much better information that it would have if it was simply given the encoding of the syntax of the OWL ontology.

5   Future Directions

It would also be possible to generalize the revised Semantic Web architecture in several ways. One could lift the requirement that systems handle lower levels of the stack, turning the Semantic Web stack into a a collection of languages with a common semantic framework. One could also loosen the requirement of a common semantic framework into simply some sort of semantic compatability. Both these generalizations involve considerable work—in the first to determine whether or not the result would balkanize the Semantic Web and thus reduce its viability, in the second to determine what sorts of semantic compatability are desirable or required.

References

[Dan Brinkley and R. V. Guha, 2000] Resource description framework (RDF) schema specification 1.0. W3C Candidate Recommendation, http://www.w3.org/TR/2000/CR-rdf-schema-20000327, March 2000.

[Dan Brinkley and R. V. Guha, 2004] RDF vocabulary description language 1.0: RDF schema. W3C Recommendation, http://www.w3.org/TR/rdf-schema, 2004.

[Dave Beckett, 2004] RDF/XML syntax specification (revised). W3C Recommendation, http://www.w3.org/TR/rdf-syntax-grammar/, 2004.

[Dean et al., 2004] Mike Dean, Guus Schreiber, Sean Bechhofer, Frank van Harmelen, Jim Hendler, Ian Horrocks, Deborah L. McGuinness, Peter F. Patel-Schneider, and Lynn Andrea Stein. OWL web ontology language: Reference. W3C Recommendation, http://www.w3.org/TR/owl-ref/, 2004.

[Graham Klyne and Jeremy Carroll, 2004] Resource description framework (RDF): Concepts and abstract syntax. W3C Recommendation, http://www.w3.org/TR/rdf-schema, February 2004.

[Hayes, 2004] Patrick Hayes. RDF semantics. W3C Recommendation, http://www.w3.org/TR/rdf-mt/, 2004.

[Horrocks et al., 2005] Ian Horrocks, Peter F. Patel-Schneider, Sean Bechhofer, and Dmitry Tsarkov. OWL Rules: A proposal and prototype implementation. *Journal of Web Semantics*, 2005.

[Ora Lassila and Ralph R. Swick, 1999] Resource description framework (RDF): Model and syntax specification. W3C Recommendation, 22 February 1999, http://www.w3.org/TR/1999/REC-rdf-syntax-19990222/, February 1999.

[Patel-Schneider et al., 2004] Peter F. Patel-Schneider, Patrick Hayes, and Ian Horrocks. OWL web ontology language: Semantics and abstract syntax. W3C Recommendation, http://www.w3.org/TR/owl-semantics/, 2004.

[Patel-Schneider, 2005] Peter F. Patel-Schneider. Building the semantic web tower from rdf straw. In *Proceedings of the Nineteenth International Joint Conference on Artificial Intelligence*. International Joint Committee on Artificial Intelligence, August 2005.

Semantic Web Architecture:
Stack or Two Towers?

Ian Horrocks[1], Bijan Parsia[2], Peter Patel-Schneider[3], and James Hendler[2]

[1] School of Computer Science,
University of Manchester, UK
www.cs.man.ac.uk/~horrocks/
[2] Maryland Information and Network Dynamics Laboratory,
University of Maryland
www.mindswap.org/~bparsia/
[3] Bell Labs Research, Murray Hill, NJ, USA
www.bell-labs.com/user/pfps/

Abstract. We discuss language architecture for the Semantic Web, and in particular different proposals for extending this architecture with a rules component. We argue that an architecture that maximises compatibility with existing languages, in particular RDF and OWL, will benefit the development of the Semantic Web, and still allow for forms of closed world assumption and negation as failure.

Up until recent times it has been widely accepted that the architecture the Semantic Web will be based on a hierarchy of languages, each language both exploiting the features and extending the capabilities of the layers below. This has been famously illustrated in Tim Berners-Lee's "Semantic Web Stack" diagram [3] (see Figure 1).

As a result of the work of the W3C Web Ontology Working Group, the "Ontology" layer has now been instantiated with the Web Ontology Language OWL [2]. Since then, attention has turned to the rules layer, and much effort has been devoted to the design of suitable rules languages. Perhaps influenced by some of this work, recently seen versions of the Semantic Web Stack diagram have illustrated a weakened version of the layering idea, with rules and ontologies (OWL) sitting side by side on top of a layer labelled as the "DLP bit of OWL/Rules" [4] (see Figure 2).

Unfortunately, this modified stack is based on some fundamental misconceptions about the semantic relationships between the various languages. In particular, the modified stack suggests that DLP [7] can be layered on top of RDFS and form a common basis for parallel Rules (presumably intended as Datalog/Logic Programming style rules) and OWL layers. This suggestion is, however, based on incorrect assumptions about the semantics of DLP. In particular, if we want Datalog style closed world semantics for Rules (in order to support Negation as Failure), as is argued by some proponents, then the resulting rules language is only a *syntactic* extension of DLP, and is *not* semantically compatible with DLP—in fact DLP is a subset of Horn rules and has standard First Order semantics.

F. Fages and S. Soliman (Eds.): PPSWR 2005, LNCS 3703, pp. 37–41, 2005.

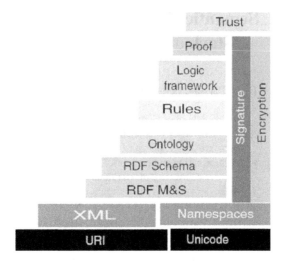

Fig. 1. Semantic Web Stack

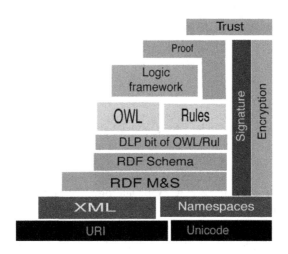

Fig. 2. Latest version of the Semantic Web Stack

Of course it is possible to treat DLP rules as having Datalog semantics (i.e., semantics based on a closed world assumption and Herbrand models [6]). In this case, however, DLP is no longer semantically compatible with OWL and so cannot be situated below OWL in the stack. In fact, when given such a semantics, DLP (and rules languages that extend DLP) are not even semantically compatible with RDF [9]. This is easy to see if we imagine querying an RDF ontology with a more expressive query language, for example one that includes counting or negation (as, for example, SQL). Given an ontology containing only a single RDF triple:

$$\langle \#pat \rangle \langle \#knows \rangle \langle \#jo \rangle.$$

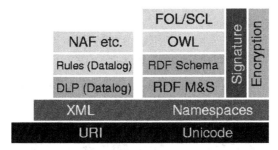

Fig. 3. Semantic Web Stack with Datalog Rules

the answer to a query asking if pat knows exactly one person would be "no" under RDF's open world semantics, but "yes" under the closed world semantics of Datalog.

It is thus more appropriate to view DLP with Datalog semantics as being layered directly on top of the XML layer. Datalog rules, and various extensions such as negation as failure (NAF) would then naturally layer on top of (this version of) DLP. Similarly, OWL and other First Order extensions (such as FOL or SCL [10]) would naturally layer on top of RDFS.[1] It has been suggested that the two different semantics (Datalog and First Order) could be unified in some overarching "Logic Framework", although it is an open research problem as to how this could be done.

This more precise analysis of the semantic relationships between the various languages demonstrates that the Datalog view of DLP and of rules actually leads to a stack like the one illustrated in Figure 1, where the Datalog languages and First Order languages are in two separate towers. The Proof and Trust layers have been omitted, as these are currently rather speculative, as has the overarching "Logic Framework", given that, as mentioned above, there is currently no suggestion as to what kind of logic might instantiate this layer.

An alternative view of DLP is as a subset of First Order Horn clauses (as proposed in [7]). In this case DLP can be seen simply as a subset of OWL (although more useful lightweight OWL subsets could be imagined, e.g., based on the $\mathcal{EL}$ description logic, which covers many important use cases, and for which all key inference problems can be solved in polynomial time [1]). A First Order rules language such as SWRL can then be layered on top of OWL. More expressive languages such as full First Order Logic (First Order Predicate Calculus) would layer naturally on top of SWRL [11].

The resulting stack is illustrated in Figure 1 (the DLP/lightweight OWL subset layer has been omitted, but could be inserted between RDFS and OWL). This language architecture has many attractive features when compared to the one illustrated in Figure 1. On the one hand, rules in this framework extend existing work on both RDFS and OWL, as well as providing a foundation for further extensions within a coherent semantic framework. Features such as closed world assumption and negation as failure (NAF) can be supported by powerful query languages—queries already have a closed world flavour (because distinguished variables can only bind to named individuals), and

---

[1] There is an issue with the meta-level features of RDFS, which has been resolved in OWL by having one language "species" that layers on top of the First Order subset of RDFS (i.e., OWL DL) and another language species that layers on top of the whole of RDFS (i.e., OWL Full).

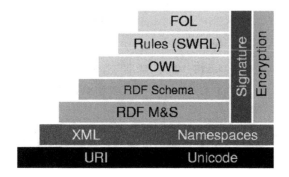

Fig. 4. Semantic Web Stack with First Order Rules

it is natural to extend this with NAF by way of query subtraction (e.g., the answer to the query "faculty(?x) and NAF professor(?x)" can be computed by subtracting the answer to the query "professor(?x)" from the answer to the query "faculty(?x)"). These features are already supported in query languages such as SPARQL [14] and nRQL [8] (the query language implemented in the Racer system). Moreover, recent work on integrating rules with OWL suggests that future versions of this framework could include, e.g., a decidable subset of SWRL, and a principled integration of OWL and Answer Set Programming [5,12,13].

On the other hand, adopting Datalog rules (and DLP with Datalog semantics) would effectively establish *two* Semantic Webs, with little or no semantic interoperability between the rules based Semantic Web and the ontology based Semantic Web, even at the RDF level. These two versions of the Semantic Web would inevitably be in competition with each other, and this would make the Semantic Web much less appealing: new users would be presented with a difficult choice as to which part to choose, and in choosing would sacrifice semantic interoperability with the other part.

References

1. F. Baader, S. Brandt, and C. Lutz. Pushing the $\mathcal{EL}$ envelope. In *Proc. of the 19th Int. Joint Conf. on Artificial Intelligence (IJCAI 2005)*, 2005. To appear.
2. Sean Bechhofer, Frank van Harmelen, Jim Hendler, Ian Horrocks, Deborah L. McGuinness, Peter F. Patel-Schneider, and Lynn Andrea Stein. OWL web ontology language reference. W3C Recommendation, 10 February 2004. Available at http://www.w3.org/TR/owl-ref/.
3. Tim Berners-Lee. WWW past & future, 2003. Available at http://www.w3.org/2003/Talks/0922-rsoc-tbl/.
4. Tim Berners-Lee. Web for real people, 2005. Available at http://www.w3.org/2005/Talks/0511-keynote-tbl/.
5. Thomas Eiter, Thomas Lukasiewicz, Roman Schindlauer, and Hans Tompits. Combining answer set programming with description logics for the semantic web. In *Proc. of the 9th Int. Conf. on Principles of Knowledge Representation and Reasoning (KR 2004)*, pages 141–151. Morgan Kaufmann, Los Altos, 2004.
6. Michael Gelfond and Vladimir Lifschitz. The stable model semantics for logic programming. In *Proceedings of the Fifth International Conference on Logic Programming*, pages 1070–1080. MIT Press, 1988.

7. Benjamin N. Grosof, Ian Horrocks, Raphael Volz, and Stefan Decker. Description logic programs: Combining logic programs with description logic. In *Proc. of the Twelfth International World Wide Web Conference (WWW 2003)*, pages 48–57. ACM, 2003.

8. Volker Haarslev, Ralf Möller, and Michael Wessel. Querying the Semantic Web with Racer+ nRQL. In *Proc. of the KI-2004 Intl. Workshop on Applications of Description Logics (ADL'04)*, 2004.

9. Patrick Hayes. RDF model theory. W3C Recommendation, 10 February 2004. Available at `http://www.w3.org/TR/rdf-mt/`.

10. Patrick Hayes and Christopher Menzel. Simple common logic. In *W3C Workshop on Rule Languages for Interoperability*, 27–28 April 2005. Washington, D.C., USA.

11. Ian Horrocks, Peter F. Patel-Schneider, Harold Boley, Said Tabet, Benjamin Grosof, and Mike Dean. SWRL: A semantic web rule language combining owl and ruleml. W3C Member Submission, 21 May 2004. Available at `http://www.w3.org/Submission/SWRL/`.

12. Boris Motik, Ulrike Sattler, and Rudi Studer. Query answering for OWL-DL with rules. In *Proc. of the 2004 International Semantic Web Conference (ISWC 2004)*, pages 549–563, 2004.

13. Riccardo Rosati. On the decidability and complexity of integrating ontologies and rules. *J. of Web Semantics*, 2005. To appear.

14. SPARQL query language for RDF. W3C Working Draft, October 2004. Available at `http://www.w3.org/TR/rdf-sparql-query/`.

Ten Theses on Logic Languages for the Semantic Web

François Bry[1] and Massimo Marchiori[2]

[1] University of Munich, Germany
http://pms.ifi.lmu.de/
[2] University of Venice, Italy, and W3C
http://www.w3.org/People/Massimo/

Abstract. This articles discusses the logic, or logic-based, languages required for a full deployment of the Semantic Web. It presents ten theses addressing

1. the kinds of logic languages needed,
2. data and data processing,
3. semantics, and
4. engineering and rendering issues.

The views reported about in this article have been presented at the *W3C Workshop on Rule Languages for Interoperability* (27-28 April 2005, Washington, D.C., USA, http://www.w3.org/2004/12/rules-ws/).

1 Languages

Thesis 1 (Diversity). *The Semantic Web requires logic languages of different kinds:*

1. *three kinds of reasoning, or deductive, languages, viz.*
   (a) constructive rules (or views),
   (b) normative rules (or integrity constraints),
   (c) descriptive specifications (or ontologies),
2. *and reactive rules.*

Constructive rules,[1] called 'views' in databases, specify how to derive new data from data already available. Constructive rules typically involve data selection and grouping. Constructive rules are often, but not always, expressed as implications of the form `new-data` ⇐ `query`. Examples of constructive rules are SQL views, Datalog or pure Prolog clauses,[2] and XSLT templates. Queries after XQuery can be seen as constructive rules with intertwined query and new-data parts. CSS rules can also be seen as constructive rules: CSS selectors are a kind of queries, declaration-blocks (or {}-blocks) specify how new, styled, data are

---

[1] The name stresses that consequences from such rules can be drawn in constructive logic, i.e. without relying on excluded middle or refutation.
[2] I.e. Prolog clauses without imperative predicates.

F. Fages and S. Soliman (Eds.): PPSWR 2005, LNCS 3703, pp. 42–49, 2005.

constructed. RDFS semantic rules are further examples of constructive rules. Inference rules[3] used in specifying proof systems, are also constructive rules (*cf.* *infra* Thesis 8).

Normative rules, called 'integrity constraints' in databases, express conditions that data must fulfill, e.g. ISBN numbers uniquely characterize books, and that must be checked when data are updated. Data schemas, especially tree grammars in their various disguises, e.g. DTD, XML Schema, RelaxNG, etc., express normative rules.[4] Normative rules can be expressed as denials and evaluated like constructive rules. A denial is a rule of the form `false` ⇐ `query` where the head `false`, or `error(...)`, etc., denotes a violation of a requirement `req` and the denial's body `query` expresses a negation of this requirement, i.e. `query` ≡ ¬`req`. E.g. the following denial expresses that ISBN numbers uniquely characterize book titles: `error(ISBN)` ⇐ `book(Title1, ISBN)` ∧ `book(Title2, ISBN)` ∧ `Title1` ≠ `Title2`.

Descriptive specifications specify data types and relationships between data types without necessarily referring to actual data. They are used in software specifications, data schemas, and ontologies. They are often expressed in logics[5] corresponding to classical logic fragments with *restricted quantifications* of the forms $\forall x : s\ F[x]$ and $\exists x : s\ F[x]$ restricting the variable x to some sort, class, entity, etc. s. Such quantifications can be expressed in classical logic as $\forall x\ s(x) \Rightarrow F[x]$ and $\exists x\ s(x) \wedge F[x]$, resp. using a conveniently defined unary predicate symbol s.

It is worth noting that, in many cases, the distinction between normative rules (integrity constraints) and descriptive specifications (ontologies) subtly depends on the use. Consider a system of rules expressing some regulation, e.g. under which conditions students are allowed to register for courses. In drawing conclusions from the regulation, or in verifying that it is consistent or non-redundant, the regulation is used as a descriptive specification – certain forms of reasoning such as excluded middle and refutation make sense and might even be indispensable. In verifying that student registrations to courses enforce the regulation, the regulation is used as integrity constraint – excluded middle and refutation do not make sense.[6]

Reactive rules specify how a data store can be modified depending on the current state of the store and, in some languages, on events. Reactive rules commonly have one of the forms `if condition then action` and `on event if condition then action`. Rules of the first kind are called *production rules*,[3] rules of the second, *ECA* (short for *Event-Condition-Action*) *rules*. In produc-

---

[3] E.g. modus ponens: If both A and $A \Rightarrow B$ are provable, then B is provable.

[4] However, variables in grammars differ from logic variables, since different occurrences of a same grammar variable represent different data instances.

[5] E.g. sorted logics and description logics.

[6] One might object that Prolog, or a Prolog-like proof-system, can used for integrity checking, integrity constraints been expressed as denials, and that the proof method of Prolog, SLD resolution, is a refutation method. In fact, as opposed to general resolution, SLD resolution can be re-expressed in constructive logic [8], i.e., without referring to refutation.

tion and ECA rules, `condition` is an (atomic or compound) query to the data store similar to a body of a constructive or normative rule, and `action` is an atomic (i.e. single) or compound update of the data store (typically consisting of insertions, removal, and/or changes in a data item). In an ECA rule, `event` denotes an *event query*, i.e. a query to events received so far. An event query can be atomic, i.e. refer to a single event, or compound, i.e. refer to composite events. In the following, the condition of a production or ECA rule is called *standard query* so as to stress its similarity with the body of a constructive or normative rule.[7]

Thesis 2 (Negation). *Non-monotonic negation[8] is the negation of choice for constructive rules (views), normative rules (integrity constraints), and reactive rules. Monotonic negation may, but must not, be offered in constructive, normative, and reactive rules. Monotonic negation is the negation of choice for descriptive specifications (ontologies).*

Non-monotonic negation, *cf.* [7] for selected articles, is the negation of choice for constructive rules (views) because data constructions depends on both, available and non-available data. Since normative rules can be expressed as constructive rules (*cf. supra* Thesis 1), non-monotonic negation is also the negation of choice for normative rules. Non-monotonic negation is the negation of choice for reactive rules, too, for both 'event queries' (i.e. the `event` parts of ECA rules) and 'standard queries' (i.e. the `condition` parts of production or ECA rules) refer to the presence or absence of data, events resp.

Monotonic negation is the negation of choice for descriptive specifications because descriptive specifications do not refer to actual data, e.g. the flights listed in a time table, but instead to meta-level specifications, e.g. conditions flights must fulfill, the negation needed in descriptive specifications does not have to refer to the absence or non-availability of such data.

Recall (*cf. supra* Thesis 1) that the same rule can be used as a normative specification (integrity constraint) or descriptive specification (ontologie). As a consequence, the choice of a negation semantics, monotonic or non-monotonic, does not necessarily depend on the syntax of negation.

Thesis 3 (Coherency and Inter-Operability). *Inter-operable logic languages of the various kinds should be striven for. Inter-operability is sustained by the following forms of coherency: syntax coherency, rendering coherency, reasoning coherency, and explanation coherency.*

Syntax coherency means that expressions from different languages with similar meanings are expressed similarly. *Rendering coherency* means that expressions from different languages are (visually or verbally) rendered (*cf. infra* Thesis 10) similarly, possibly using the same rendering methods or tools. *Reasoning coherency* means that similar forms of reasoning applied on different languages,

---

[7] [13] further discusses how constructive and reactive rules, called 'passive' and 'active' resp., relate.

[8] The negation used in concluding that flights not mentioned in a time table do not exist.

e.g. for deriving new data using constructive rules, for computing the closure of RDF specifications, or for checking normative rules, are performed using similar reasoners. Reasoning coherency is desirable both for programmers and language design, and implementation. An important aspect of reasoning coherency is to have a common semantics for non-monotonic negation in constructive, normative, and reactive rule languages. *Explanation coherency* means that similar forms of reasoning are explained, by explanation tools, relaying on similar explanation paradigms.

2   Data and Data Processing

Thesis 4 (Data Distribution and Versatility, and Meta-Level Reasoning). *A logic language for the Semantic Web must access data everywhere on the Web; be 'data versatile', i.e. capable of accessing data and meta-data in any common Web Semantic Web format – especially XML, RDF, Topic Maps, and OWL, as well as the formats of Semantic Web logic languages –, and capable of some forms of meta-level reasoning*

There has already been a number of pleas in favour of data versatile query languages, e.g. [19].

Meta-level reasoning poses interesting, but not impossible, challenges. Meta-level reasoning has bad reputation among Computational Logicians, however, conveniently, e.g. constructively, restricted, *cf.* [6] meta-level reasoning is semantically as safe, and practically as useful as higher-order functions in Functional Programming. Note that meta-level reasoning is already present, though in a limited form, on the Semantic Web: RDF Schema, the "RDF Vocabulary Description Language", is itself an RDF Vocabulary for describing terms in an RDF vocabulary.

Thesis 5 (Reasoning Paradigms). *Constructive and normative rules (views and integrity constraints) should be evaluable by both forward chaining[9] and backward chaining[10], backward chaining being the reasoning paradigm of choice. Descriptive specifications (ontologies) call for (non-constructive) reasoning, including excluded middle[11], non-contradiction[12] and refutation[13]. The reasoning paradigms of Semantic Web logic languages should support grouping, aggregation, theory reasoning, and non-monotonic negation.[14]*

On the Web, forward chaining is well-suited only for well-defined and closed sets of Web sites. Queries referring directly, or indirectly (through sub-queries triggered by constructive rules at queried Web sites) to a set of Web sites that

---

[9] Also called bottom-up reasoning.
[10] Also called top-down reasoning.
[11] At least one of A and $\neg A$ is true.
[12] At most one of A and $\neg A$ is true.
[13] If under the assumption A, a contradiction, i.e. B and $\neg B$ for some B, can be derived, then $\neg A$ is proven.
[14] Preferably with a semantics understandable without PhD in Logic!

cannot be statically[15] recognized, cannot be evaluated by forward chaining. Indeed, with such queries, forward chaining would require to compute intermediate results from all possible Web sites.Thus, on the web, backward chaining is the reasoning paradigm of choice for constructive and normative rules.

Theory reasoning, a term coined after Mark Stickel's 'theory resolution' [20], denotes enhancing a general purpose reasoning method with special reasoners where convenient, e.g., reasoning on bank accounts with a basic arithmetic 'theory reasoner' instead of the Peano axioms of Arithmetic.

Thesis 6 (Event Processing). *Event broadcasting is undesirable on the Web. Events can be exchanged between Web sites using a push, or a pull model. Pushed events can be sent as data streams, calling for streamed query evaluation methods. Evaluating event queries, e.g. the event parts of ECA rules, calls for event driven query evaluation methods.*

On the Web, events can not be broadcasted, i.e. indiscriminately sent to all sites, because this would result in too high a traffic. Events can be exchanged on the Web sites via either push, i.e. events are sent by the emitters to specific recipients, or pull methods, i.e. each site publishes the events it emits, together with the event's recipients, on a 'blackboard' which is repeatedly queried by the potential recipient sites. Such queries are called *continuous*. With the push model, event can be sent as 'data streams' [4]. Continuous queries [22,1,17,18], data streams [4], and event queries [5,2] require specific query evaluation methods.

3   Semantics

Thesis 7 (Declarative Semantics). *Logic languages for the Semantic Web, except reactive rule languages, should have declarative semantics defined as 'Tarski-style model theories'.*

Tarski-style models [12], i.e., the models of classical logic, are expressed in terms of so-called 'valuation functions' that are defined recursively on a formula's structure. They make possible to evaluate a formula independently of other formulas. Therefore, they are easy to understand, and they do not require complex operational semantics.[16]

Production and ECA rules amount to *imperative programming*, hence they are inherently not amenable to declarative semantics. However, (1) declarative semantics are possible and desirable for the 'standard query' and 'event query' languages used in production or ECA rules languages, and (2) a formal semantics amenable to reasoning on production and ECA rule programs is possible (and desirable!).

Thesis 8 (Operational Semantics). *The operational semantics of a logic language is conveniently expressed with constructive and normative rules. Back-*

---

[15] I.e. before query evaluation.

[16] Note that most declarative semantics for non-monotonic negation that do not assume stratified, or stratifiable, rules, e.g. the stable [11] and well-founded [10] semantics, do *not* have Tarski-style model theories.

tracking is useful for a fine tuning of proof construction in implementing logic languages.[17]

The operational semantics of a logic language or reasoner is usually and conveniently expressed in terms of inference rules of the form:

$$\frac{\texttt{Premise}_1 \ldots \texttt{Premise}_n}{\texttt{Conclusion}}$$

Inference rules can be seen as constructive rules in a meta-language specifying proofs for formulas of the object-level language. Thus, a constructive rules are subjacent to (the procedural semantics of) *every* rule language and reasoners. This observation has led to successful uses of the run-time system [21] of Prolog or of the Prolog language itself [14] for implementing efficient theorem provers. Normative rules, too, are convenient in specifying the procedural semantics of rule languages and reasoners for expressing constraints on the proof, or search, space. Reactive rule can be convenient in implementing logic languages and reasoners.[18]

4   Engineering and Rendering

Thesis 9 (Language Engineering). *Logic languages for the Semantic Web should be referentially transparent, strongly closed, have Web formats, and modern type systems.*[19] *The specification of abstract machines should be striven for.*

Referential transparency, i.e. within a same declaration scope two occurrences of a same expression have the same meaning, is desirable because it is *the* trait of declarativity. *Closure*, i.e. the data returned by a program are like, e.g. have formats similar to, the data accessed by programs in the same language. *Strong closure* means that the data returned by a program can be further processed by this same program. Strong closure is desirable because it eases structuring programs in sub-programs. *Web formats*, especially XML formats such as RuleML formats, are desirable for rule languages because they eases inter-changing programs on the Web, e.g., for Web services applications. *Abstract data types* and *static type checking* are desirable for Semantic Web reasoning and reactive languages as they are for any other programming languages: *"Well typed programs*

---

[17] Backtracking is however undesirable as a programming concept for high-level logic languages like the logic languages needed on the Semantic Web because it destroys the language's declarativity. The operational paradigm(s) desirable for a Semantic Web logic languages can be equivalently called 'backtracking-free logic programming' or 'set-oriented functional programming'. It is worth noting almost of the query languages proposed for RDF are of this kind.

[18] Since constructive and reactive rule languages can be used in specifying and implementing logic languages and reasoners, some claim that a single language of such a kind would be sufficient for the Semantic Web. This amounts to claiming that only one single, e.g., imperative, programming language could be sufficient for developing software.

[19] I.e., type systems supporting abstract data types and offering static type checking, parametric polymorphism, and modules.

do not go wrong. " [16] *Abstract machines* are desirable because they are essential for wide-spreading languages.

Thesis 10 (Visual and Verbal Rendering). *Logic languages for the Semantic Web should have visual and verbal renderings.*

Declarative languages are especially well-suited to visual rendering and visual rendering is very appealing to potential users of logic languages for the Semantic Web, as the many systems for graphical rendering and/or visualization of business rules amply demonstrate.

Programs used on the Web and Semantic Web should be *verbalizable*, i.e. the rules or formulas they consist of should be expressible in a controlled language [15,9], i.e. in a non-ambiguous language resembling natural language. Rules, e.g. expressing policy specifications and trust, verbalized in a controlled language would considerably help wide-spreading the (verbal as well as non-verbal forms of the) languages they are expressed in.

Acknowledgments. The ideas expressed in this article have been significantly influenced by the research project REWERSE (Reasoning on the Web with Rules and Semantics, http://rewerse.net). The authors thank their colleagues of REWERSE for many fruitful discussions on the subject of this article. This research has been funded by the European Commission and by the Swiss Federal Office for Education and Science within the 6th Framework Programme project REWERSE number 506779 (*cf.* http://rewerse.net).

References

1. Shivnath Babu and Jennifer Widom. Continuous Queries over Data Streams. *SIGMOD Record*, 2001.
2. James Bailey, François Bry, and Paula-Lavinia Pătrânjan. Composite Event Queries for Reactivity on the Web. In *Proc. 14th Int. World Wide Web Conference*, 2005.
3. Lee Brownston, Robert Farrell, Elaine Kant, and Nancy Martin. *Programming Expert Systems in OPS5: An Introduction to Rule-based Programming.* Addison-Wesley, 1985.
4. François Bry, Fatih Coskun, Serap Durmaz, Tim Furche, Dan Olteanu, and Markus Spannagel. The XML Stream Query Processor SPEX. In *Proc. 21st Int. Conf. on Data Engineering (ICDE)*, 2005.
5. Franois Bry and Paula-Lavinia Pătrânjan. Reactivity on the Web: Paradigms and Applications of the Language XChange. In *Proc. 20th Annual ACM Symp. Applied Computing (SAC)*, 2005.
6. Weidong Chen, Michael Kifer, and David Scott Warren. HILOG: A Foundation for Higher-Order Logic Programming. *Jour. of Logic Programming*, 15(3):187–230, 1993.
7. Jürgen Dix, Luís Moniz Pereira, and Teodor C. Przymusinski., editors. *Selected Papers from the Non-Monotonic Extensions of Logic Programming.* LNCS 1216. Springer-Verlag, 1996.
8. K. Doets. *From Logic to Logic Programming.* MIT Press, 1994.

9. Norbert E. Fuchs, Uta Schwertel, and Rolf Schwitter. Attempto Controlled English – Not Just Another Logic Specification Language. In *Proc. 8th Int. Workshop (LOPSTR)*, LNCS 1559. Springer-Verlag, 1999.
10. Allen Van Gelder, Kenneth A. Ross, and John S. Schlipf. The Well-Founded Semantics for General Logic Programs. *Jour. ACM*, 38(3):620–650, 1991.
11. Michael Gelfond and Vladimir Lifschitz. The Stable Model Semantics for Logic Programming. In *Proc. Int. Conf. and Symp. Logic Programming*, 1988.
12. Jerome Keisler. *Handbook of Mathematical Logic*, chapter Fundamentals of Model Theory, pages 47–103. North-Holland, 1989.
13. Rainer Manthey. Active and Passive Rules in Database Systems: How do They Relate. In *Proc. 1st Workshop on Advances in Databases and Information Systems*, 1994.
14. Rainer Manthey and François Bry. SATCHMO: A Theorem Prover Implemented in Prolog,. In *Proc. 9th Conf. on Automated Deduction*, 1988.
15. Massimo Marchiori and Janne Saarela. Query + Metadata + Logic = Metalog. In *Proc. QL '98, The Query Languages Workshop*, 1998. http://www.w3.org/TandS/QL/QL98/.
16. Robin Milner. Fuly Abstract Models of Typed λ-Calculi. *Theoretical Computer Science*, 4(1):1–22, 1977.
17. Benjamin Nguyen, Serge Abiteboul, Gregory Cobena, and Mihai Preda. Monitoring XML Data on the Web. In *Proc. ACM SIGMOD Intl. Conf. on Management of Data*, 2001.
18. Sandeep Pandey and and Soumen Chakrabarti Krithi Ramamritham. Monitoring the Dynamic Web to Respond to Continuous Queries. In *Proc. 12th Int. World Wide Web Conference*, 2003.
19. Jonathan Robie. The Syntactic Web: Syntax and Semantic on the Web. In *Proc. XML Conf. and Exposition*, 2001.
20. Mark E. Stickel. Automated Deduction by Theory Resolution. *Jour. of Automated Reasoning*, 1(4):333–355, 1985.
21. Mark E. Stickel. A Prolog Technology Theorem Prover: Implementation by an Extended Prolog Computer. *Jour. of Automated Reasoning*, 1988.
22. Douglas Terry, David Goldberg, David Nichols, and Brian Oki. Continuous Queries over Append-Only Databases. In *Proc. ACM SIGMOD Int. Conf. on Management of Data*, 1992.

Semantic and Computational Advantages of the Safe Integration of Ontologies and Rules

Riccardo Rosati

Dipartimento di Informatica e Sistemistica,
Università di Roma "La Sapienza",
Via Salaria 113, 00198 Roma, Italy
rosati@dis.uniroma1.it

Abstract. Description Logics (DLs) are playing a central role in ontologies and in the Semantic Web, since they are currently the most used formalisms for building ontologies. Both semantic and computational issues arise when extending DLs with rule-based components. In particular, integrating DLs with nonmonotonic rules requires to properly deal with two semantic discrepancies: (a) DLs are based on the Open World Assumption, while rules are based on (various forms of) Closed World Assumption; (b) The DLs specifically designed for the Semantic Web, i.e., OWL and OWL-DL, are not based on the Unique Name Assumption, while rule-based systems typically adopt the Unique Name Assumption. In this paper we present the following contributions: (1) We define *safe hybrid knowledge bases*, a general formal framework for integrating ontologies and rules, which provides for a clear treatment of the above semantic issues; (2) We present a reasoning algorithm and establish general decidability and complexity results for reasoning in safe hybrid KBs; (3) As a consequence of these general results, we close a problem left open in [18], i.e., decidability of OWL-DL with DL-safe rules.

1 Introduction

The integration of structured knowledge bases (KBs) and rules has recently received considerable attention in the research on ontologies and the Semantic Web (see e.g., [15,1]). Description Logics (DLs) [2] are playing a central role in this field, since they are currently the most used formalisms for building ontologies, and have been proposed as standard languages for the specification of ontologies in the Semantic Web [19].

Practically all the approaches in this field concern the study of description logic knowledge bases augmented with rules expressed in Datalog (and its nonmonotonic extensions). Many semantic and computational problems have emerged in this research area. Among them, we concentrate on the following main issues/goals:

(1) *OWA vs. CWA:* DLs are fragments of first-order logic (FOL), hence their semantics is based on the *Open World Assumption* (OWA) of classical logic, while rules are based on a *Closed World Assumption* (CWA), imposed by the different semantics for logic programming and deductive databases (which formalize various notions of information closure). How to integrate the OWA of DLs and the CWA of rules in a "proper" way? I.e., how to merge monotonic and nonmonotonic components from a semantic viewpoint?

F. Fages and S. Soliman (Eds.): PPSWR 2005, LNCS 3703, pp. 50–64, 2005.
© Springer-Verlag Berlin Heidelberg 2005

(2) *UNA vs. non-UNA:* some DLs, in particular the ones specifically tailored for the Semantic Web, i.e., OWL and OWL-DL, are not based on the *Unique Name Assumption* (UNA) (we recall that the UNA imposes that different terms denote different objects). On the other hand, the standard semantics of Datalog rules is based on the UNA (see e.g. [4] for a discussion on this semantic discrepancy). How to define a non-UNA-based semantics for DLs and rules? and most importantly, is it possible to reason under the non-UNA-based semantics by exploiting standard (i.e., UNA-based) Datalog engines?

(3) *decidability preservation:* as shown by the first studies in this field [16], decidability (and complexity) of reasoning is a crucial issue in systems combining DL KBs and Datalog rules. In fact, in general this combination does not preserve decidability, i.e., starting from a DL KB in which reasoning is decidable and a rule KB in which reasoning is decidable, reasoning in the KB obtained by integrating the two components may not be a decidable problem.

(4) *modularity of reasoning:* can reasoning in DL KBs augmented with rules be performed in a modular way, strongly separating reasoning about the structural component and reasoning about the rule component? This is a very desirable property, since it allows for defining reasoning techniques (and engines) on top of deductive methods (and implemented systems) developed separately for DLs [2] and for Datalog and its nonmonotonic extensions [8].

In this paper, we present an approach which addresses all the above aspects. In particular, we present *safe hybrid KBs*, which extend the framework of r-hybrid KBs presented in [21] to the treatment of KBs interpreted without the UNA. Safe hybrid KBs are constituted of a structural component, which can be expressed in any fragment of FOL (e.g., in a DL), and a relational component, corresponding to a disjunctive Datalog (Datalog$^{\neg\vee}$) program [7]. The way in which the two components interact is restricted to be *safe*. This notion of safe interaction follows (and extends) the ideas proposed in [5,16,18].

We prove that all the above listed goals are reached by safe hybrid KBs. More specifically:

- (1),(2) We show that safe hybrid KBs provide a clear formal treatment of the above semantic issues, i.e., the semantics of safe hybrid KBs does not assume unique names, and accounts for OWA on the structural component, and CWA on the relational component.

- (3) We establish decidability and complexity results for reasoning in safe hybrid KBs, which prove that, under very general conditions, the safe integration of two decidable components preserves decidability of reasoning.

- (4),(2) Our algorithm implies that reasoning in safe hybrid KBs can be done by strongly separating reasoning about the structural component and reasoning about the rule component. Furthermore, our algorithm allows for reasoning under the non-UNA-based semantics by exploiting reasoning methods and systems for standard, UNA-based, disjunctive Datalog.

- Moreover, as a consequence of these general results, we close a problem left open in [18], i.e., decidability of OWL-DL with DL-safe rules.

The paper is structured as follows. In Section 2 we define syntax and semantics of safe hybrid KBs. In Section 3 we study reasoning in safe hybrid KBs: we first define an algorithm for satisfiability of safe hybrid KBs, then address decidability and complexity of reasoning with safe hybrid KBs. We discuss related work in Section 4. Finally, we draw some conclusions in Section 5. Due to space limits, proofs of theorems are omitted in the present version of the paper.

2 Safe Hybrid KBs

In this section we define syntax and semantics of safe hybrid KBs. We introduce a monotonic, first-order semantics and a nonmonotonic semantics based on stable models.

2.1 Syntax

We denote by $\mathcal{L}$ any subset of the language of function-free first-order logic with equality (for example, a description logic language) over an alphabet of predicates $\mathcal{A} = \mathcal{A}_P \cup \mathcal{A}_R$, with $\mathcal{A}_P \cap \mathcal{A}_R = \emptyset$, and an alphabet of constants $\mathcal{C}$. Every $p \in \mathcal{A}_P$ is called a *structural predicate*. We represent the special equality predicate by the binary predicate symbol *equal* (for ease of notation, in the paper we write equality in prefixed notation), and assume that *equal* is a structural predicate, i.e., it belongs to $\mathcal{A}_P$. An *atom* is an expression of the form $r(X)$, where r is a predicate in $\mathcal{A}$ of arity n and X is a n-tuple of variables and constants. If no variable symbol occurs in X, then $r(X)$ is called a *ground atom*.

Definition 1. *A safe hybrid KB $\mathcal{H}$ is a pair $(\mathcal{T}, \mathcal{P})$, where:*

- $\mathcal{T} \subseteq \mathcal{L}$ *and no predicate in $\mathcal{A}_R$ occurs in $\mathcal{T}$. $\mathcal{L}$ is called the* structural language of *$\mathcal{H}$;*
- *$\mathcal{P}$ is a* Datalog$^{\neg\vee}$ *program over the predicate alphabet $\mathcal{A}$ and the alphabet of constants $\mathcal{C}$, i.e., a set of Datalog$^{\neg\vee}$ rules where each rule R has the form*

$$p_1(X_1) \vee \ldots \vee p_n(X_n) \leftarrow$$
$$r_1(Y_1), \ldots, r_m(Y_m), s_1(Z_1), \ldots, s_k(Z_k), not\ u_1(W_1), \ldots, not\ u_h(W_h)$$

such that $n \geq 0$, $m \geq 0$, $k \geq 0$, $h \geq 0$, each $p_i(X_i)$, $r_i(Y_i)$, $s_i(Z_i)$, $u_i(W_i)$ is an atom and:
  - *each p_i is a predicate from $\mathcal{A}$;*
  - *each r_i, u_i is a predicate from $\mathcal{A}_R$;*
  - *each s_i is a predicate from $\mathcal{A}_P$;*
  - *(safeness condition) each variable occurring in R must occur in one of the r_i's.*

If $n = 0$, we call R a constraint. *If, for all $R \in \mathcal{P}$, $n \leq 1$, $\mathcal{P}$ is called a* Datalog$^{\neg}$ *program. If, for all $R \in \mathcal{P}$, $n \leq 1$ and $h = 0$, $\mathcal{P}$ is called a* positive Datalog *program. If there are no occurrences of variable symbols in $\mathcal{P}$, $\mathcal{P}$ is called a* ground *program.*

Informally, $\mathcal{P}$ is a Datalog$^{\neg\vee}$ program with a special safeness condition: in each rule R, each variable occurring in R must occur in a positive atom in the body of R whose predicate is from $\mathcal{A}_R$, i.e., does not occur in $\mathcal{T}$. Notice that such a condition strengthens the standard Datalog range restriction condition on the use of variables in rules.

Thus, the structural component and the rule component share the predicates in $\mathcal{A}_P$ and the constants in $\mathcal{C}$, while the alphabet of predicates $\mathcal{A}_R$ is only used by $\mathcal{P}$.

2.2 Semantics

We now define two semantics for safe hybrid KBs: the first one relies on a first-order logic interpretation of both the structural and the rule component of the safe hybrid KB, while the second semantics provides a nonmonotonic meaning to rules. From now on, unless specified otherwise, we call *interpretation* a first-order interpretation of the predicates in $\mathcal{A}$ and the constants in $\mathcal{C}$. The notion of satisfaction of a first-order sentence (or a first-order theory) in a first-order interpretation is the standard one in first-order logic.

First-Order Semantics. The first-order semantics of a safe hybrid KB consists of a classical first-order interpretation not only of the structural component, but also of the rule component of the safe hybrid KB. Formally, let R be the following Datalog$^{\neg\vee}$ rule:

$$R = p_1(X_1, c_1) \vee \ldots \vee p_n(X_n, c_n) \leftarrow r_1(Y_1, d_1), \ldots, r_m(Y_m, d_m),$$
$$s_1(Z_1, e_1), \ldots, s_k(Z_k, e_k), \tag{1}$$
$$not\ u_1(W_1, f_1), \ldots, not\ u_h(W_h, f_h)$$

where each X_i, Y_i, Z_i, W_i is a set of variables and each c_i, d_i, e_i, f_i is a set of constants. Then, $FO(R)$ is the first-order sentence

$$\forall \overline{x}_1, \ldots, \overline{x}_n, \overline{y}_1, \ldots, \overline{y}_m, \overline{z}_1, \ldots, \overline{z}_k, \overline{w}_1, \ldots, \overline{w}_h.$$
$$r_1(\overline{y}_1, d_1) \wedge \ldots \wedge r_m(\overline{y}_m, d_m) \wedge s_1(\overline{z}_1, e_1) \wedge \ldots \wedge s_k(\overline{z}_k, e_k) \wedge$$
$$\neg u_1(\overline{w}_1, f_1) \wedge \ldots \wedge \neg u_h(\overline{w}_h, f_h) \rightarrow p_1(\overline{x}_1, c_1) \vee \ldots \vee p_n(\overline{x}_n, c_n)$$

Given a Datalog$^{\neg\vee}$ program $\mathcal{P}$, $FO(\mathcal{P})$ is the set of first-order sentences $\{FO(R) \mid R \in \mathcal{P}\}$.

A *FOL-model* of a safe hybrid KB $\mathcal{H}$ is an interpretation $\mathcal{I}$ such that $\mathcal{I}$ satisfies $\mathcal{T} \cup FO(\mathcal{P})$. $\mathcal{H}$ is called *FOL-satisfiable* if it has at least a FOL-model.

Finally, we define skeptical entailment under the FOL semantics. A sentence $\varphi \in \mathcal{L}$ is *FOL-entailed* by $\mathcal{H}$, denoted by $\mathcal{H} \models_{FOL} \varphi$ iff, for each FOL-model $\mathcal{I}$ of $\mathcal{H}$, $\mathcal{I}$ satisfies φ.

Notice that the above first-order semantics of rules does not distinguish between negated atoms in the body and disjunction in the head of rules: e.g., according to such semantics, the rules $A \leftarrow B, not\ C$ and $A \vee C \leftarrow B$ have the same meaning.

Nonmonotonic Semantics. An alternative semantics to safe hybrid KBs is based on a nonmonotonic interpretation of the rule component, according to the notion of *stable model* [10]. This is the semantics commonly adopted in Disjunctive Logic Programming (DLP) and in Disjunctive Datalog [7]. We now formalize such a semantics in the framework of safe hybrid KBs.

Given an interpretation $\mathcal{I}$, we denote by $\mathcal{I}_R$ the projection of $\mathcal{I}$ to $\mathcal{A}_R$ and $\mathcal{C}$, i.e., $\mathcal{I}_R$ is obtained from $\mathcal{I}$ by restricting it to the interpretation of the predicates in $\mathcal{A}_R$ and the constants in $\mathcal{C}$. Analogously, we denote by $\mathcal{I}_P$ the projection of $\mathcal{I}$ to $\mathcal{A}_P$ and $\mathcal{C}$, and denote $\mathcal{I}$ as $\mathcal{I}_P \cup \mathcal{I}_R$.

The *ground instantiation of $\mathcal{P}$ with respect to $\mathcal{C}$*, denoted by $gr(\mathcal{P}, \mathcal{C})$, is the program obtained from $\mathcal{P}$ by replacing every rule R in $\mathcal{P}$ with the set of rules obtained by applying all possible substitutions of variables in R with constants in $\mathcal{C}$.

Given an interpretation $\mathcal{I}$ of an alphabet of predicates $\mathcal{A}' \subset \mathcal{A}$ and the constants $\mathcal{C}$, and a ground program $\mathcal{P}_g$ over the predicates in $\mathcal{A}$, the *projection of $\mathcal{P}_g$ with respect to* $\mathcal{I}$, denoted by $\Pi(\mathcal{P}_g, \mathcal{I})$, is the ground program obtained from $\mathcal{P}_g$ as follows. For each rule $R \in \mathcal{P}_g$:

- delete R if there exists an atom $r(t)$ in the head of R such that $r \in \mathcal{A}'$ and $t^{\mathcal{I}} \in r^{\mathcal{I}}$;
- delete each atom $r(t)$ in the head of R such that $r \in \mathcal{A}'$ and $t^{\mathcal{I}} \notin r^{\mathcal{I}}$;
- delete R if there exists an atom $r(t)$ in the body of R such that $r \in \mathcal{A}'$ and $t^{\mathcal{I}} \notin r^{\mathcal{I}}$;
- delete each atom $r(t)$ in the body of R such that $r \in \mathcal{A}'$ and $t^{\mathcal{I}} \in r^{\mathcal{I}}$;

Informally, the projection of $\mathcal{P}_g$ with respect to $\mathcal{I}$ corresponds to evaluating $\mathcal{P}_g$ with respect to $\mathcal{I}$, thus eliminating from $\mathcal{P}_g$ every atom whose predicate is interpreted in $\mathcal{I}$. Thus, when $\mathcal{A}' = \mathcal{A}_P$, all occurrences of structural predicates are eliminated in the projection of $\mathcal{P}_g$ with respect to $\mathcal{I}$, according to the evaluation in $\mathcal{I}$ of the atoms with structural predicates occurring in $\mathcal{P}_g$.

Then, we introduce the notions of minimal model and stable model of a Datalog$^{\neg\vee}$ program where the UNA is not adopted.[1] Given two interpretations $\mathcal{I}_1$, $\mathcal{I}_2$ of the set of predicates $\mathcal{A}$ and the set of constants $\mathcal{C}$, we write $\mathcal{I}_1 \subset_{\mathcal{A},\mathcal{C}} \mathcal{I}_2$ if (i) for each $p \in \mathcal{A}$ and for each tuple t of constants from $\mathcal{C}$, if $t^{\mathcal{I}_1} \in p^{\mathcal{I}_1}$ then $t^{\mathcal{I}_2} \in p^{\mathcal{I}_2}$, and (ii) there exist $p \in \mathcal{A}$ and tuple t of constants from $\mathcal{C}$ such that $t^{\mathcal{I}_1} \notin p^{\mathcal{I}_1}$ and $t^{\mathcal{I}_2} \in p^{\mathcal{I}_2}$.

Given a positive ground Datalog$^{\neg\vee}$ program $\mathcal{P}$ over an alphabet of predicates $\mathcal{A}_R$ and an interpretation $\mathcal{I}$, we say that $\mathcal{I}$ is a *minimal model* of $\mathcal{P}$ if $\mathcal{I}$ satisfies $FO(\mathcal{P})$ and there is no interpretation $\mathcal{I}'$ such that $\mathcal{I}'$ satisfies $FO(\mathcal{P})$ and $\mathcal{I}' \subset_{\mathcal{A}_R,\mathcal{C}} \mathcal{I}$.

Given a ground Datalog$^{\neg\vee}$ program $\mathcal{P}$ and an interpretation $\mathcal{I}$ for $\mathcal{P}$, the *GL-reduct* [10] of $\mathcal{P}$ with respect to $\mathcal{I}$, denoted by $GL(\mathcal{P}, \mathcal{I})$, is the positive ground program obtained from $\mathcal{P}$ as follows. For each rule $R \in \mathcal{P}$: (i) delete R if there exists a negated atom $not\ r(t)$ in the body of R such that $t^{\mathcal{I}} \in r^{\mathcal{I}}$; (ii) delete each negated atom $not\ r(t)$ in the body of R such that $t^{\mathcal{I}} \notin r^{\mathcal{I}}$.

Given a ground Datalog$^{\neg\vee}$ program $\mathcal{P}$ and an interpretation $\mathcal{I}$, $\mathcal{I}$ is a *stable model* for $\mathcal{P}$ iff $\mathcal{I}$ is a minimal model of $GL(\mathcal{P}, \mathcal{I})$.

Given a safe hybrid KB $\mathcal{H} = (\mathcal{T}, \mathcal{P})$, we say that an interpretation $\mathcal{I}$ is a *NM-model* for $\mathcal{H}$ if the following conditions hold: (i) $\mathcal{I}_P$ satisfies $\mathcal{T}$; (ii) $\mathcal{I}_R$ is a stable model for $\Pi(gr(\mathcal{P}, \mathcal{C}), \mathcal{I}_P)$. $\mathcal{H}$ is called *NM-satisfiable* (or simply *satisfiable*) if $\mathcal{H}$ has at least a NM-model.

Finally, we define skeptical entailment in safe hybrid KBs under the nonmonotonic semantics, which is analogous to the previous notion of entailment under the first-order semantics. We say that a sentence $\varphi \in \mathcal{L}$ is *NM-entailed* by $\mathcal{H}$, denoted by $\mathcal{H} \models_{NM} \varphi$ iff, for each NM-model $\mathcal{I}$ of $\mathcal{H}$, $\mathcal{I}$ satisfies φ.

In other words, the nonmonotonic semantics for a safe hybrid KB $\mathcal{H} = (\mathcal{T}, \mathcal{P})$ is obtained in the following way. Take a first-order interpretation $\mathcal{I} = \mathcal{I}_P \cup \mathcal{I}_R$ such that $\mathcal{I}_P$ satisfies $\mathcal{T}$; then, evaluate $\mathcal{P}$ in $\mathcal{I}_P$, obtaining the program $\Pi(gr(\mathcal{P}, \mathcal{C}), \mathcal{I}_P)$; if $\mathcal{I}_R$ represents a stable model for such a program, then $\mathcal{I}$ is a NM-model for $\mathcal{H}$.

---

[1] Observe that the notions of minimal model and stable model presented here slightly differs from the standard ones for Datalog$^{\neg\vee}$, since they are expressed in a more general framework in which unique names are not assumed. Consequently, the interpretation of constants must be considered in the definition of minimal and stable model.

It can be shown that satisfiability of safe hybrid KBs under the first-order semantics can be reduced to satisfiability under the nonmonotonic semantics (due to space limits, we are not able to provide details about this aspect in the paper). Therefore, in the rest of the paper, we study safe hybrid KBs under the nonmonotonic semantics. In particular, when we speak about satisfiability of safe hybrid KBs we always mean satisfiability under the nonmonotonic semantics.

OWA vs. CWA. We now briefly comment on how the OWA of the structural part and the CWA of the relational part coexist in safe hybrid KBs.

The key point is the fact that, in safe hybrid KBs, structural predicates and relational predicates are interpreted in a different way. More precisely, the semantics of the relational part is defined starting from a given interpretation of the structural component: given an interpretation $\mathcal{I}$ of $\mathcal{T}$, we compute the stable models of the projection of $\mathcal{P}_g$ with respect to $\mathcal{I}$. In this way, it is possible to interpret relational predicates under a CWA (actually, the stable model semantics), while keeping the interpretation of structural predicates open, i.e., based on the classical FOL semantics.

Example 1. Let $\mathcal{H}$ be the safe hybrid KB where the following structural component $\mathcal{T}$ defines an ontology about persons:

$$\forall x.PERSON(x) \rightarrow \exists y.FATHER(y,x) \wedge MALE(y)$$
$$\forall x.MALE(x) \rightarrow PERSON(x)$$
$$\forall x.FEMALE(x) \rightarrow PERSON(x)$$
$$\forall x.FEMALE(x) \rightarrow \neg MALE(x)$$
$$MALE(Bob)$$
$$PERSON(Mary)$$
$$PERSON(Paul)$$

and the rule component $\mathcal{P}$ defines nonmonotonic rules about students, as follows:

$$boy(X) \leftarrow enrolled(X,c1), PERSON(X), not\ girl(X)\ [R1]$$
$$girl(X) \leftarrow enrolled(X,c2), PERSON(X)\ [R2]$$
$$boy(X) \vee girl(X) \leftarrow enrolled(X,c3), PERSON(X)\ [R3]$$
$$FEMALE(X) \leftarrow girl(X)\ [R4]$$
$$MALE(X) \leftarrow boy(X)\ [R5]$$
$$enrolled(Paul,c1)$$
$$enrolled(Mary,c1)$$
$$enrolled(Mary,c2)$$
$$enrolled(Bob,c3)$$

It can be easily verified that all *NM*-models for $\mathcal{H}$ satisfy the following ground atoms:

- *boy(Paul)* (since rule R1 is always applicable for $X = Paul$ and R1 acts like a *default rule*, which can be read as follows: if X is a person enrolled in course $c1$, then X is a boy, unless we know for sure that X is a girl)
- *girl(Mary)* (since rule R2 is always applicable for $X = Mary$)
- *boy(Bob)* (since rule R3 is always applicable for $X = Bob$, and, by rule R4, the conclusion *girl(Bob)* is inconsistent with $\mathcal{T}$)

– *MALE*(*Paul*) (due to rule R5)
– *FEMALE*(*Mary*) (due to rule R4)

Notice that $\mathcal{H} \models_{NM} FEMALE(Mary)$, while $\mathcal{T} \not\models_{FOL} FEMALE(Mary)$. In other words, adding a rule component has indeed an effect on the conclusions one can draw about structural predicates. Such an effect also holds under the first-order semantics of safe hybrid KBS, since it can be immediately verified that in this case $\mathcal{H} \models_{FOL}$ *FEMALE*(*Mary*). □

Among other things, the above example shows that, in safe hybrid KBs, the information flow is bidirectional: not only the structural component constrains the forms of the stable models of the rule component (through the structural predicates in the body of the rules), but also vice versa, since the rule component imposes constraints that the models of the structural components must satisfy. Hence, the rule component has an effect on the conclusions that can be drawn from the structural component, since it filters out those models $\mathcal{I}$ of the structural component for which the program $\Pi(gr(\mathcal{P}, \mathcal{C}), \mathcal{I})$ has no stable models.

UNA vs. Non-UNA. The semantic issue concerning the UNA is treated in safe hybrid KBs in the following way:

– The equality predicate is a structural predicate, therefore its semantics is "under control" of the structural KB, and is interpreted under the classical FOL semantics. In particular, equality is not involved in the computation of stable models, since stable models of the relational part are defined based only on a particular interpretation of the equality predicate;
– Nevertheless, new equalities may be imposed by the relational component (just like any other structural predicate), since rules may have equality atoms in the head.

Example 2. Let $\mathcal{H} = (\mathcal{T}, \mathcal{P})$ where $\mathcal{P}$ is the program constituted by the fact $r(a, b)$ and the rule $equal(X, Y) \leftarrow r(X, Y)$, and suppose $\mathcal{T} \cup \{equal(a, b)\}$ is satisfiable. Then, $\mathcal{H}$ is satisfiable, and $equal(a, b)$ holds in every model for $\mathcal{H}$. Indeed, the effect of the relational component is to eliminate from the set of models of $\mathcal{H}$ all the interpretations $\mathcal{I}$ of the structural predicates in which $a^{\mathcal{I}} \neq b^{\mathcal{I}}$, since for such interpretations the projection of $\mathcal{P}_g$ with respect to $\mathcal{I}$ is a program that has no stable models. □

3   Reasoning in Safe Hybrid KBs

We now study satisfiability in safe hybrid KBs, i.e., the basic reasoning task in this framework (entailment can be easily reduced to unsatisfiability). We first define an algorithm for deciding satisfiability of safe hybrid KBs, and prove its correctness; Then, based on such an algorithm, we analyze decidability and complexity of reasoning in safe hybrid KBs; Finally, we prove decidability of OWL-DL with DL-safe rules.

Algorithm. We start by providing some preliminary definitions. First, we introduce the notion of *rectification* of a Datalog$^{\neg \vee}$ program [6], which will be needed in the algorithm to properly handle the effects of the non-UNA-based semantics of the structural component on the relational component.

Definition 2. *Let R be a Datalog$^{\neg\vee}$ rule. We denote by rectify(R) the Datalog$^{\neg\vee}$ rule obtained from R as follows:*

1. *for each variable X which occurs $n \geq 2$ times in R, and for each $i \in \{1, \ldots, n\}$, replace the i-th occurrence in R of the variable X with the new variable symbol X^i;*
2. *for each variable X which occurs $n \geq 2$ times in R, and for each $i \in \{2, \ldots, n\}$, add the atom equal(X^{i-1}, X^i) to the body of the rule.*
3. *for each constant c occurring in R and not occurring within the predicate equal, replace every occurrence of c with the new variable symbol X^c, and add the atom equal(X^c, c) to the body of the rule.*

Given a Datalog$^{\neg\vee}$ program $\mathcal{P}$, we denote by rectify$(\mathcal{P})$ the program rectify$(\mathcal{P}) = \bigcup_{R \in \mathcal{P}}$ rectify(R).

Then, we introduce a notion of grounding of a relational component of a safe hybrid KB. Given a Datalog$^{\neg\vee}$ program $\mathcal{P}$, we denote by $C_\mathcal{P}$ the set of constant symbols occurring in $\mathcal{P}$, and denote by $\mathcal{A}_P/\mathcal{P}$ the set of predicates from $\mathcal{A}_P$ occurring in $\mathcal{P}$. We assume that $\mathcal{A}_P$ always contains the equality predicate, even if such a predicate does not actually occur in $\mathcal{P}$.

Definition 3. *Let $\mathcal{H} = (\mathcal{T}, \mathcal{P})$ be a safe hybrid KB. The grounding of the structural predicates in $\mathcal{P}$, denoted by $gr_p(\mathcal{P})$ is the set of ground atoms*

$$\{m(t) \mid m \in \mathcal{A}_P/\mathcal{P} \text{ and } m \text{ has arity } k \text{ and } t \text{ is a } k\text{-tuple of constants of } C_\mathcal{P}\}$$

The idea behind the above definition is that, in the case of safe hybrid KBs, $gr_p(\mathcal{P})$ identifies the set of *all* the relevant instantiations of the predicates in $\mathcal{A}_P$ needed to decide satisfiability of the rule component of the safe hybrid KB $\mathcal{H}$: In fact, due to the safeness condition in the program rules, it turns out that we can restrict the grounding of the rules only to the instantiations which substitute each variable with a symbol in $C_\mathcal{P}$ (notice that, since we assume that $\mathcal{A}_P/\mathcal{P}$ always contains the equality predicate, $gr_p(\mathcal{P})$ always contains all the atoms representing the equality between two constants in $C_\mathcal{P}$).

Thus, we can divide the set of all interpretations for $\mathcal{T}$ into equivalence classes, based on the way in which such interpretations evaluate the ground atoms in $gr_p(\mathcal{P})$. Each such equivalence class can be represented by a partition (G_P, G_N) of $gr_p(\mathcal{P})$. More precisely, G_P is the set of ground atoms in $gr_p(\mathcal{P})$ satisfied by the interpretations in the equivalence class, while G_N is the set of atoms in $gr_p(\mathcal{P})$ which are not satisfied by such interpretations.

However, not all the partitions of $gr_p(\mathcal{P})$ represent a guess of the ground atoms that is compatible with the KB $\mathcal{T}$. The following definition formalizes the notion of consistency of a partition of ground atoms with respect to $\mathcal{T}$.

Definition 4. *A partition (G_P, G_N) of $gr_p(\mathcal{P})$ is consistent with $\mathcal{T}$ iff the first-order theory $\mathcal{T} \cup \{m(t) \mid m(t) \in G_P\} \cup \{\neg m(t) \mid m(t) \in G_N\}$ is satisfiable.*

Informally, the above definition indicates that, if a partition is consistent with $\mathcal{T}$, then there exists at least one interpretation that both satisfies $\mathcal{T}$ and evaluates the atoms in $gr_p(\mathcal{P})$ according to the partition (G_P, G_N).

Algorithm Safe-Hybrid-Sat($\mathcal{H}$)
Input: safe hybrid KB $\mathcal{H} = (\mathcal{T}, \mathcal{P})$
Output: true if $\mathcal{H}$ is satisfiable, false otherwise
begin
    if there exists partition (G_P, G_N) of $gr_p(\mathcal{P})$
    such that
        (a) (G_P, G_N) is consistent with $\mathcal{T}$ **and**
        (b) $rectify(\mathcal{P}(G_P, G_N))$ has a standard stable model
    then return true
    else return false
end

Fig. 1. The algorithm Safe-Hybrid-Sat

Finally, we denote by $\mathcal{P}(G_P, G_N)$ the Datalog$^{\neg\vee}$ program

$$\mathcal{P}(G_P, G_N) = \mathcal{P} \cup G_P \cup \{\leftarrow r(t) \mid r(t) \in G_N\}$$

In Figure 1 we report the algorithm Safe-Hybrid-Sat for deciding satisfiability of a safe hybrid KB $\mathcal{H} = (\mathcal{T}, \mathcal{P})$. The algorithm formalizes the idea that a way to decide satisfiability of $\mathcal{H}$ is to look for a partition of $gr_p(\mathcal{P})$ that is consistent with $\mathcal{T}$ and such that the program $rectify(\mathcal{P}(G_P, G_N))$ has a *standard* stable model, i.e., a stable model according to the standard, UNA-based semantics of Datalog$^{\neg\vee}$ [7].

More precisely, we reduce reasoning in the absence of UNA to reasoning in the presence of UNA in the relational component as follows:

– a partition (G_P, G_N) of $gr_p(\mathcal{P})$ fixes an interpretation of the equality predicate for the constants in $\mathcal{C}_\mathcal{P}$ (since all ground atoms stating equality between constants in $\mathcal{C}_\mathcal{P}$ belong to $gr_p(\mathcal{P})$);
– now, the program $\mathcal{P}(G_P, G_N)$ takes into account such an interpretation of equality by adding the corresponding facts and constraints to $\mathcal{P}$. However, to correctly model the absence of the UNA, each rule must be transformed (rectified) as in Definition 2. In fact, it can be shown [6] that the transformation of a rule produced by the rectification precisely corresponds to allow for unification of terms via the equality predicate under UNA, thus simulating the absence of the UNA in the actual semantics for safe hybrid KBs.

Example 3. Let $\mathcal{H} = (\mathcal{T}, \mathcal{P})$ where $\mathcal{P}$ is the following program:

$$\begin{aligned}
equal(X, Y) &\leftarrow r(X, Y), r(X, Z)\\
t(X) &\leftarrow s(X, X)\\
r(a, b)&\\
r(a, c)&\\
s(b, c)&
\end{aligned}$$

and for simplicity suppose that $\mathcal{T}$ is the empty theory. Let G_P, G_N be as follows:

$$G_P = \{equal(b, c), equal(c, b), equal(a, a), equal(b, b), equal(c, c)\}$$
$$G_N = \{equal(a, c), equal(c, a), equal(a, b), equal(b, a)\}$$

First, (G_P, G_N) is consistent with $\mathcal{T}$, since it does not violate the semantics of *equal* (i.e., the fact that *equal* is an equivalence relation). Then, $rectify(\mathcal{P}(G_P, G_N))$ is the following program:

$$equal(X^1, Y^1) \leftarrow r(X^2, Y^2), r(X^3, Z), equal(X^1, X^2), equal(X^2, X^3), equal(Y^1, Y^2)$$
$$t(X^1) \leftarrow s(X^2, X^3), equal(X^1, X^2), equal(X^2, X^3)$$
$$r(X^a, X^b) \leftarrow equal(X^a, a), equal(X^b, b)$$
$$r(X^a, X^c) \leftarrow equal(X^a, a), equal(X^c, c)$$
$$s(X^b, X^c) \leftarrow equal(X^b, b), equal(X^c, c)$$
$$\leftarrow equal(a, c)$$
$$\leftarrow equal(c, a)$$
$$\leftarrow equal(a, b)$$
$$\leftarrow equal(b, a)$$

$$equal(b, c)$$
$$equal(c, b)$$
$$equal(a, a)$$
$$equal(b, b)$$
$$equal(c, c)$$

It is immediate to verify that, for instance, the facts $s(b, b)$, $t(b)$, $s(c, c)$, $t(c)$ belong to the only standard stable model of $rectify(\mathcal{P}(G_P, G_N))$. It is also easy to see that the only other guess (G_P, G_N) that is both satisfiable at step (a) and at step (b) of the algorithm is the one in which $G_N = \emptyset$, i.e., the three constants are assumed as equal. In fact, every other guess is either unsatisfiable at step (a) of the algorithm (since it violates the fact that *equal* must be an equivalence relation) or is such that there are no stable models for $rectify(\mathcal{P}(G_P, G_N))$ (since $equal(b, c) \in G_N$ and therefore the first rule of the program is violated). $\square$

The algorithm Safe-Hybrid-Sat is sound and complete with respect to the non-monotonic semantics defined in Section 2.2, as stated by the following theorem.

Theorem 1. *Let* $\mathcal{H} = (\mathcal{T}, \mathcal{P})$ *be a safe hybrid KB. Then,* $\mathcal{H}$ *is satisfiable iff Safe-Hybrid-Sat($\mathcal{H}$) returns* true.

We remark that the algorithm reduces reasoning in safe hybrid KBs to standard reasoning in the structural component (step (a)) and to standard reasoning in Datalog$^{\neg\vee}$ (step (b)). Therefore, not only the algorithm is modular, but also it allows for reusing deductive techniques (and implemented systems) developed for the structural language and for Datalog$^{\neg\vee}$ [8].

Decidability and Complexity. We now study decidability and complexity issues in the framework of safe hybrid KBs. We start by recalling a decidability and complexity result for Datalog$^{\neg\vee}$ programs under standard (UNA-based) stable model semantics.

Proposition 1 ([7]). *Satisfiability of Datalog$^{\neg\vee}$ programs under standard stable model semantics is NEXPTIME^{NP}-complete. Moreover, satisfiability of Datalog$^{\neg}$ programs under standard stable model semantics is NEXPTIME-complete.*

Then, it can be shown that satisfiability of Datalog$^{\neg\vee}$ programs under standard stable model semantics can be reduced to satisfiability in safe hybrid KBs. Consequently, the following hardness result follows.

Theorem 2. *Satisfiability of safe hybrid KBs is NEXPTIME^{NP}-hard. Moreover, it is NEXPTIME-hard if the rule component is a Datalog$^{\neg}$ program.*

We now prove a very general result on the decidability of reasoning in safe hybrid KBs.

Theorem 3. *Let $\mathcal{H} = (\mathcal{T}, \mathcal{P})$ be a safe hybrid KB. If establishing consistency of a partition of $gr_p(\mathcal{P})$ with $\mathcal{T}$ is decidable, then satisfiability of $\mathcal{H}$ is a decidable problem.*

Proof. First, observe that the set $gr_p(\mathcal{P})$ is finite, therefore the number of partitions of $gr_p(\mathcal{P})$ is finite. Then, since by hypothesis establishing consistency of a partition (G_P, G_N) with $\mathcal{T}$ is decidable, for each such partition (G_P, G_N) condition (a) of the algorithm can be verified in a finite amount of time; moreover, since $rectify(\mathcal{P}(G_P, G_N))$ is a finite Datalog$^{\neg\vee}$ program, from Proposition 1 it follows that condition (b) of the algorithm can also be verified in a finite amount of time.   □

We remark that, starting from a logic $\mathcal{L}$ in which reasoning is decidable, it is very often the case that deciding satisfiability of a theory of an $\mathcal{L}$-KB augmented with a finite set of ground literals is still decidable, and therefore that reasoning in safe hybrid KBs made of $\mathcal{L}$ theories as structural components is decidable. In this sense, the previous theorem can be read as a very strong result, stating that the framework of safe hybrid KBs generally preserves decidability of reasoning.

Decidability of OWL-DL with DL-Safe Rules. The DL that currently plays a central role in the Semantic Web is $\mathcal{SHOIN}(\mathbf{D})$: as mentioned in Section 1, it is equivalent to OWL-DL [19], which is a W3C recommendation language for ontology representation in the Semantic Web. Reasoning in $\mathcal{SHOIN}(\mathbf{D})$, and hence in OWL-DL, is decidable, as stated by the following property.

Proposition 2 ([14,22]). *Satisfiability of $\mathcal{SHOIN}(\mathbf{D})$ KBs is NEXPTIME-complete.*

Based on Theorem 3, it is possible to prove that reasoning in $\mathcal{SHOIN}(\mathbf{D})$ safe hybrid KBs is decidable, and to provide a computational characterization of the problem.

Theorem 4. *Let $\mathcal{H} = (\mathcal{T}, \mathcal{P})$ be a safe hybrid KB where $\mathcal{T}$ is a $\mathcal{SHOIN}(\mathbf{D})$ KB and $\mathcal{P}$ is a Datalog$^{\neg\vee}$ program. Deciding satisfiability of $\mathcal{H}$ is NEXPTIME^{NP}-complete. Moreover, if $\mathcal{P}$ is a Datalog$^{\neg}$ program, deciding satisfiability of $\mathcal{H}$ is NEXPTIME-complete.*

As a corollary of the above theorem, we close an open problem in [18], i.e., decidability of satisfiability of $\mathcal{SHOIN}(\mathbf{D})$ with DL-safe rules. This problem exactly corresponds in our framework to deciding satisfiability of a safe hybrid KB composed of a $\mathcal{SHOIN}(\mathbf{D})$ KB and a positive Datalog program: as a corollary of the above results, it immediately follows that satisfiability in such safe hybrid KBs is decidable and is NEXPTIME-complete.

4   Related Work

Although in various forms, the notion of safe integration has been taken into account since the earliest studies concerning the extension of DLs with rules. The first formal proposal for the integration of Description Logics and rules is $\mathcal{AL}$-log [5]. $\mathcal{AL}$-log is a framework which integrates KBs expressed in the description logic $\mathcal{ALC}$ and positive Datalog programs. Then, disjunctive $\mathcal{AL}$-log was proposed in [20] as an extension of $\mathcal{AL}$-log, based on the use of Datalog$^{\neg\vee}$ instead of positive Datalog, and on the possibility of using binary predicates (roles) besides unary predicates (concepts) in rules. When choosing $\mathcal{ALC}$ as the structural language, the framework of safe hybrid KBs captures disjunctive $\mathcal{AL}$-log and can be seen as a generalization of it: indeed, differently from safe hybrid KBs, in disjunctive $\mathcal{AL}$-log structural predicates can occur only in the bodies of rules, which restricts the information flow only from the structural KB to the rule KB, but not vice versa.

This line of research was carried on by the work on CARIN [16], which established several fundamental decidability results concerning non-safe interaction between DL-KBs and rules. Some of such results clearly indicate that, in case of unrestricted interaction between the structural component and the rule component in hybrid KBs, decidability of reasoning holds only if at least one of the two component KBs has very limited expressive power: e.g., in order to retain decidability of reasoning, allowing recursion in the rule KB imposes very severe restrictions on the expressiveness of the structural KB.

The framework of $\mathcal{AL}$-log has been extended in a different way in [18]. There, the problem of extending OWL-DL with positive Datalog programs is analyzed. The interaction between OWL-DL and rules is restricted through a safeness condition which is exactly the one adopted in safe hybrid KBs. With respect to disjunctive $\mathcal{AL}$-log, in [18] a more expressive structural language and a less expressive rule language are adopted: moreover, the information flow is bidirectional, i.e., structural predicates may appear in the head of rules. As we have shown in Section 3, such a framework is perfectly captured by safe hybrid KBs.

The work presented in [11] can also be seen as an approach based on a form of safe interaction between the structural DL-KB and the rules: in particular, a rule language is defined such that it is possible to encode a set of rules into a semantically equivalent DL-KB. As a consequence, such a rule language is very restricted.

A different approach is presented in [13,12], which proposes Conceptual Logic Programming (CLP), an extension of answer set programming (i.e., Datalog$^{\neg\vee}$) towards infinite domains. In order to keep reasoning decidable, a syntactic restriction on CLP program rules is imposed. This approach is related to integrating DLs and rules, since the authors also show that CLPs can embed expressive DL-KBs, which in turn implies decidability of adding CLP rules to such DLs. However, the syntactic restriction on CLP rules, whose purpose is to impose a "forest-like" structure to the models of the program, is different from the safeness conditions analyzed so far, which makes it impossible to compare this approach with safe hybrid KBs (and with the approaches previously mentioned).

Another approach for extending DLs with Datalog$^{\neg}$ rules is presented in [9]. Differently from safe hybrid KBs and from the other approaches above described, this proposal allows for specifying in rule bodies *queries* to the structural component, where every query also allows for specifying an input from the rule component, and thus for an information flow from the rule component to the structural component. The meaning of such queries in rule bodies is given at the meta-level, through the notion of skeptical entailment in the DL-KB. Thus, from the semantic viewpoint, this form of interaction-via-entailment between the two components is more restricted than in safe hybrid KBs (and in the similar approaches previously mentioned); on the other hand, such an increased separation in principle allows for more modular reasoning methods, which are able to completely separate reasoning about the structural component and reasoning about the rule component. However, in this paper we have shown that an analogous form of modularization of reasoning is possible also in the presence of a semantically richer form of interaction between the two components of a safe hybrid KB.

An approach for the combination of defeasible reasoning with Description Logics is presented in [1], under a safe interaction-via-entailment scheme which is semantically analogous to the one proposed in [9]. Besides the differences with our approach (and with the studies on nonmonotonic extensions of DL-KBs previously mentioned) concerning the semantics of nonmonotonic rules, a main characteristic of these proposals consists in the fact the information flow is unidirectional, i.e., it goes from the structural component to the rule component.

Generally speaking, it is difficult to provide a satisfactory semantic account for non-safe interaction between DL-KBs and nonmonotonic rules, due to the classical, open world semantics of DL-KBs, and the closed world assumption underlying non-monotonic systems. For instance, [17] illustrates the problems in providing a semantic account for non-safe interaction of ontologies and $\text{Datalog}^{\neg\vee}$ programs.

Finally, [4] proposes OWL Flight, a logic programming based formalism for the Semantic Web. A detailed comparison of the relative expressive abilities of OWL Flight and OWL-DL is made, which proves the adequacy of the proposed approach for Semantic Web applications. Although based on logic program rules, the purpose of this approach is different from ours and from the ones mentioned above, and does not actually deal with the problem of integrating DLs with rules.

5   Conclusions

In this paper we have formally demonstrated that the form of safe interaction introduced in [5] and extended in various forms by [20,18] can be generally applied, and constitutes a good choice for the design of integrated KBs when we want to keep expressive power both in the structural component and in the rule component, and when decidability and complexity of (sound and complete) reasoning is a crucial aspect. Indeed, in general, such safe interaction preserves decidability of reasoning and, in many cases, does not increase the complexity of reasoning, i.e., reasoning in the integrated KB is computationally no harder than reasoning separately in the two components.

Moreover, we have shown that such a form of safe interaction allows for a clear formal treatment of hybrid KBs in which the UNA is not adopted, and in which we want the OWA on the structural component and the CWA on the rule component.

A possible further extension of the present work is towards the study of *data complexity* in the framework of safe hybrid KBs, following the lines of [3], which analyzes data complexity for $\mathcal{AL}$-log. Moreover, it should be interesting to analyze whether tighter forms of interaction between the structural and the rule component can be defined, relaxing, on the one hand, the safeness condition of safe hybrid KBs, while preserving, on the other hand, their nice computational properties. Finally, it would be very interesting to study *data* complexity in the framework of safe hybrid KBs, continuing the research presented in [3], which analyzes data complexity for $\mathcal{AL}$-log.

Acknowledgments. This research has been partially supported by the projects IN-FOMIX (IST-2001-33570) and INTEROP Network of Excellence (IST-508011) funded by the EU, and by the project HYPER, funded by IBM through a Shared University Research (SUR) Award grant.

References

1. Grigoris Antoniou. A nonmonotonic rule system using ontologies. In *Proc. of RuleML 2002*, volume 60 of *CEUR Workshop Proceedings*, 2002.
2. Franz Baader, Diego Calvanese, Deborah McGuinness, Daniele Nardi, and Peter F. Patel-Schneider, editors. *The Description Logic Handbook: Theory, Implementation and Applications*. Cambridge University Press, 2003.
3. Marco Cadoli, Luigi Palopoli, and Maurizio Lenzerini. Datalog and description logics: Expressive power. In *Proc. of DBPL'97*, 1997.
4. Jos de Bruijn, Ruben Lara, Axel Polleres, and Dieter Fensel. OWL DL vs. OWL flight: conceptual modeling and reasoning for the semantic web. In *Proc. of WWW 2005*, pages 623–632, 2005.
5. Francesco M. Donini, Maurizio Lenzerini, Daniele Nardi, and Andrea Schaerf. $\mathcal{AL}$-log: Integrating Datalog and description logics. *J. of Intelligent Information Systems*, 10(3):227–252, 1998.
6. Oliver M. Duschka, Michael R. Genesereth, and Alon Y. Levy. Recursive query plans for data integration. *J. of Logic Programming*, 43(1):49–73, 2000.
7. Thomas Eiter, Georg Gottlob, and Heikki Mannilla. Disjunctive Datalog. *ACM Trans. on Database Systems*, 22(3):364–418, 1997.
8. Thomas Eiter, Nicola Leone, Cristinel Mateis, Gerald Pfeifer, and Francesco Scarcello. The KR system dlv: Progress report, comparison and benchmarks. In *Proc. of KR'98*, pages 636–647, 1998.
9. Thomas Eiter, Thomas Lukasiewicz, Roman Schindlauer, and Hans Tompits. Combining answer set programming with description logics for the semantic web. In *Proc. of KR 2004*, pages 141–151, 2004.
10. Michael Gelfond and Vladimir Lifschitz. Classical negation in logic programs and disjunctive databases. *New Generation Computing*, 9:365–385, 1991.
11. Benjamin N. Grosof, Ian Horrocks, Raphael Volz, and Stefan Decker. Description logic programs: combining logic programs with description logic. In *Proc. of WWW 2003*, pages 48–57, 2003.
12. Stijn Heymans, Davy Van Nieuwenborgh, and Dirk Vermeir. Semantic web reasoning with conceptual logic programs. In *Proc. of RuleML 2004*, pages 113–127, 2004.
13. Stijn Heymans and Dirk Vermeir. Integrating description logics and answer set programming. In *Proc. of PPSWR 2003*, pages 146–159, 2003.
14. Ian Horrocks and Peter F. Patel-Schneider. Reducing OWL entailment to Description Logic satisfiability. In *Proc. of ISWC 2003*, pages 17–29, 2003.
15. Ian Horrocks and Peter F. Patel-Schneider. A proposal for an OWL rules language. In *Proc. of WWW 2004*, pages 723–731, 2004.

16. Alon Y. Levy and Marie-Christine Rousset. Combining Horn rules and description logics in CARIN. *Artificial Intelligence*, 104(1–2):165–209, 1998.

17. Jing Mei, Shengping Liu, Anbu Yue, and Zuoquan Lin. An extension to OWL with general rules. In *Proc. of RuleML 2004*, pages 155–169, 2004.

18. Boris Motik, Ulrike Sattler, and Rudi Studer. Query answering for OWL-DL with rules. In *Proc. of ISWC 2004*, pages 549–563, 2004.

19. Peter F. Patel-Schneider, Patrick J. Hayes, Ian Horrocks, and Frank van Harmelen. OWL web ontology language; semantics and abstract syntax. W3C candidate recommendation, http://www.w3.org/tr/owl-semantics/, november 2002.

20. Riccardo Rosati. Towards expressive KR systems integrating Datalog and description logics: Preliminary report. In *Proc. of DL'99*, pages 160–164. CEUR Electronic Workshop Proceedings, http://ceur-ws.org/Vol-22/, 1999.

21. Riccardo Rosati. On the decidability and complexity of integrating ontologies and rules. *Journal of Web Semantics*, 2005. To appear.

22. Stephan Tobies. *Complexity Results and Practical Algorithms for Logics in Knowledge Representation*. PhD thesis, LuFG Theoretical Computer Science, RWTH-Aachen, Germany, 2001.

Logical Reconstruction of RDF and Ontology Languages*

Jos de Bruijn[1], Enrico Franconi[2], and Sergio Tessaris[2]

[1] Digital Enterprise Research Institute,
University of Innsbruck,
Austria
jos.debruijn@deri.org
[2] Faculty of Computer Science,
Free University of Bozen-Bolzano, Italy
lastname@inf.unibz.it

Abstract. In this sketchy paper we introduce a logical reconstruction of the RDF family of languages and the OWL-DL family of languages. We prove that our logical framework is equivalent to the standard W3C definitions of RDF and OWL-DL/Lite. The main aim is to have a unified model theoretic semantics for both worlds. As a consequence we get various complexity results and a model theoretic semantics for basic SPARQL.

1 Introduction

The main aim of this sketchy paper is to recast the RDF model theory in a more classical logic framework, and to use this characterisation to shed new light on the ontology languages layering in the semantic web, and to lay down the logic based semantics of SPARQL. In particular, we will show how the models of RDF can be related to the models of DL based ontology languages, without requiring any change on the existing syntactic or semantic definitions in the RDF and OWL-DL realms.

We first introduce the notion of herbrand and canonical models for RDF graphs, and we use this notion to characterise RDF entailment. RDF herbrand models can also be seen as classical first order structures, that we call FO interpretations. These structures provide the semantic bridge between RDF and classical logics, such as description logics (DL) based languages (e.g., OWL-DL). The intuition beyond FO interpretations is that it singles out the concepts and the individuals from an RDF herbrand model – possibly in a polymorphic way when the same node is given both the meaning as a class and as an individual.

Once we have characterised RDF graphs in terms of their herbrand models, it is possible to understand the notion of logical implication between RDF graphs and classical logic formulas. At the end of this paper we analyse the problem

---

* This work has been partially supported by the EU projects KnowledgeWeb, Interop, Tones, Sekt, and Asg.

F. Fages and S. Soliman (Eds.): PPSWR 2005, LNCS 3703, pp. 65–71, 2005.

of querying RDF graphs with OWL-DL ontologies. We prove an important reduction result. That is, given an RDF graph S and a query Q, the answer set
of Q to S (as defined by W3C) is the same as the answer of Q to S given the
empty KB. This shows a complete interoperability between RDF and OWL-DL.
For example, in absence of ontologies, it would be possible to use OWL-QL to
answer queries to RDF graphs, or to use SPARQL to answer queries to ABoxes.

In this paper we assume that the reader is familiar with the definitions associated to RDF.

2   RDF Model Theory Revisited

In this paper we consider an extended notion of RDF graph, in which we are
less restrictive on the kind of triples. In particular we allow

- literals in subject positions;
- blank nodes in property positions.

Note that the first kind of extension has been already considered by W3C
working groups (e.g. see Section 2.2 of [Prud'hommeaux and Seaborne, 2005]).
All the results shown in this paper still holds for the standard definition of
RDF graph. From now on, by *RDF graph* we intend the extended definition.
Also note that reification is not considered as not being part of the standard
semantic definition of RDF.

We indicate with $\mathcal{RDF}_U$ the set of all RDF URI references together the set
of all literals in their canonical representation[1]. An RDF graph is said to be *well
typed* if doesn't contain the triple

$$\langle \texttt{"xxx"^^rdf:XMLLiteral}, \texttt{rdf:type}, \texttt{rdf:XMLLiteral} \rangle$$

where `"xxx"^^rdf:XMLLiteral` is an ill-typed XML literal string (see the RDF
semantic conditions in Section 3.1 of [Hayes, 2004]).

We first define the notion of herbrand and canonical models for an RDF
graph.

Definition 1. *(Herbrand and canonical models)*
*A herbrand model of an RDF graph S is a well typed ground instantiation of the
graph obtained by replacing each bnode in the completed S with some element
in $\mathcal{RDF}_U$.*
A graph is completed *if it is augmented by the RDF axiomatic triples, it is
extended by applying the property RDF entailment and grounded lg rules (see
sections 3.1, 7.1 and 7.2 in [Hayes, 2004])[2], and all the literals are in their
canonical representation.*

---

[1] The canonical representation of a literal is a chosen representative of all the literals
associated to the same value, if the literal is non ill-typed, otherwise it is the literal
itself.

[2] Note that, since we allow literals as subject in RDF triples, we need to add a sym-
metric lg rule acting on literals in the subject of a triple.

The canonical model $\widehat{S}$ of an RDF graph S is the herbrand model of S obtained by replacing each distinct bnode in S with a distinct fresh URI – that is, a skolem constant not appearing elsewhere in S nor in the context in which S is used (e.g. in queries).

Note that a herbrand model is always finite if the RDF graph is finite, that a ground RDF graph has a unique herbrand model that it is also its canonical model, and that a herbrand model is a ground RDF graph.

As the following theorem shows, the herbrand models of an RDF graph contain *explicitly* all the information entailed by the graph itself.

Theorem 2. *(RDF entailment)*
An RDF graph S entails an RDF graph $\mathcal{E}$ (as defined in [Hayes, 2004]), written $S \vdash \mathcal{E}$, if and only if some herbrand model of $\mathcal{E}$ is a subgraph of the canonical model of S.

Corollary 3. *(Complexity of entailment)*

1. *RDF entailment is NP-complete in the size of the RDF graphs.*
2. *RDF entailment is polynomial in the size of the entailing graph S.*
3. *RDF entailment is polynomial in the size of the graphs if $\mathcal{E}$ is acyclic or ground.*

The proofs are based on a reduction to the problem of conjunctive query containment, and by using the interpolation lemma in [Hayes, 2004].

The above theorem and corollary (without the polynomiality results) have been already sketched in [Gutierrez *et al.*, 2004]. However, the results in [Gutierrez *et al.*, 2004] are imprecise since the role of axiomatic triples and the completion (as defined here) are neglected, and literals are not taken in careful account.

2.1   The Semantics of Basic SPARQL

Let's now consider SPARQL queries on RDF graphs. If we restrict our attention to SPARQL query basic graph patterns [Prud'hommeaux and Seaborne, 2005], we can define the semantics of query answering in the usual logic based way (as, e.g., is defined for classical relational databases, or for description logics). We also disallow in this paper the answer to a query to contain blank nodes. Relaxing this restriction raises several issues regarding the redundancy of answer, which are not taken into account in [Prud'hommeaux and Seaborne, 2005].

Definition 4. *(Semantics of basic SPARQL)*
A SPARQL query basic graph pattern to an RDF graph S is a (possibly ground) RDF graph $Q_{\mathbf{x}}$ where, in addition to URIs and bnodes, variables are allowed; the elements in the set $\mathbf{x}$ (possibly empty) of n variables of a query are called distinguished variables, *and the bnodes play the role of* non-distinguished *variables. The answer set of $Q_{\mathbf{x}}$ is the set of all substitutions of the distinguished variables with some arbitrary URI from $\mathcal{RDF}_U$, such that the for each substitution the instantiated query is entailed by S, i.e.,*

$$\{\langle c_1 \ldots c_n \rangle \in (\mathcal{RDF}_U)^n \mid \mathcal{S} \vdash \mathcal{Q}_{[x_1 \mapsto c_1, \ldots, x_n \mapsto c_n]}\}.$$

Note that according to our extended definition of RDF graphs we allow blank nodes and variables in property position.

Corollary 5. *(Complexity of SPARQL)*
Query answering for SPARQL query basic graph patterns is polynomial in data complexity.

Again, the proof follows from an encoding of the problem as a conjunctive query containment problem. Note that the above definition together with the correspondence stated in Theorem 2 suggests an implementation of query answering for SPARQL based on the canonical models.

The result of Corollary 5 has been already sketched in [Gutierrez *et al.*, 2004] for a richer query language, with the same imprecision we mentioned before.

2.2   The FO Model Theory for RDF

A *FO interpretation* (first order interpretation) of an RDF graph shows how models of RDF can be seen as interpretations of classical first order logic.

Definition 6. *(FO interpretation of an RDF herbrand model)*
A FO interpretation of an RDF herbrand model (say, $\mathcal{I}_{RDF}$) is a first order type structure $\mathcal{I}(\mathcal{I}_{RDF}) = \langle \Delta, .^{\mathcal{I}_O}, .^{\mathcal{I}_C}, .^{\mathcal{I}_R} \rangle$, where Δ is an abstract domain corresponding to $\mathcal{RDF}_U$. The interpretation of the elements of $\mathcal{I}_{RDF}$ is given by the interpretation functions $.^{\mathcal{I}_O}, .^{\mathcal{I}_C}, .^{\mathcal{I}_R}$, whose domain is $\mathcal{RDF}_U$, and the range is respectively all elements of Δ, all subsets of Δ, and all binary relations over Δ. The interpretation functions state which of the elements of the graph play the role of individuals, concepts, and roles.
For each $u \in \mathcal{RDF}_U$, $\mathcal{I}(\mathcal{I}_{RDF})$ should be such that:

$$u^{\mathcal{I}_O} = u$$
$$u^{\mathcal{I}_C} = \{o \mid \langle o, \boldsymbol{rdf\!:\!type}, u \rangle \in \mathcal{I}_{RDF}\}$$
$$u^{\mathcal{I}_R} = \{(o_1, o_2) \mid \langle o_1, u, o_2 \rangle \in \mathcal{I}_{RDF}\}$$

An URI reference is associated to more than one syntactic type, e.g., an URI may refer to an individual and to a class at the same time: polymorphic meanings of URIs are allowed. However note that, just like in the case of contextual predicate calculus (as defined in [Chen *et al.*, 1993]), in the above definition there is no semantic interaction between the distinct occurrences of the same URI as a concept name, or as a role name, or as an individual. This absence of interaction is required for classical first order (description) logic fragments such as OWL-Lite or OWL-DL. For example, given the triple $\langle \mathtt{ex\!:\!o}, \mathtt{rdf\!:\!type}, \mathtt{ex\!:\!o} \rangle$ within an RDF herbrand model, in the FO interpretation associated to it the URI $\mathtt{ex\!:\!o}$ is interpreted as both an individual and a concept, and the individual $\mathtt{ex\!:\!o}$ is in the extension of the concept $\mathtt{ex\!:\!o}$.

We say that the FO interpretations of an RDF graph are the FO interpretations of its herbrand models. The main theorem of this Section states that we can correctly define RDF entailment and queries using a classical logic with FO interpretations.

Theorem 7. *(FO entailment and query)*

1. *An RDF graph $\mathcal{S}$ entails an RDF graph $\mathcal{E}$ (as defined in [Hayes, 2004]), written as $\mathcal{S} \vdash \mathcal{E}$, if and only if the set of all the FO interpretations of $\mathcal{S}$ is included in the set of all the FO interpretations of $\mathcal{E}$, written $\mathcal{S} \models \mathcal{E}$.*
2. *The answer set of a SPARQL query basic graph pattern $\mathcal{Q}_{\mathbf{x}}$ to an RDF graph $\mathcal{S}$, as defined in Definition 4, is equal to*

$$\{\langle c_1 \ldots c_n \rangle \in (\mathcal{RDF}_U)^n \mid \mathcal{S} \models \mathcal{Q}_{[x_1 \mapsto c_1, \ldots, x_n \mapsto c_n]}\}.$$

3 Classical Logic Interoperability

In this Section we define the interoperability between RDF graphs and classical logics. We show how a tower of classical logics (e.g., from OWL-Lite to OWL-DL, to full first order logic, or any arbitrary logic equipped with classical first order models) can be built on top of the language of RDF: the interoperability is grounded on the notion of FO interpretations.

First, we need to define the notion of non high order graphs, that basically do not have bnodes in any property or class position.

Definition 8. *(Non-high order RDF graph)*
An RDF graph is non-high order if bnodes and variables are not in property position of any triple, nor in object position of rdf:type triples.

Note that herbrand models and canonical models are always non-high order RDF graphs, since they are always ground graphs.

Definition 9. *(Classical logic translation)*
The classical logic translation FO$(\mathcal{S})$ of a non-high order RDF graph $\mathcal{S}$ is a predicate logic formula, where URIs and literals are constants and blank nodes are existentially quantified variables, and the body is a conjunction of the ground binary atomic formulas in correspondence with the triples of $\mathcal{S}$, where the binary atomic formulas of the kind "rdf:type(a, b)" are replaced by ground unary atomic formulas of the kind "$a(b)$".

We now introduce the general problem of reasoning and query answering in a classical logic $\mathcal{C}$ given an RDF graph. We require that in $\mathcal{C}$ the interpretation of well-typed literals is subject to the Unique Name Assumption.

Definition 10. *(Classical logic RDF extension)*

1. *The logical implication problem in a classical logic $\mathcal{C}$ given an RDF graph $\mathcal{S}$ is defined as follows:*

$$\mathsf{FO}(\widehat{\mathcal{S}}), \phi \models_{\mathcal{C}} \psi$$

where ϕ and ψ are formulas in $\mathcal{C}$, and $\models_{\mathcal{C}}$ is entailment in $\mathcal{C}$.

2. *The query answering problem in a classical logic $\mathcal{C}$ given an RDF graph $\mathcal{S}$ is defined as follows:*

$$\{\langle c_1 \ldots c_n \rangle \in (\mathcal{RDF}_U)^n \mid \mathsf{FO}(\widehat{\mathcal{S}}), \phi \models_{\mathcal{C}} \psi_{[x_1 \mapsto c_1, \ldots, x_n \mapsto c_n]}\}.$$

where ϕ is a formula in $\mathcal{C}$ and $\psi_{\mathbf{x}}$ is an open formula in $\mathcal{C}$ (expressing the query) with $\mathbf{x}$ being the free (distinguished) variables, and $\models_{\mathcal{C}}$ is entailment in $\mathcal{C}$.

The above general definition of reasoning and querying given an RDF graph is actually an abstraction of basic reasoning and querying for RDF graphs only, as the following reduction theorem shows. In this way, we believe that the classical logic RDF extension presented above is a meaningful way to build up logical languages on top of RDF, and it is a formal justification of the semantic web tower of languages proposed by Tim Berners-Lee.[3]

Theorem 11. *(Reduction theorem)*

1. *Given an RDF graph $\mathcal{S}$ and a non-high order graph $\mathcal{E}$, $\mathcal{S} \vdash \mathcal{E}$ if and only if $\mathsf{FO}(\widehat{\mathcal{S}}) \models_{\mathcal{C}} \mathsf{FO}(\mathcal{E})$*
2. *Given an RDF graph $\mathcal{S}$ and a SPARQL non-high order query basic graph pattern $\mathcal{Q}_{\mathbf{x}}$, its answer set is equal to*

$$\{\langle c_1 \ldots c_n \rangle \in (\mathcal{RDF}_U)^n \mid \mathsf{FO}(\widehat{\mathcal{S}}) \models_{\mathcal{C}} \mathsf{FO}(\mathcal{Q}_{[x_1 \mapsto c_1, \ldots, x_n \mapsto c_n]})\}.$$

The proof of the reduction theorem is based on the following lemma.

Lemma 12. *(Canonical entailment)*
An RDF graph $\mathcal{S}$ entails an RDF graph $\mathcal{E}$ (as defined in [Hayes, 2004]), i.e., $\mathcal{S} \vdash \mathcal{E}$, if and only if the FO interpretation corresponding to the canonical model of $\mathcal{S}$ is in the set of all the FO interpretations of $\mathcal{E}$.

This lemma together with the reduction theorem justifies the use of datalog-like implementations for SPARQL.

3.1   The Case of OWL-DL

The results presented so far have several immediate consequences when considering the interoperability between OWL-DL/Lite with RDF.

First of all, it is possible to have an implementation for free of a query evaluation engine for SPARQL non-high order query basic graph patterns, using any of the existing description logics based query system available. In fact, it is enough to encode the (arbitrary) RDF graph to query as an ABox in the system (by considering its canonical model), and to query it by encoding the SPARQL non-high order query basic graph pattern as a standard conjunctive query. The reduction theorem above guarantees that we will get the correct answer.

---

[3] This paper focuses on RDF; for the sake of simplicity, we ignore RDFS in the semantic web tower. Including RDFS is currently subject of our research work.

Moreover, it is possible to extend the query problem of an RDF graph in SPARQL to the query problem of an RDF graph given an ontology in OWL-DL, again by exploiting standard description logics based query systems. This is achieved by just adding the encoding of the RDF graph to query as an ABox.

This work also shows how it is possible to give a semantics to OWL-DL based on RDF, generalising the recommended semantics given in [Peter-Schneider *et al.*, 2004]. Our proposal is fully compatible with the W3C recommended semantics, but removes some of the non necessary limitations related to the polymorphism of URIs. As a matter of fact, [Patel-Schneider *et al.*, 2004] would allow interoperation and queries only with RDF graphs not containing any meta information (for example, of the kind represented by the triple $\langle$ex:o, rdf:type, ex:o$\rangle$); a similar kind of restriction has been proposed in [Antoniou and van Harmelen, 2004](called *type separation*) and in [Pan and Horrocks, 2003] (where a more liberal stratification is proposed).

References

[Antoniou and van Harmelen, 2004] Grigoris Antoniou and Frank van Harmelen. *A Semantic Web Primer*. MIT Press, 2004.

[Chen *et al.*, 1993] Weidong Chen, Michael Kifer, and David Warren. HILOG: a foundation for higher-order logic programming. *Journal of Logic Programming*, 15(3):187–230, February 1993.

[Gutierrez *et al.*, 2004] C. Gutierrez, C. Hurtado, and A. Mendelzon. Foundations of semantic web databases. In *Proceedings of the 2004 ACM SIGART SIGMOD SIGART Symposium on Principles of Database Systems (PODS'04)*, 2004.

[Hayes, 2004] Patrick Hayes. RDF semantics. Technical report, W3C, February 2004. W3C recommendation, URL http://www.w3.org/TR/rdf-mt/.

[Pan and Horrocks, 2003] Jeff Pan and Ian Horrocks. RDFS(FA) and RDF MT: Two semantics for RDFS. In *Proc. 2003 International Semantic Web Conference (ISWC 2003)*, 2003.

[Patel-Schneider *et al.*, 2004] Peter F. Patel-Schneider, Patrick Hayes, and Ian Horrocks. OWL web ontology language semantics and abstract syntax. Technical report, W3C, February 2004. W3C recommendation, URL http://www.w3.org/TR/owl-semantics/.

[Prud'hommeaux and Seaborne, 2005] Eric Prud'hommeaux and Andy Seaborne. SPARQL query language for RDF. Technical report, W3C, April 2005. W3C working draft, URL http://www.w3.org/TR/rdf-sparql-query/.

Marriages of Convenience: Triples and Graphs, RDF and XML in Web Querying

Tim Furche, François Bry, and Oliver Bolzer

Institute for Informatics,
University of Munich,
Oettingenstraße 67,
80538 München, Germany
http://pms.ifi.lmu.de/

Abstract. Metadata processing is recognized as a central challenge for database research in the next decade. Already, novel desktop data management and search applications (cf. Apple's Spotlight and Microsoft's WinFS) are enabled by rich metadata. Efficient and effective access to such data becomes a crucial issue for more and more application scenarios. In this article, we focus on metadata represented in RDF. A number of query languages for RDF have been presented in recent years. This article argues that most of these approaches fail to address properly two core issues: the provision of rich operators and constructs to adequately support RDF's graph data model and the ability to intertwine access to metadata (in RDF format) and data (in XML format). To address this points, two XML views over RDF data are expressed in the query language Xcerpt and discussed. Furthermore, it is shown how these views together with Xcerpt's rich graph patterns allow the succinct expression of complex, but common queries against RDF graphs.

1   Introduction

The 'Semantic Web' is an endeavor widely publicized in [1], envisioning the current Web, which consists of (X)HTML and documents in other XML formats, extended by metadata specifying the meaning of these documents in forms usable by both human beings and computers.

The integral processing of data and metadata is recognized as a central challenge for the next decade (cf., e.g., Pat Selinger's ICDE 2005 Keynote) not only as a contribution to the Semantic Web vision, but also on a smaller scale as part of the next generation of desktop data management (cf. Apple's Spotlight and Microsoft's WinFS that aim at extending current file storage and desktop search with extensive metadata facilities).

In the (Semantic) Web context, a number of formalisms have been proposed for representing metadata, in particular RDF, Topic Maps, and OWL. This article concentrates concentrate on RDF as the most widely used formalism. This article illustrates first steps towards integrating access to standard Web data in XML format and RDF metadata: First, as argued above, integrated

F. Fages and S. Soliman (Eds.): PPSWR 2005, LNCS 3703, pp. 72–84, 2005.

access to standard Web data in XML and metadata in RDF is essential. A framework to access RDF data through XML views is proposed. Second, this article argues that the currently predominant treatment of RDF data as flat triples is, although easy to comprehend, not the only and often not the best way of considering RDF data. Rather, a view of the RDF data directly as a graph is not only natural and closer to the RDF data model, but also allows for easy expression of graph patterns using much the same constructs as for navigating in XML data. This is particularly evident in face of incomplete information about the precise graph structure. Third, this article argues that querying RDF data is often most conveniently achieved if queries are composed in terms of both the triple and the graph view of RDF. Finally, this article argues that many applications call for queries combining object data in (X)HTML or XML and metadata in RDF. Thus, it is convenient to "marry" triple and graphs as well as RDF and XML in querying the Semantic Web.

The proposed framework is realized by rules in the XML query language Xcerpt that allow (a) the easy conversion between the two views on RDF and (b) the 'serialization transparent' querying of RDF, i.e., the querying of RDF in many of the over a dozen serialization formats for RDF proposed in recent years.

2   Preliminaries

2.1   RDF and RDF Schema: Metadata Representation in the Semantic Web

RDF [2] is the prevalent standard for representing metadata in the (Semantic) Web. RDF data is sets of 'triples' or 'statements' of the form (*Subject, Property, Object*). RDF's data model (as defined in [3]) is a directed graph, whose nodes correspond to statements' subjects and objects and whose arcs correspond to statements' property (thus relating subjects with objects). Nodes are labeled by either (1) URIs describing (Web) resources, or (2) literals (i.e. scalar data such as strings or numbers), or (3) are unlabeled, being so-called anonymous or 'blank nodes'. Blank nodes are commonly used to group or 'aggregate' properties. Edges are always labeled by URIs indicating the type of relation between its subject and object.

RDFS allows one to define so-called 'RDF Schemas' or 'ontologies', similar to object-oriented data models. Based on an RDFS, 'inference rules' can be specified, for instance the transitivity of the class hierarchy, or the type of an untyped resource that has a property associated with a known domain.

RDF can be *serialized* in various formats, the most frequent being XML. Early approaches to RDF serialization have raised considerable criticism due to their complexity. As a consequence, a surprisingly large number of RDF serialization have been proposed, cf. [4] for a survey of serialization formats.

Figure 1 shows the running example for this article, a (simplified) representation of an RDF graph as used, e.g., in a book recommender system.

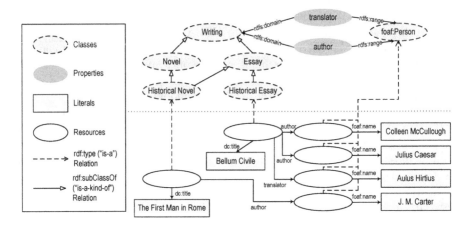

Fig. 1. Sample Data: representation as a (simplified) RDF graph

2.2   Xcerpt, a Versatile Web Query Language

Xcerpt [5,6] is a query language designed after principles given in [7] for querying both data on the standard Web (e.g., XML and HTML data) and data on the Semantic Web (e.g., RDF, Topic Maps, etc. data).

Xcerpt is 'data versatile', i.e. a same Xcerpt query can access and generate, as answers, data in different Web formats. Xcerpt is 'strongly answer-closed', i.e. it not only gives rise to construct answers in the same data formats as the data queries, but also to include in a query program data generated by this same query program. Xcerpt's queries are pattern-based and give rise to incompletely specify the data to retrieve by (1) not explicitly specifying all children of an element, (2) specifying descendant elements at indefinite depths (restrictions in the form of regular path expressions being possible), and (3) specifying optional query parts. Xcerpt's evaluation of incomplete queries is based on a novel form algorithm called 'simulation unification'. Xcerpt's processing of XML documents is graph-oriented, i.e., aware of the reference mechanisms (e.g., ID/IDREF attributes and links) of XML. Xcerpt is rule-based: An Xcerpt rule expresses how data queried can be re-assembled into new data items.

Xcerpt Programs consist of at least one 'goal' and some (possibly zero) 'rules'. Rules and goals contain query and construction patterns, called 'terms'. Terms represent tree- or graph-like structures. The children of a node may either be 'ordered' (as in a XHTML document or in RDF sequence containers), i.e. the order of occurrence is relevant, or 'unordered', i.e. the order of occurrence is irrelevant and may be ignored (as in the case of RDF statements). In the term syntax, an ordered term specification is denoted by square brackets [ ], an un-ordered term specification by curly braces { }. Terms may contain the *reference constructs* ^id ('referring' occurrence of the identifier id) and id @ t ('defin-ing' occurrence of the identifier id). Using reference constructs, terms can form cyclic (rooted) graph structures.

Terms can be either data, query, or construct terms. *Data terms* represent XML documents and the data items of a semistructured database. They are similar to *ground* functional programming expressions and logical atoms. A *database* is a (multi-)set of data terms (e.g. the Web). A non-XML syntax has been chosen for Xcerpt to improve readability, but there is a one-to-one correspondence between an XML document and a data term.

Query terms are (possibly incomplete) patterns matched against Web resources represented by data terms. In many ways, they are like forms or examples for the queried data (in the style of the 'query-by-example' paradigm [8]), but also

- may be *incomplete in breadth*, i.e., contain 'partial' as well as 'total' term specifications: A term t using a partial term specification for its subterms matches with all such terms that (1) contain matching subterms for all subterms of t and that (2) might contain further subterms without corresponding subterms in t. Partial term specification is denoted by double (square or curly) brackets. In contrast, a term t using a total term specification does not match with terms that contain additional subterms without corresponding subterms in t.
- may be augmented by *variables* for selecting data items, possibly with 'variable restrictions' using the $\rightarrow$ construct (read **as**), which restricts the admissible bindings to those subterms that are matched by the restriction pattern.
- may contain *query constructs* like position matching (using **position**), subterm negation (using **without**), optional subterms (using **optional**), regular expressions for namespaces, labels, and text, and conditional or unconditional path traversal (using **desc**).
- may contain further constraints on the variables in a so-called *condition box*, beginning with the keyword **where**.

Construct terms serve to reassemble variables (the bindings of which are specified in query terms) so as to construct new data terms. Again, they are similar to the latter, but augmented by variables (acting as place holders for data selected in a query) and the grouping construct **all** (which serves to collect all instances that result from different variable bindings). Occurrences of **all** may be accompanied by an optional sorting specification.

Rules or construct-query rules relate a construct term to a query consisting of arbitrary boolean expressions using only **AND**, **OR**, and **NOT** to connect query terms. They have the form

```
CONSTRUCT query term FROM and { query term, or { query term, ... }, ... } END
```

An Xcerpt rule may contain one or several references to *resources* (expressed using **in** and **resource**).

Rules can be seen as 'views' specifying how to obtain documents shaped in the form of the construct term by evaluating the query against Web resources (e.g. an XML document or a database).

Xcerpt rules may be *chained* like active or deductive database rules to form complex query programs, i.e., rules may query the results of other rules.

3   Two Perspectives on RDF

This section introduces two different perspectives on RDF: (1) a flat, almost relational view and (2) a graph view reminiscent of semi-structured data. Existing
approaches for RDF querying are classified along these perspectives briefly.

To illustrate these two perspectives, the selection query "Select all *Essays*
together with their *authors* (i.e. author URIs and corresponding names)" is
used against the data of Figure 1. This simple, but natural query requires a
(unconditional) traversal of the sub-classes of Essay, to find also books classified
as, e.g., *Historical Essay*.

3.1   RDF Triples: A Flat, Relational View

The following Xcerpt program expresses the above query on a triple view of the
RDF data:

```
 1 DECLARE ns-prefix rdf = "http://www.w3.org/1999/02/22−rdf−syntax−ns#"
   DECLARE ns-prefix books = "http://example.org/books#"
 3 GOAL
     result [
 5     all essay [
         id [ var Essay ],
 7       all author [
           id [ var Author ],
 9         all name [ var AuthorName ]
     ] ] ]
11 FROM
     and{ RDFS-TRIPLE [
13       var Essay, rdf:type{{}}, books:Essay{{}}        ],
         RDF-TRIPLE [
15       var Essay, books:author{{}}, var Author          ],
         RDF-TRIPLE [
17       var Author, books:authorName{{}}, var AuthorName ] }
   END
```

The query pattern (between **FROM** and **END**) is a conjunction of queries against
the RDF triples represented in the predicate RDF-TRIPLE using the prefixes
declared in line 1 and 2. Notice that the first conjunct actually uses RDFS-
TRIPLE. This view of the RDF data contains all basic triples plus the ones
entailed by the RDFS semantics (cf. [9] for a detailed description). Using RDFS-
TRIPLE instead of RDF-TRIPLE ensures that also resources actually classified in
a sub-class of books:Essay are returned.

In the construct pattern (between **GOAL** and **FROM**), one of the strengths of
combining XML and RDF querying in Xcerpt is shown: Following the W3C's
requirements for an RDF data access language, yet in contrast to most other
RDF query languages, it is possible to construct arbitrary XML: E.g., here, a
list of all essays with their authors grouped inside is constructed. Indeed, when
constructing structured data such as RDF and XML, grouping is among the
most essential constructs, cf. [10,11] on grouping in an XML context. For RDF
querying, this points towards the need for similarly powerful, declarative, and
explicit grouping constructs, as provide in Xcerpt's **all**.

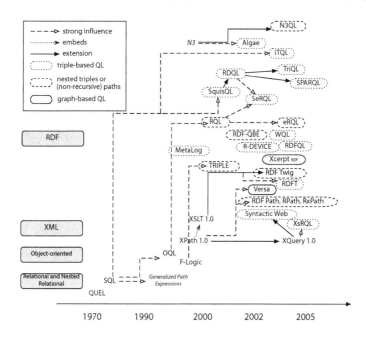

Fig. 2. RDF Query Languages: historical overview and classification

Except for the construction of arbitrary XML, a similar (triple) view of RDF is taken in most of the current RDF query languages (cf. Figure 2), most notably in RDQL and the W3C's SPARQL [12], and also in [13], an approach for querying RDF with XQuery: A query is composed of conjunctions (and in some languages including our proposal disjunctions) of "triple patterns", i.e., triples with variables indicating queried data. Using multiple occurrences of same variables more complex conditions can be expressed, e.g., for traversing paths in the RDF data or even for restricting a resource using several of its properties.

While familiar from SQL, this style leads for RDF data to hard-to-read and lengthy queries that also pose problems for evaluation (cf., e.g., [14]). Furthermore, queries involving (conditional or unconditional) traversals of unknown length in the RDF graph can often not be expressed in query languages using this style and, if it is provided, requires recursive views, rules, or functions (e.g., in [13]). This applies to the traversal of the subclasses of *Essay* needed in the sample query. This is a serious limitation of triple-based RDF query languages, as such queries are frequent (especially when considering ontological data in RDFS or other ontology languages) and recursive views or similar mechanisms make optimization and efficient evaluation of such queries hard or even impossible.

The previous observations lead us to an alternative view of RDF that is both closer to its actual data model and can make better use of the advanced features of an XML query language such as the traversal of arbitrary length paths in tree or graph data.

3.2   RDF Graphs: A Semi-structured View

For this view of RDF, Xcerpt's treatment of XML as graph data is an advantage over XML query languages such as XPath or XQuery, which consider XML as strictly tree shaped, providing no direct support for (ID/IDREF or similar) references in the data model. Although there have been proposals for slicing an (acyclic) RDF graph into trees (cf. Figure 2) for processing them with XSLT or XQuery (e.g., [15]), these approaches invariantly suffer (a) from choosing an appropriate slicing and (b) from the (in general) exponential blow-up of the tree view of an acyclic RDF graph.

In Xcerpt, a graph view of RDF is rather natural as the following Xcerpt program expressing the same query as above, but on the graph instead of the triple view, demonstrates:

```
   DECLARE ns-prefix rdf = "http://www.w3.org/1999/02/22-rdf-syntax-ns#"
2  DECLARE ns-prefix books = "http://example.org/books#"
   GOAL
4    result [
       all essay [
6        id [ var Essay ],
         all author [
8          id [ var Author ],
           all name [ var AuthorName ]
10   ] ] ]
   FROM
12   RDFS-GRAPH {{
       var Essay {{
14       rdf:type {{ books:Essay {{ }} }},
         books:author {{
16         var Author {{ books:name {{ var AuthorName }} }}
         }}
18     }} }}
   END
```

The RDF graph view is represented in the RDF-GRAPH predicate. Here, the RDFS-GRAPH view is used that extends RDF-GRAPH as RDFS-TRIPLE extends RDF-TRIPLE. Triples are represented similar to striped RDF/XML: each resource is a direct child element in RDF-GRAPH with a sub-element for each statement with that resource as object. The sub-element is labeled with the URI of the predicate and contains the object of the statement. As Xcerpt's data model is a rooted *graph* this can be represented without duplication of resources.

In contrast to the previous query against the RDF triple view, no conjunction is used but rather a nested pattern that naturally reflects the structure of the RDF graph. The more complex a query, the more evident the advantage of the graph view becomes: instead of having to use multiple occurrences of same variables for relating parts of the query, that relation is represented in the structure of the query itself (represented in the textual version of the query shown above by nesting and indentation).

Path traversals of arbitrary length can be expressed using traversal operators such as descendant. E.g., to find all subclasses of a given class one can use Xcerpt's qualified descendant **desc**(rdfs:subClassOf<rdfs:Class>)* that is similar to regular path expressions or conditional XPath. Similarly, other constructs for querying XML data with incomplete information about the structure of the queried data can be used for RDF as well.

The following Xcerpt rule illustrate the use of a conditional descendant. It computes all persons that have a common ancestor and includes any such common ancestor, if it is the 'nearest' common ancestor, i.e., there is no other common ancestor on the path to the two persons. Since all persons have at least foaf:Person as common ancestor, the query also excludes all resources reached by rdf:type relations.

```
     DECLARE ns-prefix rdf = "http://www.w3.org/1999/02/22-rdf-syntax-ns#"
 2   DECLARE ns-prefix books = "http://example.org/books#"
     GOAL
 4     result [
         all related-persons [
 6           var Person1,
             var Person2,
 8           all via { var Resource }
           ]
10     }
     FROM
12     RDFS-GRAPH {{
         var Resource @ /.*/ {{
14         desc(!/rdf:type/)* var Person1 {{ rdf:type { foaf:Person {{}} } }},
           desc(!/rdf:type/)* var Person2 {{ rdf:type { foaf:Person {{}} } }},
16         without desc /.*/ {{
             desc(!/rdf:type/)* var Person1 {{ }},
18           desc(!/rdf:type/)* var Person2 {{ }},
           }}
20       }}
       }}
22   END
```

Such explicit query constructs make optimization and evaluation of a frequent class of queries easier than relying on recursive views or similar generic mechanisms as required on the triple view. Considering the efficient evaluation of queries against such a graph view of RDF data, there are results on the efficient evaluation of queries against graph-shaped semi-structured data, cf. [16]. Ongoing work by the authors targets efficient evaluation methods for implementing Xcerpt queries against graph-shaped data. We believe it likely that at least for some interesting subsets of Xcerpt queries efficient evaluation methods against graph-shaped data can be found.

Nevertheless, only a surprisingly small number of RDF query languages consider a graph-view of RDF and provide expressive traversal operators, aside of Xcerpt most notably Versa [17,18]. In contrast to the proposal presented in this paper, Versa uses an unfamiliar syntax instead of established traversal operators from XML and generalized path expressions.

Graph Merging. In contrast to conventional data such as XML or relational data, RDF data from different and heterogeneous sources can be easily merged, as nodes in an RDF graph can be and mostly (with the exception of blank and literal nodes) are identified by URIs, i.e., globally valid identifiers. On the first glance, it might seem that merging two RDF graphs is more difficult if

considering the graph view of RDF. However, this crucial use case can be solved
in Xcerpt easily on either view.

On parsing RDF data, Xcerpt annotates the RDF data with provenance
information similar to recent proposals on named graphs [19] and their use in
RDF query languages [20]: In the case of the triple view, a origin attribute is
added to each RDF-TRIPLE term indicating the URI of the data's origin resource.
In the case of the graph view, the same procedure could be taken. Alternatively,
a single origin attribute for an entire RDF graph can be used by adding it to
the RDF-GRAPH term. While this sacrifices some flexibility, it saves considerable
space.

The following Xcerpt program shows the construction of the merged triples
from the base triples. Notice, how the outer **all** groups only over the variables
Subject, Property, and Object (as they occur free in that **all**, i.e., nested
inside that **all** without another **all** in between). Therefore, a RDF-TRIPLE is
created for each combination of subject, property, and object occurring in the
base triples (from either graph) with a origin attribute that is a concatenation of
the values of all origin attributes of base triples. If a statement occurred in both
graphs the origin attribute will thus point to two resources.

```
   CONSTRUCT
 2   merged-triples {{
       all RDF-TRIPLE [
 4       attributes {{ origin { all var Origin }, all var OtherAttributes }},
           var Subject, var Property, var Object
 6     ]
     }}
 8 FROM
     RDF-TRIPLE [
10     attributes {{ origin {{ var Origin }}, var OtherAttributes }}
       var Subject, var Property, var Object
12   ]
   END
```

If only named graph provenance (i.e., provenance for entire RDF graphs) is
needed, the following rule illustrate the merging of two RDF graphs using the
graph view:

```
 1 CONSTRUCT
     RDF-GRAPH {
 3     all var Resources {{
         all var Statements {{ }}
 5     }}
     }
 7 FROM
     and {
 9     RDF-GRAPH {{
         var Resource {{
11         optional var Statements → /.*/ {{ }}
         }}
13     }}
     }
15 END
```

Notice, how the query can simply ignore where the resources come from. Dupli-
cate resources and statements are eliminated implicitly during the grouping.

3.3   Marrying Triples and Graphs

A final observation on the two views on RDF is that they are not mutually exclusive. In fact, conversion between the two views can be performed by the following, linear Xcerpt view:

```
1  CONSTRUCT
     RDF-GRAPH {
3      all var Subject @ var Subject {
         all optional var Predicate {  ^var Object   },
5        all optional var Predicate {  var Literal   }
       } }
7  FROM
     or{
9      RDF-TRIPLE[
         var Subject,   var Predicate{},
11       optional var Literal as literal{{}},
         optional var Object {{}} where { var Object != 'literal'}
13     ],
       RDF-TRIPLE[
15       /.*/:/.*/{{}},   /.*/:/.*/{{}},   var Subject{{}}
       ]  }
17 END
```

Notice the use of the **optional** keyword in lines 11 and 12. This indicates that the contained part of the pattern does not have to occur in the data, but if it does occur the contained variables are bound appropriately. In lines 3 and 4 the actual graph structure is constructed: by using the operators @ and ^ a (possibly cyclic) link can be constructed.

Indeed, the framework for RDF access in Xcerpt discussed in this article provides both views, thus allowing the query author to decide which view is more appropriate for his liking and requirements.

4   Marrying XML and RDF

Providing integrated access to RDF and XML is a crucial issue for the success of the Semantic Web. This is reflected by a number of proposals for such integrated access: As discussed above, [13] and [15] share with the work presented in this article the aim to extend XML query languages with access to RDF data, but are limited to a triple or tree view of RDF. In [21] the dual approach has been taken: mapping XML data into RDF. However, [21] only preserves a subset of the information represented in the XML data and requires schema-specific mapping rules to be defined prior to accessing the information. Reconciling the RDF and XML data models has been considered in [22] and [23]. Whereas the first essentially defines a new data model, the latter proposes a new node type for XML as means for handling RDF edges.

In the remainder of this section, the mapping from RDF into XML discussed in this article is further detailed.

4.1   A Marriage Contract: Issues When Mapping RDF into XML

The mapping proposed here, although it has some similarities with [23], differs from all of the above noticeably: Figure 3 illustrates the mapping from an ex-

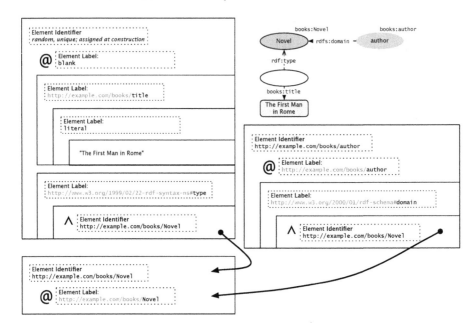

Fig. 3. Excerpt of RDF Graph represented in XML

cerpt of the sample RDF graph into three (top-level) XML elements (i.e., direct children of **RDF-GRAPH**). The following Xcerpt data term is a textual representation of the data in Figure 3:

```
1  DECLARE ns-prefix rdf = "http://www.w3.org/1999/02/22 rdf syntax ns#"
   DECLARE ns-prefix rdfs = "http://www.w3.org/2000/01/rdf-schema#"
3  DECLARE ns-prefix books = "http://example.org/books#"
   RDF-GRAPH {
5    id1 @ blank {
       books:title { literal { "The First Man in Rome" } },
7      rdf:type { ^books:Novel }
     },
9    books:author @ books:author {
       rdfs:domain { ^books:Novel }
11   },
     books:Novel @ books:Novel {},
13   ...
   }
```

Notice how both edges and nodes from the RDF graph are represented as XML elements. However, nodes can still be distinguished as they are either blank nodes (without namespace) literal nodes (again without namespace) or named resources in which case both their element identifier and element label are set to the URI identifying the resource. In contrast, elements for edges never have an identifier (as they can not be referenced by another part of the data). This mapping results in a 'stripped' representation of the RDF graph: the children of elements representing nodes (i.e., resources) are always elements representing edges and vice versa. One might question the use of resource URIs both as labels and identifiers of nodes. However, while element labels are more convenient for querying, unique identifiers for the elements are needed (for establishing graph references). Since URIs already provide uniqueness, they are also used for this purpose. [23] suggest the use of RDF types (i.e., the URI of the resource associated with rdf:type) as element labels when mapping RDF to XML. However, this approach is not able to map all RDF graphs as RDF resources may be classified by distinct types (that may not be related at all in the type hierarchy).

The XML mapping allows additional information about the RDF statements, e.g., provenance information, to be recorded alongside.

4.2   Serialization Transparency

Aside of providing the above discussed two views on RDF, Xcerpt's rules are also convenient for making the language 'serialization transparent'. For each RDF serialization, a set of rules expresses a translation from or into that serialization. Exemplary rules for RDF/XML and RXR can be found in [9], similar functions for parsing RDF/XML in XQuery are described in [13].

5   Conclusion and Outlook

In this article, a brief overview of a framework for RDF querying in the XML query language Xcerpt is presented highlighting in particular the need for reconsideration of the triple view as the only perspective on RDF available in the established RDF query languages. We believe that a richer view of RDF more akin to XML data with graph-shape not only makes the integration of data and metadata easier but also leads in many cases to more succinct queries without sacrificing efficiency.

Acknowledgments. This research has been funded by the European Commission and by the Swiss Federal Office for Education and Science within the 6th Framework Programme project REWERSE number 506779 (cf. http:// rewerse.net).

References

1. Berners-Lee, T., Hendler, J., Lassila, O.: The Semantic Web—A new form of Web content that is meaningful to computers will unleash a revolution of new possibilities. Scientific American (2001)
2. Manola, F., Miller, E., McBride, B.: RDF primer. Recommendation, W3C (2004)
3. Klyne, G., Carroll, J., McBride, B.: Resource Description Framework (RDF): Concepts and Abstract Syntax. W3C. (2004)
4. Bry, F., Furche, T., Badea, L., Koch, C., Schaffert, S., Berger, S.: Identification of Design Principles for a (Semantic) Web Query Language. Deliverable I4-D1, REWERSE (2004)
5. Schaffert, S., Bry, F.: Querying the Web Reconsidered: A Practical Introduction to Xcerpt. In: Proc. Extreme Markup Languages. (2004)

6. Schaffert, S.: Xcerpt: A Rule-Based Query and Transformation Language for the Web. Dissertation/Ph.D. thesis, University of Munich (2004)
7. Bry, F., Furche, T., Badea, L., Koch, C., Schaffert, S., Berger, S.: Querying the Web Reconsidered: Design Principles for Versatile Web Query Languages. Journal of Semantic Web and Information Systems 1 (2005)
8. Zloof, M.M.: Query-by-Example: A Data Base Language. IBM Systems Journal 16 (1977)
9. Bolzer, O.: Towards Data-Integration on the Semantic Web: Querying RDF with Xcerpt. Diplomarbeit/Master thesis, University of Munich (2005)
10. Paparizos, S., Al-Khalifa, S., Jagadish, H.V., Lakshmanan, L.V., Nierman, A., Srivastava, D., Wu, Y.: Grouping in XML. In: EDBT Workshop on XML Data Management. Number 2490 in LNCS, Springer-Verlag (2002)
11. Beyer, K.S., Cochrane, R., Colby, L.S., Ozcan, F., Pirahesh, H.: XQuery for Analytics: Challenges and Requirements. In: Int. Workshop on XQuery Implementation, Experience and Perspectives <XIME-P/>. (2004)
12. Prud'hommeaux, E., Seaborne, A.: SPARQL Query Language for RDF. Working Draft, W3C (2005)
13. Robie, J.: The Syntactic Web: Syntax and Semantics on the Web. In: XML. (2001)
14. Hung, E., Deng, Y., Subrahmanian, V.S.: RDF Aggregate Queries and Views. In: Int. Conf. on Data Engineering. (2005)
15. Walsh, N.: RDF Twig: accessing RDF graphs in XSLT. In: Extreme Markup Languages. (2003)
16. Schenkel, R., Theobald, A., Weikum, G.: HOPI: A Efficient Connection Index for Complex XML Document Collections. In: Extending Database Technology. (2004)
17. Olson, M., Ogbuji, U.: Versa Specification. Online only (2003)
18. Ogbuji, U.: Versa by example. Online only (2004)
19. Carroll, J., Bizer, C., Hayes, P., Stickler, P.: Named Graphs, Provenance and Trust. Technical Report HPL-2004-57, HP Labs (2004)
20. Bizer, C.: TriQL—A Query Language for Named Graphs. Online only (2004)
21. Koffina, I., Serfiotis, G., Christophides, V., Tannen, V., Deutsch, A.: Integrating XML data sources using RDF/S schemas: The ICS-FORTH Semantic Web Integration Middleware (SWIM). In: Dagstuhl Seminar on Semantic Interoperability and Integration. Number 04391 in Dagstuhl Seminar Proceedings, IBFI (2005)
22. Patel-Schneider, P., Simeon, J.: The Yin/Yang Web: XML Syntax and RDF Semantics. In: Int. World Wide Web Conference. (2002)
23. Boley, H.: The Rule Markup Language: RDF-XML Data Model, XML Schema Hierarchy, and XSL Transformations. In: Int. Conf. on Applications of Prolog. (2001)

Descriptive Typing Rules for Xcerpt

Sacha Berger[1], Emmanuel Coquery[2],
Włodzimierz Drabent[3,4], and Artur Wilk[4]

[1] Institute for Computer Science, University of Munich, Germany
`sacha.berger@ifi.lmu.de`
[2] INRIA Rocquencourt and Conservatoire des Arts et Métiers, France
`Emmanuel.Coquery@inria.fr`
[3] IPI PAN, Polish Academy of Sciences, Warszawa, Poland
[4] IDA, Linköping University, 581-83 Linköping, Sweden
{`wdr, artwi`}`@ida.liu.se`

Abstract. We present typing rules for the Web query language Xcerpt. The rules provide a descriptive type system: the typing of a program is an approximation of its semantics. The rules can also be seen as an abstract form of a type inference algorithm (presented in previous work), and as a stage in a formal soundness proof of the algorithm. The paper considers a substantial fragment of Xcerpt; the main restriction is that we deal with data terms corresponding to trees (instead of general graphs), and we do not deal with Xcerpt rule chaining. We provide a formal semantics for the fragment of Xcerpt and a soundness theorem for the presented type system.

1 Introduction

This article presents a type system for the Web and Semantic Web query language Xcerpt [12,6,11], formalized using typing rules in the spirit of [7]. It is an extension and reformulation of the type system presented in the earlier work [13,8]. The type system is *descriptive*, this means a typing approximates the semantics of a program (in an untyped programming language). In descriptive typing, type inference means finding an approximation of the semantics of the given program; type checking means proving program correctness with respect to a specification expressed by means of types. In our case, for a given Xcerpt program and a type of data (i.e. the set of data objects to which the program may be applied) the type system provides a type of the program's results (i.e. a superset of the set of the program's results). This is type inference; if a type of expected results is given then type checking can be performed by checking if the obtained type of results is a subset of the the given one. The main intended application of the proposed type system is discovering errors in Xcerpt programs.

In the previous work [13,8] two descriptive type systems for an Xcerpt fragment[1] have been presented. They are formulated by means of algorithms. This

---

[1] The main Xcerpt features excluded are: data terms corresponding to general graphs (which are not trees), grouping constructs (**all**, **some**), negation, and programs consisting of multiple query rules.

F. Fages and S. Soliman (Eds.): PPSWR 2005, LNCS 3703, pp. 85–100, 2005.

is rather complicated and makes any formal reasoning about the type system difficult. In the present paper we generalize the simpler of these type systems to a bigger fragment of Xcerpt (grouping constructs are added). An important difference is that we formulate the type system by means of derivation rules. The rules are similar to proof rules of logic, rules used in operational semantics, and those used in prescriptive typing [7]. Employing rules makes it possible to specify a type system in a formal and concise way. Such approach facilitates formal reasoning; we confirm this by presenting a soundness proof of the type system in a full version of this paper [2]. The rules may be seen as an abstraction of an algorithm; they abstract from lower level details. Thus – we believe – this formulation of a type system is also easier to understand by humans than the previous one.

To facilitate a soundness proof we provide a formal semantics (based on [13,6,11]) of the fragment of Xcerpt. The semantics is substantially simpler than that of a full Xcerpt [11] (as it does not use the notion of simulation unification), and may be of separate interest.

Similarly to other work related to Xcerpt [12,11] we use *data terms* as an abstraction of semi-structured data [1] of the Web. Data terms generalize the notion of a term: the number of arguments of a symbol is not fixed, moreover a symbol may have an (unordered) set of arguments, instead of an ordered sequence. (This paper does not deal with data terms representing graphs which are not trees). As a formalism to define types we use *type definitions* [13,4]. They are similar to unranked tree automata [3] (and equivalent formalisms), but deal also with the case of unordered children of a tree node. The types defined by type definitions roughly correspond to the sets of documents defined by various schema languages like DTD, XML Schema or Relax NG.[10]

Our descriptive type system uses rules in a similar way as prescriptive type systems [7] do. We expect that this should make possible a formal comparison of the two approaches, and maybe even combining their advantages, thus obtaining a system that can be used for detecting errors, checking program composition and providing a base for documentation. (There is no general agreement about what exactly descriptive and prescriptive typing mean. Roughly speaking, the former deals with an untyped programming language and types approximate program semantics, while in the latter the language is typed and types are an important part of its semantics.)

The article is organized as follows: First, data terms and type definitions are introduced. A short introduction of Xcerpt is given afterwards, explaining a substantial fragment of the language and the semantics of the fragment. Then, in Section 4 the type system for the Xcerpt fragment is introduced, by (1) motivating the idea of descriptive types for Xcerpt, and (2) providing typing rules in the spirit of [7], specifying the type system inductively based on the syntax of Xcerpt.

2   Modelling XML Data

We model XML data using a formalism of data terms similar to that defined in [12]. Data terms can be seen as mixed trees which are labelled trees where children of a node are either linearly ordered or unordered. This is related to existence of two basic concepts in XML: *tags* which are nodes of an ordered tree and *attributes* that attach attribute-value mappings to nodes of a tree. These mappings are represented as unordered trees. Unordered children of a node may also be used to abstract from the order of elements, when this order is inessential. We assume that there is no syntactic difference between XML tag names and attribute names and they both are labels of nodes in our mixed trees (and symbols of our data terms). The infinite alphabet of labels will be denoted by $\mathcal{L}$.

A content of an element is a sequence of other elements or **basic constants**. Basic constants are basic values such as attribute values and all "free" data appearing in an XML document – all data that is between start and end tag except XML elements, called PCDATA (short for *parseable character data*) in XML jargon. Basic constants occur as strings in XML documents but they can play a role of data of other types depending on an adequate definition in DTD (or other schema languages) e.g. IDREF, CDATA,.... The set of basic constants will be denoted by $\mathcal{B}$. In our notation we will enclose all basic constants in quotation marks " ".

XML documents are represented as *data terms*.

Definition 1. *A **data term** is an expression defined inductively as follows:*

- *Any basic constant is a data term,*
- *If l is a label and $t_1, \ldots, t_n$ are $n \geq 0$ data terms, then $l[t_1, \ldots, t_n]$ and $l\{t_1, \ldots, t_n\}$ are data terms.*

The linear ordering of children of the node with label l is denoted by enclosing them by brackets $[\,]$, while unordered children are enclosed by braces $\{\}$.

A **subterm** of a data term t is defined inductively: t is a subterm of t, and any subterm of t_i ($1 \leq i \leq n$) is a subterm of $l'[t_1, \ldots, t_n]$ and of $l'\{t_1, \ldots, t_n\}$. Data terms $t_1, \ldots, t_n$ will be sometimes called the arguments of l', or the **direct subterms** of $l'[t_1, \ldots, t_n]$ (and of $l'\{t_1, \ldots, t_n\}$). The **root** of a data term t, denoted $root(t)$, is defined as follows . If t is of the form $l[t_1, \ldots, t_n]$ or $l\{t_1, \ldots, t_n\}$ then $root(t) = l$; for t being a basic constant we assume that $root(t) = \$$.

2.1 Type Definitions

Here we introduce a formalism for specifying a class of decidable sets of data terms representing XML documents. It is a certain simplification of the formalism of [4]. First we specify a set of **type names** $\mathcal{T} = \mathcal{C} \cup \mathcal{S} \cup \mathcal{V}$ which consist of

- **type constants** from the alphabet $\mathcal{C}$
- **special type names** from the alphabet $\mathcal{S}$
- **type variables** from the alphabet $\mathcal{V}$

We associate each type name T with a set $[\![T]\!]$ (the *type denoted by T*) of data terms which are allowed values assigned to T. For T being a type constant or a special type name, the elements of $[\![T]\!]$ are basic constants.

Type constants correspond to an XML schema language base types. The set of type constants is fixed and finite. In our examples we will use a type constant $\#$ assuming that $[\![\#]\!]$ is the set of non empty strings of characters. This is similar to #PCDATA in DTD. In our notation, type constants and special type names are sequences of letters beginning with character $\#$.

Each type variable T is associated with a set of data terms $[\![T]\!]$ which is specified in a way similar to that of [4] and described below. Similarly, each special type name T is associated with a finite set $[\![T]\!]$ of basic constants.

First we introduce some auxiliary notions. The empty string will be denoted by ϵ. A *regular expression* over an alphabet Σ is ε, ϕ, any $a \in \Sigma$ and any $r_1 r_2$, $r_1 | r_2$ and r_1^*, where r_1, r_2 are regular expressions. A language $L(r)$ of strings over Σ is assigned to each regular expression r in the standard way (see e.g. [9]). In particular, $L(\phi) = \emptyset$, $L(\varepsilon) = \{\epsilon\}$ and $L(r_1 | r_2) = L(r_1) \cup L(r_2)$.

Definition 2. *A* **regular type expression** *is a regular expression over the alphabet of type names $\mathcal{T}$. We abbreviate a regular expression $r^n | r^{n+1} | \cdots | r^m$, where $n \leq m$, as $r^{(n:m)}$, $r^n r^*$ as $r^{(n:\infty)}$, rr^* as r^+, and $r^{(0:1)}$ as $r^?$. A regular type expression of the form*

$$r_1 \cdots r_k$$

where $k \geq 0$, each r_i is $T_i^{(n_{i,1}:n_{i,2})}$, $0 \leq n_{i,1} \leq n_{i,2} \leq \infty$ for $i = 1, \ldots, k$, and $T_1, \ldots, T_k$ are distinct type names, will be called a **multiplicity list**.

Multiplicity lists will be used to specify multisets of type names. We use $types_D(r)$ to denote the set of all type names occurring in the regular expression r.

Definition 3. *A* **type definition** *is a set D of rules of the form*

$$T \to l[r], \quad T \to l\{s\}, \quad or \quad T' \to c_1 | \ldots | c_n,$$

where T is a type variable, T' a special type name, l a label, r a regular type expression, s a multiplicity list, and $c_1, \ldots, c_n$ are basic constants. A rule $U \to G \in D$ will be called a **rule for** *U in D. We require that for any type name $U \in \mathcal{V} \cup \mathcal{S}$ occurring in D there is exactly one rule for U in D.*

If the rule for a type variable T in D is as above then l will be called the **label** *of T (in D) and denoted $label_D(T) = l$. For T being a type constant or a special type name we define $label_D(T) = \$$. The regular expression in a rule for type variable T is called the* **content model** *of T.*

Example 4. Consider type definition D:

$$Cd \to cd[\text{Title Artist}^+ \#\text{Category}^?]$$
$$Title \to title[\# \text{ Subtitle}^?]$$
$$Subtitle \to subtitle[\#]$$
$$Artist \to artist[\#]$$
$$\#Category \to \text{pop} \mid \text{rock} \mid \text{classic}$$

D contains a rule for each of type variables: *Cd, Title, Subtitle, Artist* and a rule for special type name $\#Category$. Labels occurring in D are: *cd, title, subtitle, artist*, and *pop, rock, classic* are basic constants.

Type definitions are a kind of grammars, they define sets by means of derivations, where a type variable T is replaced by the right hand side of the rule for T and a regular expression r is replaced by a string from $L(r)$; if T is a type constant or a special type name then it is replaced by a basic constant from respectively $[\![T]\!]$, or from the rule for T. This can be concisely formalized as follows (treating type definitions similarly to tree automata).

Definition 5. *Let D be a type definition. We will say that a data term t is* **derived** *in D from a type name T, iff there exists a mapping ν from the subterms of t to type names such that $\nu(t) = T$ and for each subterm u of t*

- *if u is a basic constant then $\nu(u) \in \mathcal{C}$ and $u \in [\![\nu(u)]\!]$ or $\nu(u) \in \mathcal{S}$ and there exists a rule $\nu(u) \to \cdots |u| \cdots$ in D.*
- *otherwise $\nu(u) = U \in \mathcal{V}$ and*
  - *there is a rule $U \leftarrow l[r] \in D$, $u = l[t_1, \ldots, t_n]$, and $\nu(t_1) \cdots \nu(t_n) \in L(r)$,*
  - *or there is a rule $U \leftarrow l\{r\} \in D$, $u = l\{t_1, \ldots, t_n\}$, and $\nu(t_1) \cdots \nu(t_n)$ is a permutation of a string in $L(r)$.*

The set of the data terms derived in D from a type name T will be denoted by $[\![T]\!]_D$.

Example 6. For the type definition D from the previous example, we have that the data term

$$t = cd[\,title[\text{"Stop"}],\ artist[\text{"Sam Brown"}],\ \text{"pop"}\,]$$

is derived from the type variable Cd. The type names assigned to the three arguments of cd are, respectively, $Title$, $Artist$, $\#Category$, and the type constant $\#$ is assigned to the constants "Stop", and "Sam Brown".

Notice that if T is a type constant then $[\![T]\!]_D = [\![T]\!]$. If it is clear from the context which type definition is considered, we will often omit the subscript in the notation $[\![\ ]\!]_D$ and similar ones. For U being a set of type names $\{T_1, \ldots, T_n\}$, we define a set of data terms $[\![U]\!] = [\![T_1]\!] \cup \ldots \cup [\![T_n]\!]$. For a regular type expression r we define $[\![r]\!] = \{\, d_1, \ldots, d_n \mid d_1 \in [\![T_1]\!], \ldots, d_n \in [\![T_n]\!]$ for some $T_1, \ldots, T_n \in L(r)\,\}$. Notice that if $D \subseteq D'$ are type definitions then $[\![T]\!]_D = [\![T]\!]_{D'}$ for any type name T occurring in D.

3   Xcerpt – Introduction

Xcerpt is a rule-based query and transformation language for XML (see [11,6,12,5]). It employs patterns instead of paths to query XML and semi-structured data. This approach stems from logic programming. A query term is matched against a data term from a database. A successful matching results in binding the variables in the query term to certain subterms of the data term. This operation is called simulation unification.

We consider here a somehow simplified version of Xcerpt. We focused on core Xcerpt features to make our type system simpler and easier to understand.

The main difference is that our data terms represent trees while in full Xcerpt terms are used to represent graphs (by adding unique identifiers to some tree nodes and introducing nodes which are references to these identifiers). Other neglected Xcerpt features in respect to the Xcerpt version described in [12,11] are: functions and aggregations, non-pattern conditions, optional subterms, position specifications, negation, regular expressions and label variables. Moreover, we restrict ourselves to Xcerpt programs containing only one query rule.

We provide a formal semantics to the chosen fragment of Xcerpt. The semantics of query terms is from [13], the rest of the semantics is based on [11].

We assume that a database is a data term or a multiset of data terms. There are two other kinds of terms in Xcerpt: query terms and construct terms. The role of query terms is to be matched against a database. Construct terms are used in constructing data terms which are query results.

Definition 7. Query terms *are inductively defined as follows:*

- *Any basic constant is a query term.*
- *A variable X is a query term.*
- *If q is a query term, then* desc q *is a query term.*
- *If X is a variable and q is a query term, then $X \rightsquigarrow q$ is a query term.*
- *If l is a label and $q_1, \ldots, q_n$ $(n \geq 0)$ are query terms, then $l[q_1, \ldots, q_n]$, $l\{q_1, \ldots, q_n\}$, $l[[q_1, \ldots, q_n]]$ and $l\{\{q_1, \ldots, q_n\}\}$ are query terms (called* rooted *query terms).*

For a rooted query term $q = l\alpha q_1, \ldots, q_n\beta$, where $\alpha\beta$ are parentheses $[\,]$, $[[\,]]$, $\{\}$ or $\{\{\}\}$, $root(q) = l$ and $q_1, \ldots, q_n$ are the child *subterms of q. If q is a basic constant then $root(q) = \$$.*

To informally explain the role of query terms, consider a query term $q = l\alpha q_1, \ldots, q_m\beta$ and a data term $d = l'\alpha'd_1, \ldots, d_n\beta'$, where $\alpha, \beta, \alpha', \beta'$ are parentheses. In order to q match d it is necessary that $l = l'$. Moreover the child subterms $q_1, \ldots, q_m$ of q should match certain child subterms of d. Single parentheses in d ($[\,]$ or $\{\}$) mean that $m = n$ and each q_i should match some (distinct) d_j. Double parentheses mean that $m \leq n$ and $q_1, \ldots, q_m$ are matched against some m terms out of $d_1, \ldots, d_n$. Curly braces ($\{\}$ or $\{\{\}\}$) in q mean that the order of the child subterms in d does not matter; square brackets in q mean that $q_1, \ldots, q_m$ should match (a subsequence of) $d_1, \ldots, d_n$ in the same order.

A variable matches any data term, desc q matches a data term d whenever q matches some subterm of d. A query term $X \rightsquigarrow q$ matches any data term matched by q. A side effect of a query term X or $X \rightsquigarrow q$ matching a data term d is that variable X obtains a value d.

Now we formally define which query terms match which data terms and what are the resulting assignments of data terms to variables. We do not follow the original definition of simulation unification. Instead we define a notion of answer substitution for a query term q and a data term d. As usually, by a *substitution* (of data terms for variables) we mean a set $\theta = \{X_1/d_1, \ldots, X_n/d_n\}$, where $X_1, \ldots, X_n$ are distinct variables and $d_1, \ldots, d_n$ are data terms; its domain $dom(\theta)$ is $\{X_1, \ldots, X_n\}$, its application to a (query) term is defined in a standard way.

Definition 8 ([13]). *A substitution θ is an* answer substitution *(shortly, an **answer**) for a query term q and a data term d if q and d are of one of the forms below and the corresponding condition holds. (In what follows $m, n \geq 0$, X is a variable, l is a label, $q, q_1, \ldots$ are query terms, and $d, d_1, \ldots$ data terms; set notation is used for multisets, for instance $\{d, d\}$ and $\{d\}$ are different multisets).*

q	d	condition on q and d
b	b	b is a basic constant
$l[q_1, \ldots, q_n]$	$l[d_1, \ldots, d_n]$	θ is an answer for q_i and d_i, for each $i = 1, \ldots, n$
$l[[q_1, \ldots, q_m]]$	$l[d_1, \ldots, d_n]$	for some subsequence $d_{i_1}, \ldots, d_{i_m}$ of $d_1, \ldots, d_n$ (i.e. $0 < i_1 < \ldots < i_m \leq n$) θ is an answer for q_j and d_{i_j}, for each $j = 1, \ldots, m$,
$l\{q_1, \ldots, q_n\}$	$l\{d_1, \ldots, d_n\}$ or $l[d_1 \cdots d_n]$	for some permutation $d_{i_1}, \ldots, d_{i_n}$ of $d_1, \ldots, d_n$ (i.e. $\{d_{i_1}, \ldots, d_{i_n}\} = \{d_1, \ldots, d_n\}$) θ is an answer for q_j and d_{i_j} for each $j = 1, \ldots, m$,
$l\{\{q_1, \ldots, q_m\}\}$	$l\{d_1, \ldots, d_n\}$ or $l[d_1, \ldots, d_n]$	for some $\{d_{i_1}, \ldots, d_{i_m}\} \subseteq \{d_1, \ldots, d_n\}$ θ is an answer for q_j and d_{i_j} for each $j = 1, \ldots, m$,
X	d	$X\theta = d$
$X \leadsto q$	d	$X\theta = d$ and θ is an answer for q and d
desc q	d	θ is an answer for q and some subterm d' of d

We say that q matches d if there exists an answer for q, d.

Thus if q is a rooted query term (or a basic constant) and $root(q) \neq root(d)$ then no answer for q, d exists. If $q = d$ then any θ is an answer for q, d. A query $l\{\{\}\}$ matches any data term with the label l. If θ, θ' are substitutions and $\theta \subseteq \theta'$ then if θ is an answer for q, d then θ' is an answer for q, d. If a variable X occurs in a query term q then queries $X \leadsto q$ and $X \leadsto \text{desc}\, q$ match no data term, provided that $q \neq X$ and q is not of the form $\text{desc} \cdots \text{desc}\, X$.

Example 9. Query term $q_1 = a[c\{\{d[], "e"\}\}, f[[g[], h\{"i"\}]]]$ matches data terms $a[c\{"e", d[], g[]\}, f[g[], l[], h["i"]]]$ and $a[c[d[], g[], "e"], f[g[], h["i"]]]$. In contrast, data terms $f[h["i"], g[]]$ and $f\{g[], h["i"]\}$ are not matched by $f[[g[], h\{"i"\}]]$. Query term $q_2 = \text{desc}\, w\{\{\}\}$ matches data terms $a[b\{w[]\}]$ and $w["s"]$. Query term $q_2 = a[[X_1 \leadsto c[[d\{\}]], X_2, "p"]]$ matches $a["s", c[d\{\}, "r"], h\{j[]\}, "p"]$, with an answer which binds X_1 to $c[d\{\}, "r"]$ and X_2 to $h\{j[]\}$.

Each answer for a query term q binds all the variables of the query to some data terms. For any such answer θ' (for q and d) there exists an answer $\theta \subseteq \theta'$

(for q and d) binding exactly these variables. We will call such answers *non redundant*. From Definition 8 one can derive an algorithm which produces non redundant answers for a given q and d. Construction of the algorithm is rather simple, we skip the details. Non redundant answers are actually those of interest; we consider a more general class of answers to simplify Definition 8.

A **targeted query term** is a pair $\mathtt{in}(db, q)$, of a URI and a query term. We assume that the URI locates on the Web a data term $d(db)$. An answer substitution for q and $d(db)$ is called an answer substitution for $\mathtt{in}(db, q)$ (and an arbitrary data term).

Definition 10. *A* **query** *is inductively defined as follows.*

- *Any query term and any targeted query term is a query.*
- *If $Q_1, \ldots, Q_n$ ($n \geq 0$) are queries then $\mathtt{and}(Q_1, \ldots, Q_n)$ and $\mathtt{or}(Q_1, \ldots, Q_n)$ are queries.*
  A substitution θ is an answer substitution *for $\mathtt{and}(Q_1, \ldots, Q_n)$ (respectively for $\mathtt{or}(Q_1, \ldots, Q_n)$) and a data term d iff θ is an answer substitution for each of (some of) $Q_1, \ldots, Q_n$ and d.*

A query can be transformed into equivalent one in *disjunctive normal form* $\mathtt{or}(Q_1, \ldots, Q_n)$, where each Q_i is of the form $\mathtt{and}(Q_{i1}, \ldots, Q_{ik_i})$ and each Q_{ij} is a (targeted) query term (cf. [11, Proposition 6.4]).

Definition 11. *A* **construct term** *and the set $FV(c)$ of free variables of a construct term c are defined recursively. If b is a basic constant, X a variable, l a label, $c, c_1, \ldots, c_n$ construct terms ($n \geq 0$), and k a natural number then*

$$b, \quad X, \quad l[c_1, \ldots, c_n], \quad l\{c_1, \ldots, c_n\}, \quad \mathtt{all}\ c, \quad \mathtt{some}\ k\ c,$$

are construct terms. $FV(b) = \emptyset$, $FV(X) = \{X\}$, $FV(l[c_1, \ldots, c_n]) = FV(l\{c_1, \ldots, c_n\}) = \bigcup_{i=1}^{n} FV(c_i)$, $FV(\mathtt{all}\ c) = FV(\mathtt{some}\ k\ c) = \emptyset$.

Notice that any data term is a construct term. (Also, a construct term without any $\mathtt{all}$ and $\mathtt{some}$ construct is a query term).

Before we define the notion of a query rule and its result we need to provide some auxiliary definitions. By a substitution set we mean a set of substitutions of data terms for variables, e.g. of answers for a query and a data term.

Definition 12. *Given a substitution set Θ and a set V of variables, such that $V \subseteq dom(\theta)$ for each $\theta \in \Theta$, the equivalence relation $\simeq_V \subseteq \Theta \times \Theta$ is defined as: $\theta_1 \simeq \theta_2$ iff $\theta_1(X) = \theta_2(X)$ for all $X \in V$. The set of equivalence classes of $\simeq_V$ is denoted by $\Theta/\simeq_V$.*

The concatenation of two sequences S_1, S_2 of data terms will be denoted by $S_1 \circ S_2$. We do not distinguish between a data term d and the one element sequence with the element d.

Definition 13. *Let c be a construct term and Θ be a substitution set containing the same assignments for the free variables $FV(c)$ of c (i.e. $\theta_1 \simeq_{FV(c)} \theta_2$ for any $\theta_1, \theta_2 \in \Theta$). The application $\Theta(c)$ of the substitution set Θ to c is a sequence of data terms defined as follows*

- $\Theta(b) = b$, *where b is a basic constant*
- $\Theta(X) = X\theta$, *where $\theta \in \Theta$*
- $\Theta(l\{c_1, \ldots, c_n\}) = l\{\Theta(c_1) \circ \cdots \circ \Theta(c_n)\}$
- $\Theta(l[c_1, \ldots, c_n]) = l[\Theta(c_1) \circ \cdots \circ \Theta(c_n)]$
- $\Theta(\texttt{all } c') = \Theta_1(c') \circ \cdots \circ \Theta_k(c')$, *where $\{\Theta_1, \ldots, \Theta_k\} = \Theta/{\simeq}_{FV(c')}$*
- $\Theta(\texttt{some } k \ c') = \Theta_1(c') \circ \cdots \circ \Theta_m(c')$, *where $\{\Theta_1, \ldots, \Theta_m\} \subseteq \Theta/{\simeq}_{FV(c')}$ and $m = k$ if $|\Theta/{\simeq}_{FV(c')}| \geq k$ or $m = |\Theta/{\simeq}_{FV(c')}|$ otherwise.*

For a construct term c containing neither $\texttt{all}$ nor $\texttt{some}$, $\Theta(c) = c\theta$ for any $\theta \in \Theta$. Notice that $\Theta(c)$ is defined uniquely unless c contains $\texttt{all}$ or $\texttt{some}$ (and $\Theta(c)$ is defined uniquely up to reordering provided c does not contain $\texttt{some}$). Notice also that $\Theta(c)$ is a one element sequence unless c is of the form $\texttt{all } c'$ or $\texttt{some } k \ c'$.

Definition 14. *A* **construct-query rule** *(shortly,* query rule*) is an expression of the form $c \leftarrow Q$, where c is a construct term not of the form $\texttt{all } c'$ or $\texttt{some } k \ c'$, Q is a query and every variable occurring in c also occurs in Q. Moreover, if $\texttt{or}(Q_1, \ldots, Q_n)$ is a disjunctive normal form of Q then every variable of c occurs in each Q_i, for $i = 1, \ldots, n$. The construct term c will be sometimes called the* head *and Q the* body *of the rule.*

If Θ is the set of all answers for Q and a data term d, and $\Theta' \in \Theta/{\simeq}_{FV(c)}$ then $\Theta'(c)$ is a **result** *for query $c \leftarrow Q$ and d.*

Each result of a query rule is a data term, as an answer for a query term binds all the variables of the rule to data terms.

Example 15. Consider a database which is a data term:

$catalogue[\ cd[\ title["Empire\ Burlesque"],\ artist["Bob\ Dylan"],\ year["1985"]\ ],$
$\qquad\qquad cd[\ title["Hide\ your\ heart"],\ artist["Bonnie\ Tyler"],\ year["1988"]\ ],$
$\qquad\qquad cd[\ title["Stop"],\ artist["Sam\ Brown"],\ year["1988"]\ ]\ ]$

Here is a rule which extracts titles and artists for the CD's issued in 1988 and presents the results in a changed form (title as name and artist as author). *TITLE* and *ARTIST* are variables.

$result[\ name[TITLE],\ author[ARTIST]\ ]\ \leftarrow$
$\qquad\qquad catalogue\{\{\ cd\{title[TITLE],\ artist[ARTIST],\ year["1988"]\ \}\}\}$

The results returned by the rule are:

$\qquad\qquad result[\ name["Hide\ your\ heart"],\ author["Bonnie\ Tyler"]\ ]$
$\qquad\qquad result[\ name["Stop"],\ author["Sam\ Brown"]\ ]$

The next query rule is similar. It uses $\texttt{all}$ for grouping all the results together and another $\texttt{all}$ for grouping together the CD's from the same year.

$\qquad results[\ \texttt{all } result[\ cds[\ \texttt{all } name[TITLE]\ ],\ year[YEAR]\ ]\ ]\ \leftarrow$
$\qquad\qquad catalogue\{\{\ cd\{\{\ title[TITLE],\ year[YEAR]\ \}\}\}\}$

The rule returns the following result:

$results[\ result[\ year["1988"],\ cds[\ title["Hide\ your\ heart"\ ],\ title["Stop"]\ ]\ ],$
$\qquad result[\ year["1985"],\ cds[\ title["Empire\ Burlesque"\ ]\ ]\ ]\ ].$

4   Reasoning About Types of Xcerpt Query Results

4.1   Motivation

In this section we study the relation between types of databases and types of query results. Assume that the only information available about the database is that it is a data term (or a set of data terms) from a given type $[\![T_{\mathrm{DB}}]\!]$ (or from a given union of types $[\![T_1]\!] \cup \ldots \cup [\![T_n]\!]$). One may want to know what query results are possible for such database. We show how to compute (a superset of) the set of such results The set will be expressed as a type, specified by a type definition. We will usually call it the query result type.

Computing the query result type may serve some additional purposes. 1. If this type is empty, then the query will never give an answer for a data term from $[\![T_{\mathrm{DB}}]\!]$. An algorithm checking this property is obtained by combining computing query result type with checking emptiness of a type. 2. If some specification of the intended type of results exists, one may check if the query is correct w.r.t. the specification, by checking whether the computed type of the results is included in the specified one. 3. If we use a data term d as the body of the query, then computing the result type is also a check whether $d \in [\![T_{\mathrm{DB}}]\!]$. Namely $d \in [\![T_{\mathrm{DB}}]\!]$ iff the result type is not empty. 4. The algorithm computing the query result type produces as a side effect the types of the variables of the queries. For each variable from the query it gives a set containing every value that can be assigned to the variable (when querying a data term from type $[\![T_{\mathrm{DB}}]\!]$). This provides additional information about the behaviour of the query. We may consider specifications of the types of the query variables. A query is correct w.r.t. such a specification if for every variable the computed type is a subset of the specified type.

Example 16. Consider the type definition D from Example 4 and a construct-query rule Q:

$$result[\,name[\,TITLE], \; author[ARTIST]\,] \leftarrow$$
$$cd\{\!\{\; TITLE, \; ARTIST \leadsto artist\{\!\{\}\!\}, \; "rock" \;\}\!\}$$

The intention of the rule is to collect titles and authors of all the CD's of the rock category. When the query term of the rule is matched against a database of type Cd, the variables $TITLE, ARTIST$ are bound to data terms of types, respectively, $Title, Artist$ or $Artist, Artist$. As the variable $TITLE$ is intended to take values only of type $Title$, the query is incorrect w.r.t. our expectations. The type $Result$ of the query result can be described by the following type definition $D' = D \cup \{\, Result \rightarrow result[Name\,Author],\; Name \rightarrow name[\,Title|Artist],\; Author \rightarrow author[Artist]\,\}$.

4.2   Variable-Type Mappings

In this section we assume a fixed type definition D (describing the type of the database).

To represent a set of answers (for a query term and a set of data terms) we will use a mapping $\Gamma \colon V \to \mathcal{E}$ (called a *variable-type mapping*), where V is the set of variables occurring in the considered query rule and $\mathcal{E}$ is a set of expressions. $\mathcal{E}$ contains 0, 1, the type names from D, and expressions of the form $T_1 \cap T_2$, where $T_1, T_2 \in \mathcal{E}$. Each expression E from $\mathcal{E}$ denotes a set $[\![E]\!]$ of data terms. $[\![1]\!]$ denotes the set of all data terms, $[\![0]\!] = \emptyset$, $[\![T]\!] = [\![T]\!]_D$ for any type name T, and $[\![T_1 \cap T_2]\!] = [\![T_1]\!] \cap [\![T_2]\!]$. The set of substitutions corresponding to a mapping $\Gamma: V \rightarrow \mathcal{E}$ is

$$substitutions_D(\Gamma) = \{ \theta \mid \forall_{X \in V}\ \theta X \in [\![\Gamma(X)]\!] \}.$$

(According to our convention, we will often skip the index $_D$.) Notice that if $\theta \in substitutions(\Gamma)$ then $V \subseteq dom(\theta)$ and if $\theta \subseteq \theta'$ then $\theta' \in substitutions(\Gamma)$. For a set Ψ of variable-type mappings we define $substitutions(\Psi) = \bigcup_{\Gamma \in \Psi} substitutions(\Gamma)$.

For $Y_1, \ldots, Y_k \in V$, $T_1, \ldots, T_k \in \mathcal{E}$, mapping $[Y_1 \mapsto T_1, \ldots, Y_k \mapsto T_k]: V \rightarrow \mathcal{E}$ is defined as

$$[Y_1 \mapsto T_1, \ldots, Y_k \mapsto T_k](X) = \begin{cases} T_i \text{ if } X = Y_i \\ 1 \ \text{ otherwise.} \end{cases}$$

We will not distinguish between expressions $T \cap 1$ and T, and between $T \cap 0$ and 0 (where $T \in \mathcal{E}$).

Inclusion of types induces a partial order $\sqsubseteq$ on the mappings from $V \rightarrow \mathcal{E}$, as follows. If Γ and Γ' are such mappings then $\Gamma \sqsubseteq \Gamma'$ iff $[\![\Gamma(X)]\!] \subseteq [\![\Gamma'(X)]\!]$ for each variable $X \in V$. Notice that $\Gamma \sqsubseteq \Gamma'$ is equivalent to $substitutions(\Gamma) \subseteq substitutions(\Gamma')$.

4.3   Typing Rules for Xcerpt

The rules presented in this section provide a descriptive type system for Xcerpt: the typing of a program is an approximation of its semantics. An algorithm computing a type of results for a given Xcerpt query rule can be easily derived from the presented rules as they can be seen as an abstract version of the algorithm. Below we present the rules for query terms, queries, construct terms and query rules. In the Appendix we prove correctness of the typing system.

Query Terms. The rules in this subsection provide a way to derive facts of the form $D \vdash q : T \triangleright \Gamma$, where D is a type definition, q a query term, T a type name, and Γ a variable-type mapping. The intention is that if q is applied to a data term $d \in [\![T]\!]$ then the resulting substitution is in $substitutions(\Gamma)$ for some Γ such that $D \vdash q : T \triangleright \Gamma$ can be derived.

$$\frac{b \in [\![T]\!]}{D \vdash b : T \triangleright \Gamma} \qquad \text{(CONST)}$$

where b is a basic constant.

$$\frac{\Gamma \sqsubseteq [X \mapsto T]}{D \vdash X : T \triangleright \Gamma} \qquad \text{(VAR)}$$

$$\frac{D \vdash q : T \triangleright \Gamma \qquad \Gamma \sqsubseteq [X \mapsto T]}{D \vdash X \rightsquigarrow q : T \triangleright \Gamma} \qquad \text{(As)}$$

$$\frac{D \vdash q : T \triangleright \Gamma}{D \vdash \mathtt{desc}\ q : T \triangleright \Gamma} \qquad \text{(Descendant)}$$

$$\frac{D \vdash \mathtt{desc}\ q : T' \triangleright \Gamma}{D \vdash \mathtt{desc}\ q : T \triangleright \Gamma} \qquad \text{(Descendant Rec)}$$

where $T' \in types(r)$ and r is the content model of T.

$$\frac{D \vdash q_1 : T_1 \triangleright \Gamma \quad \cdots \quad D \vdash q_n : T_n \triangleright \Gamma}{D \vdash l\ \alpha q_1, \cdots, q_n \beta : T \triangleright \Gamma} \qquad \text{(Pattern)}$$

where the rule for T in D is of the form $T \to l[\,r\,]$
  or it is of the form $T \to l\{\,r\,\}$ and ($\alpha\beta = \{\}$ or $\alpha\beta = \{\{\}\}$),
  s is r with every type name U replaced by $U|\epsilon$,
  $T_1 \cdots T_n \in L(r)$ if $\alpha\beta = [\,]$,
  $T_1 \cdots T_n \in L(s)$ if $\alpha\beta = [[\,]]$,
  $T_1 \cdots T_n \in perm(L(r))$ if $\alpha\beta = \{\}$,
  $T_1 \cdots T_n \in perm(L(s))$ if $\alpha\beta = \{\{\}\}$.
Here $perm(L)$ stands for the language of permutations of the strings from a language L.

Queries. From the rules below one can derive facts of the form $D \vdash Q : U \triangleright \Gamma$, where Q is a query, U a finite set of type names and Γ a variable-type mapping. If θ is an answer substitution for Q and a data term from $\llbracket U \rrbracket$ then $\theta \in substitutions(\Gamma)$ for some Γ such that $D \vdash q : T \triangleright \Gamma$ can be derived.

In general a query may be applied to data terms produced by query rules of an Xcerpt program. As their results may be of different types, we consider here a set of types U instead of a single type T.

$$\frac{D \vdash q : T \triangleright \Gamma \qquad T \in U}{D \vdash q : U \triangleright \Gamma} \qquad \text{(Query Term)}$$

$$\frac{D \vdash q : T \triangleright \Gamma}{D \vdash \mathtt{in}(db, q) : U \triangleright \Gamma} \qquad \text{(Targeted Query Term)}$$

where $d(db)$ is of type T (formally $d(db) \in \llbracket T \rrbracket$).

$$\frac{D \vdash Q_1 : U \triangleright \Gamma \quad \cdots \quad D \vdash Q_n : U \triangleright \Gamma}{D \vdash \mathtt{and}(Q_1, \ldots, Q_n) : U \triangleright \Gamma} \qquad \text{(And Query)}$$

$$\frac{D \vdash Q : U \triangleright \Gamma}{D \vdash \mathtt{or}(\ldots, Q, \ldots) : U \triangleright \Gamma} \qquad \text{(Or Query)}$$

Construct Terms. To formulate typing rules for construct terms we need an equivalence relation on mappings:

Definition 17. *Given a type definition D, a set of variable-type mappings Ψ and a set V of variables, such that $V \subseteq dom(\Gamma)$ for each $\Gamma \in \Psi$, the relation $\sim_V \subseteq \Psi \times \Psi$ is defined as: $\Gamma_1 \sim_V \Gamma_2$ iff $[\![\Gamma_1(X)]\!] \cap [\![\Gamma_2(X)]\!] \neq \emptyset$ for all $X \in V$. The set of equivalence classes of the transitive closure $\overset{*}{\sim}_V$ of $\sim_V$ is denoted by $\Psi/\overset{*}{\underset{\sim_V}{}}$.*

The following rules allow to derive facts of the form $D \vdash c : \Psi \triangleright S$, where c is a construct term, Ψ is a set of variable-type mappings (for which the types are defined by D) and S is a regular type expression. The intention is that if applying a substitution set Θ to c results in a data term sequence $\Theta(c) = d_1, \ldots, d_n$ and $substitutions(\Theta) \subseteq substitutions(\Psi)$ then $D \vdash c : \Psi \triangleright S$ can be derived such that each $d_i \in [\![T_i]\!]$ and $T_1 \cdots T_n \in L(S)$. To derive $D \vdash c : \Psi \triangleright S$ it is necessary that $\Gamma(X) \neq 1$ for any $\Gamma \in \Psi$ and any variable X occurring in c. For correctness of the rules it is required that for any $\Gamma_1, \Gamma_2 \in \Psi$, $\Gamma_1 \overset{*}{\sim}_{FV(c)} \Gamma_2$.

$$\frac{(T_c \to c) \in D}{D \vdash c : \Psi \triangleright T_c} \tag{Const}$$

where c is a basic constant.

$$\frac{[\![T_1]\!] = [\![\Gamma_1(X)]\!] \quad \cdots \quad [\![T_n]\!] = [\![\Gamma_n(X)]\!]}{D \vdash X : \{\Gamma_1, \ldots, \Gamma_n\} \triangleright T_1 \mid \cdots \mid T_n} \tag{Var}$$

$$\frac{D \vdash c_1 : \Psi \triangleright S_1 \quad \cdots \quad D \vdash c_n : \Psi \triangleright S_n \quad (T_c \to l\alpha S_1 \cdots S_n \beta) \in D}{D \vdash l\alpha c_1, \ldots, c_n \beta : \Psi \triangleright T_c} \tag{Pattern}$$

$$\frac{D \vdash c : \Psi_1 \triangleright S_1 \quad \cdots \quad D \vdash c : \Psi_n \triangleright S_n \quad \{\Psi_1, \ldots, \Psi_n\} = \Psi/\overset{*}{\underset{\sim_{FV(c)}}{}}}{D \vdash \mathsf{all}\ c : \Psi \triangleright (S_1 \mid \cdots \mid S_n)^+} \tag{All}$$

$$\frac{D \vdash c : \Psi_1 \triangleright S_1 \quad \cdots \quad D \vdash c : \Psi_n \triangleright S_n \quad \{\Psi_1, \ldots, \Psi_n\} = \Psi/\overset{*}{\underset{\sim_{FV(c)}}{}}}{D \vdash \mathsf{some}\ k\ c : \Psi \triangleright (S_1 \mid \cdots \mid S_n)^{(1:k)}} \tag{Some}$$

Xcerpt Query Rules. For a given type definition D, query Q and a set U of types names, the rules introduced above nondeterministically generate variable type mappings. Now we describe which sets of generated mappings are sufficient for the purpose of approximating the semantics of query-rules.

Definition 18. *Let D be a type definition. Let Q be a query term and W a type name, or Q a query and W a set of type names. A set $\{\Gamma_1, \ldots, \Gamma_n\}$ of variable-type mappings is **complete** for Q and W wrt. D if*

- *$D \vdash Q : W \triangleright \Gamma_i$ for $i = 1, \ldots, n$, and*
- *whenever $D \vdash Q : W \triangleright \Gamma$, there exists $i \in \{1, \ldots, n\}$ such that $\Gamma \sqsubseteq \Gamma_i$.*

From the following rule one can derive facts of the form $D \vdash (c \leftarrow Q) : U \rhd S_1 \mid \cdots \mid S_n$ where $c \leftarrow Q$ is a query rule, U is a finite set of type names and S_i are regular type expressions. The intention is that if we apply a query rule $c \leftarrow Q$ to a database of a type $\llbracket U \rrbracket$ then we obtain results belonging to the set $\llbracket S_1 \mid \cdots \mid S_n \rrbracket$.

$$\frac{D \vdash c : \Psi_1 \rhd S_1 \quad \cdots \quad D \vdash c : \Psi_n \rhd S_n \quad \{\Psi_1, \ldots, \Psi_n\} = \Psi /_{\approx_{FV(c)}}}{D \vdash (c \leftarrow Q) : U \rhd S_1 \mid \cdots \mid S_n} \text{ (QUERY RULE)}$$

where Ψ is complete for Q and U wrt. D.

Example 19. Consider type definition $D = \{T \to l[A^* B C], A \to a, B \to b, C \to c, R_1 \to a[A^+ A], R_2 \to a[A^+ B], R_3 \to a[(A \mid B)^+ C]\}$ and the query rule

$$a \, [\, \mathtt{all}\, X, Y\,] \; \leftarrow \; l\,[[\,X, Y\,]]$$

abbreviated as $c_0 \leftarrow q$. We apply the query rule to a set of types $U = \{T, A, B, C\}$. First we need to find a complete set of mappings Ψ_0 for q and U. If we apply the query term q to the type T using the rules for query terms we can derive facts $D \vdash q : T \rhd \Gamma_i$ for $i = 1, \ldots, 4$, where $\Gamma_1 = [X \mapsto A, Y \mapsto A]$, $\Gamma_2 = [X \mapsto A, Y \mapsto B]$, $\Gamma_3 = [X \mapsto A, Y \mapsto C]$ and $\Gamma_4 = [X \mapsto B, Y \mapsto C]$. If we apply the query term q to the type A, B or C we cannot derive anything using the rules. Hence, the rules for queries allow us to derive $D \vdash q : U \rhd \Gamma_i$ for $i = 1, \ldots, 4$. The set $\Psi_0 = \{\Gamma_1, \Gamma_2, \Gamma_3, \Gamma_4\}$ is complete for q and U. Since $FV(c_0) = \{Y\}$, $\Psi_0 /_{\approx_{FV(c_0)}} = \{\Psi_1, \Psi_2, \Psi_3\}$, where $\Psi_1 = \{\Gamma_1\}$, $\Psi_2 = \{\Gamma_2\}$, $\Psi_3 = \{\Gamma_3, \Gamma_4\}$. Now we apply each of Ψ_i to the construct term c_0. Using the rules for construct terms we can derive the following facts: $D \vdash c_0 : \Psi_1 \rhd R_1$, $D \vdash c_0 : \Psi_2 \rhd R_2$ and $D \vdash c_0 : \Psi_3 \rhd R_3$. Using the rule (QUERY RULE) we can derive $D \vdash c_0 \leftarrow q : U \rhd R_1 \mid R_2 \mid R_3$. It means that if the rule $c_0 \leftarrow q$ is applied to a data term from $\llbracket U \rrbracket$ all the obtained results are in the set $\llbracket R_1 \mid R_2 \mid R_3 \rrbracket$.

The following theorem expresses the correctness of the typing rules wrt. the semantics given in section 3. More precisely, it expresses the existence of a typing derivation for a rule whenever it has a result for some data term d in the type denoted by a set U of type names. It also expresses that any derivation of a query rule $(c \leftarrow Q)$ wrt. a set of type names U is a correct approximation of the set of results for $(c \leftarrow Q)$ and any data term in the type denoted by U.

Theorem 20. *Let D be a type definition and $(c \leftarrow Q)$ be a query rule, where for each targeted query term $\mathtt{in}(db, q)$ in Q there is a type name T in D such that $d(db) \in \llbracket T \rrbracket$. Let U be a set of type names and d a data term such that $d \in \llbracket U \rrbracket$.*
If a result for $(c \leftarrow Q)$ and d exists then there exist S and D' such that $D' \supseteq D$ and $D' \vdash (c \leftarrow Q) : U \rhd S$.
If there exists S such that $D \vdash (c \leftarrow Q) : U \rhd S$ and if d' is a result for $(c \leftarrow Q)$ and d, then $d' \in \llbracket S \rrbracket$.

Proof. See an extended version of this article [2].

5   Conclusion

This paper presents a descriptive type system for a substantial fragment of the Web and Semantic Web query language Xcerpt. The type system provides approximation of the semantics of Xcerpt programs. For a given Xcerpt query rule it provides a type of its results (i.e. a superset of the set of the results) under the assumption that the query rule is applied to data of a given type. The main contribution of the paper is a formalization of the type system of [13] by means of typing rules and a soundness theorem for the type system. The employed formal semantics of the Xcerpt fragment may be of separate interest.

A topic for the future work is formalization by means of typing rules of the more precise typing algorithm presented in [8]. The current work should also be generalized to the omitted features of Xcerpt. Dealing with some of them, e.g. negation or terms representing graphs, seems to be difficult and needs further investigation. Moreover the type system should be extended to Xcerpt programs containing more than one query rule.

Another interesting topic for the future work is a comparison between the descriptive typing approach (to which our work belongs) and the prescriptive approach [7,8]. As our type system is presented by means of typing rules similar to the typing rules of prescriptive type systems, the differences and similarities between two approaches can be better understood.

The work on a prototype implementation of the type system for Xcerpt is in progress. The algorithm corresponding to the presented typing rules has been implemented as an additional module in Xcerpt prototype. We plan to implement the more precise version of the algorithm and also to extend the prototype to be able to handle all constructs used in Xcerpt.

Acknowledgement. This research has been partially funded by the European Commission and by the Swiss Federal Office for Education and Science within the 6th Framework Programme project REWERSE number 506779 (cf. http://rewerse.net).

References

1. Serge Abiteboul, Peter Buneman, and Dan Suciu. *Data on the Web: from relations to semistructured data and XML.* Morgan Kaufmann Publishers Inc., San Francisco, CA, USA, 2000.
2. S. Berger, E. Coquery, W. Drabent, and A. Wilk. Descriptive Typing Rules for Xcerpt and their Soundness. Technical report, REWERSE, 2005. Available at http://rewerse.net/publications.html/#REWERSE-TR-2005-01.
3. A. Brüggemann-Klein, M. Murata, and D. Wood. Regular tree and regular hedge languages over unranked alphabets. Technical Report HKUST-TCSC-2001-0, The Hongkong University of Science and Technology, April 2001.
4. François Bry, Wlodzimierz Drabent, and Jan Maluszynski. On subtyping of tree-structured data: A polynomial approach. In *International Workshop, PPSWR 2004, St. Malo, France, September, 2004, Proceedings*, number 3208 in LNCS, pages 1–18, 2004.

5. François Bry, Tim Furche, Liviu Badea, Christoph Koch, Sebastian Schaffert, and Sacha Berger. Identification of Design Principles. Deliverable I4-D2, REWERSE, 2004. At `http://rewerse.net/publications.html/#REWERSE-DEL-2004-I4-D2`.

6. François Bry and Sebastian Schaffert. An Entailment Relation for Reasoning on the Web. In *Proceedings of Rules and Rule Markup Languages for the Semantic Web, Sanibel Island (Florida), USA (20th October 2003)*, LNCS, 2003.

7. Luca Cardelli. Type Systems. In Allen B. Tucker, editor, *The Handbook of Computer Science and Engineering, Second Edition*, chapter 97-1. CRC Press, 2004.

8. Horatiu Cirstea, Emmanuel Coquery, Włodzimierz Drabent, François Fages, Claude Kirchner, Luigi Liquori, Benjamin Wack, and Artur Wilk. Types for REWERSE reasoning and query languages. Deliverable I3-D4, REWERSE, 2005. Available at `http://rewerse.net/publications.html/#REWERSE-DEL-2005-I3-D4`.

9. J. E. Hopcroft and J. D. Ullmann. *Introduction to Automata Theory, Languages and Computation*. Addison-Wesley, 1979.

10. M. Murata, D. Lee, M. Mani, and K. Kawaguchi. Taxonomy of XML schema languages using formal language theory. Submitted, 2003.

11. Sebastian Schaffert. *Xcerpt: A Rule-Based Query and Transformation Language for the Web*. PhD thesis, University of Munich, 2004.

12. Sebastian Schaffert and François Bry. Querying the Web Reconsidered: A Practical Introduction to Xcerpt. In *Proceedings of Extreme Markup Languages 2004, Montreal, Quebec, Canada (2nd–6th August 2004)*, 2004.

13. A. Wilk and W. Drabent. On types for XML query language Xcerpt. In *International Workshop, PPSWR 2003, Mumbai, India, December 8, 2003, Proceedings*, number 2901 in LNCS, pages 128–145. Springer Verlag, 2003.

A General Language for Evolution and Reactivity in the Semantic Web

José Júlio Alferes[1], Ricardo Amador[1], and Wolfgang May[2]

[1] Centro de Inteligência Artificial - CENTRIA, Universidade Nova de Lisboa
[2] Institut für Informatik, Universität Göttingen

Abstract. In this paper we define the basic concepts for a general language for evolution and reactivity in the Semantic Web. We do this by exposing an UML model that specifies an ontology for the language. The proposed language is based on Event-Condition-Action rules, where different languages for events (including languages for composite events), for conditions (queries) and actions (including complex actions) may be composed, this way catering for language heterogeneity (besides heterogeneity on the data-model) that we think is essential for dealing with evolution and reactivity in the Semantic Web.

1 Introduction

The Web and the Semantic Web, as we see it, can be understood as a "living organism" combining autonomously evolving data sources, each of them possibly reacting to events it perceives. The dynamic character of such a Web requires declarative languages and mechanisms for specifying the evolution of the data. This vision of the Web, as well as a state of the art overview of related areas, is described in our previous work [17].

Rather than a Web of data sources, we envisage a Web of Information Systems, where each such system, besides being capable of gathering information (querying, both on persistent data, as well as on volatile data such as occurring events), is capable of updating persistent data, communicating the changes, requesting changes of persistent data in other systems, and being able to react to requests from other systems. As a practical example, consider a set of data (re)sources in the Web of travel agencies, airline companies, train companies, etc. It should be possible to query the resources about timetables, availability of tickets, etc. But in such an evolving Web, it should also be possible for a train company to report on late trains, and travel agencies (and also individual clients) be able to detect such an event and react upon it, by rescheduling travel plans, notifying clients that in turn could have to cancel hotel reservations and book other hotels, or try alternatives to the late trains, etc.

The importance of being able to update the Web has long been acknowledged, and several languages exist (e.g. XUpdate [24], XML-RL [15], XPathLog [16]) for just that. More recently some reactive languages have been proposed, that not only allow for updating Web data as the above ones, but are also capable

F. Fages and S. Soliman (Eds.): PPSWR 2005, LNCS 3703, pp. 101–115, 2005.

of dealing-with/reacting-to some forms of events, evaluate conditions, and upon that act by updating data. These are the cases of the XML active rules of [6], of Active XQuery [5], of the Event-Condition-Action (ECA) language for XML defined in [2], and RDFTL [18], which is an ECA reactive language on RDF data. The common aspect of all of these languages is the use of ECA (declarative) rules for specifying reactivity and evolution. Such kind of rules (also known as triggers, active rules, or reactive rules), that have been widely used in other fields (e.g. active databases [19,23]) have the general form **on** *event* **if** *condition* **do** *action*. They are intuitively easy to understand, and provide a well-understood formal semantics: when an event (atomic or composite) occurs, evaluate a condition, and if the condition is satisfied then execute an action (or a sequence of actions, a program, a transaction, or even start a process).

In fact, we agree with the arguments exposed for the definition of the above languages in what regards adopting ECA rules for dealing with evolution and reactivity in the Web (declarativity, modularity, maintainability, etc). But in our opinion, these languages fall short in various aspects, when the goal is aimed at the general view of an evolving Web as described above. Namely, they do not provide for more complex events and actions and, most important, they do not deal with heterogeneity at the level of the language. Autonomous web nodes will use different formalisms for ECA rules, and also different formalism for events, conditions and actions, depending on the requirements of their applications.

In general, actions are more than just simple updates to Web data (be it XML or RDF data). As said above, besides that, actions can be notifications to other resources, update requests of other resources, can be composition of simpler actions (like: do this, and then do that), or even transactions whose ACID properties ensure that either all actions in a transaction are performed, or nothing is done. In our view, a general language should cater for such richer actions. Moreover, events may in general be more than simple atomic events in Web data, as in the above languages. First, there are atomic events other than physical changes in Web data: events may be received messages, or even "happenings" in the global Web, which may require complex event detection mechanisms (e.g (once) any train to St. Wendel is delayed ...). Moreover, as in active databases [10,25], there may be more complex (composite) events. For example, we may want a rule to be triggered when there is a flight cancellation and then the notification of a new reservation whose price is much higher than the previous (e.g. to complain to the airline company). In this respect, there is some preliminary work on composite events in the Web [3], but that only considers composition of events of modification of XML-data in a single document.

The quite recent work on the language XChange [8] already aims at having more complex actions and events for evolution and reactivity on the Web and, in our opinion, is an important contribution in this direction. However, having in mind the requirements we set up for the general evolving Semantic Web, there are still some important aspects, that are not yet dealt with by XChange, namely that of language heterogeneity.

The problem of language heterogeneity will definitely appear when dealing with evolution and reactivity on the Web. This calls for more general languages. In such an open and heterogeneous environment as the Web, it is difficult to assume that there will be *a single* event language, or *a single* way to deal with actions. Our view is that a general language for evolution and reactivity in the Web should allow for the usage of different event languages, different condition languages, and different action languages, considering ontological descriptions and mappings for these languages. Each of these different (sub)languages should adhere to some minimal requirements (e.g. dealing with variables), but it should be as free as possible. The task of the general ECA language is then to combine these various (sub)languages for reacting and performing evolution in the (Semantic) Web. This requirement is far from the goals of XChange, which is based on a concrete language for all the components of ECA.

Moreover, the ECA rules do not only operate on the Semantic Web, but are themselves also part of it. In general, especially if one wants to reason about evolution, ECA rules (and their components) must be communicated between different nodes, and may themselves be subject to being updated. For that, the ECA rules themselves must be represented as data in the (Semantic) Web. This need calls for a (XML) Markup Language of ECA Rules. A markup proposal for active rules can be found already in RuleML [4], but it does not tackle the complexity of events, actions, and the generality of rules, as described here. Moreover, to deal with the requirements of heterogeneity and of reasoning about rules, an ontology of ECA rules and (sub)ontologies for events, conditions and actions, with rules possibly specified in RDF/OWL, is required.

In this paper we define the basic concepts of a general language for evolution and reactivity in the Semantic Web that responds to the requirements just exposed. Rather than presenting an RDF/OWL ontology, in this paper we present a UML 2.0 [14] model. By doing this, we not only consubstantiate the language concepts, but also provide an abstract syntax for it, which is already a step for having a markup (XML) language for general ECA rules. For defining such a markup, it is worth noting that the UML model we present is mappable into XMI [13], this directly providing an XML representation. The modelling of the language starts in Section 2, where the global aspects are spelled out, and the composition between the components is discussed. The common structure of the (sub)languages for the rule components discussed in Section 3. Then, in Section 4, the specific aspects of each of the E, C, and A components is discussed and an illustrative concrete (instantiation) of each of these (sub)languages is given. We end the paper by mentioning ongoing and future work.

2   Global Aspects for a General ECA Language

In order to cope with the Semantic Web heterogeneity, the target of development and definition of languages for (ECA) rules, for events, for conditions and for actions should be a semantic approach, i.e. an approach based on an (extensible) ontology for rules, events, conditions and actions that also allows for reasoning about these concepts.

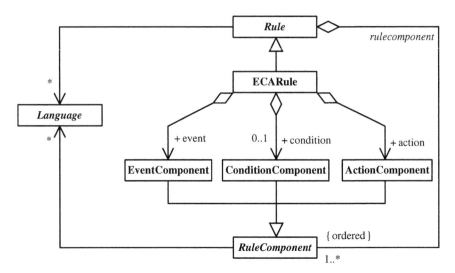

Fig. 1. General UML model for ECA rules

At a quite abstract level a rule is an aggregation of rule components, and an ECA rule can be described by the UML diagram given in Figure 1. As expected, an ECA rule has 3 different components: event, condition and action. The condition is optional, in the sense that it can be omitted, or that languages may allow to integrate the evaluation of the condition with the event component, or with the action component. This model can be readily extended by adding a fourth component (also optional) – the post-condition (another *Condition*) – resulting in a variation usually called ECAP rules. In most cases, this post-condition can be omitted by allowing the action language to test for conditions inside the action part. But it may have particular relevance when considered together with cascading reactions and transactional rules, in which case the post-condition allows the declarative specification of restrictions that must apply after the whole transaction, given by the action, is successfully executed. This will be further detailed in Section 4.3 below, when discussing languages for the action part.

Current databases already support active concepts by triggers (e.g., SQL) where the distinction between events, conditions and actions is not necessarily explicit. Such rules can be handled as *opaque* rules of a given language that are understood as a whole by an underlying system. Note that there exist well-defined mappings into the above ECA model.

When defining (ECA) rules, language heterogeneity has to be considered not only at the global rule level, but also at the rule component level. As stated before, several reactive rule languages have already been proposed (e.g. XChange [8], RDFTL [18]), introducing heterogeneity at the rule level. A generic approach for rules in the Semantic Web must be able to cover *all* such explicit language proposals. In most of these proposals there exists a pattern of language reuse, usually a query (sub)language that already exists (e.g. XQuery) is

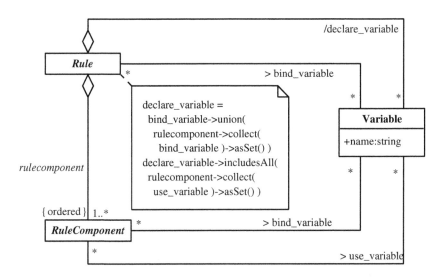

Fig. 2. Rules and Variables

chosen for the condition and either an existing update (sub)language is chosen
(e.g. XQuery+Updates [21]) or an extension is built over the query language
(e.g. Xcerpt [20]) in order to obtain a new (sub)language (e.g. XChange [8]) for
the action component. Finally, an event (sub)language is defined (often based
on an existing one from the field of Active Databases, e.g. the SQL3 standard).

A general approach requires a clean distinction between the three components
E, C, and A on the ontology level of the rules (as shown in Figure 1). Given
this, additional heterogeneity is provided by using and combining different event,
condition, and action (sub)languages according to a global ECA schema. Each
language is identified by its namespace which then contains markup elements of
the specific languages. To achieve language heterogeneity at the rule component
level, there must be a precise convention between all languages how the different
parts of a rule can exchange information and interact with each other. This is
achieved by a set of "bindable" names (logical variables), cf. Figure 2.

A variable must be bound only once to a value; in case that an already bound
variable is "bound" again, the values must coincide, i.e., yielding an analogous
semantics as in logic programming (this e.g. allows for an event component
that in some cases binds a variable which is then used as a join variable in the
condition, and in others is bound by the latter). The OCL constraints in Figure 2
guarantee that the variables of the rule are exactly those bound either in the
Rule or in a *RuleComponent*. The binding mechanism can be extended with a
type system.

The actual handling (and its markup) of variables will be discussed below for
a simple case of rules, and later in Sections 3 and 4. We currently recommend to
be explicit with declaring variables that are used or bound in a rule component,
although in most cases it will be possible to derive this from the markup and
the languages' ontologies.

Rules with Opaque Components. At the most basic level, each rule component has a textual specification (again called *opaque*) that is to be understood by some language engine. In this case it is marked up as text content of an eca:opaque element that references the language via its lang attribute (see Example 1). Additionally, since variable bindings must be communicated and binding/using cannot be derived from the opaque text, this information must be given explicitly. Thus, the eca:opaque element must list all variables that are used or bound by it (i.e., whose bindings must be exchanged with the engine), also optionally giving their names (e.g., for embedding JDBC where variables are only named ?1, ?2 etc.). Variables can be bound by opaque parts by (i) matching them – logic programming style, or (ii) assigning the result set of a query to them.

Example 1. Consider an ECA rule expressing the idea that whenever a flight is cancelled, every customer who has a reservation for this flight must be notified, preferably by SMS. Using XML rule markup with opaque rule components (using different languages), this rule could take the following form:

```
<eca:rule xmlns:eca="http://www.eca.org/eca-ml"
    xmlns:datalog="http://www.lp.org/datalog"
    xmlns:xpath="http://www.w3.org/XPath"
    xmlns:pseudocode="http://www.pseudocode-actions.nop" >
  <eca:bind-variable name="Reservations" >
    http://www.reservations.nop/actual.xml
  </eca:bind-variable>
  <eca:variable name="Flight" />
  <eca:variable name="Customers" />
  <eca:event>
    <eca:opaque lang='datalog'>
      <eca:bind-variable name="Flight" use="F" mode="match" />
      flight_cancelation(F)    <!-- matches literal against event in datalog -->
    </eca:opaque>
  </eca:event>
  <eca:condition>
    <eca:opaque lang='xpath'>
      <eca:use-variable name="Flight" use="$Flight" />
      <eca:use-variable name="Reservations" use="$Reservations" />
      <eca:bind-variable name="Customers" mode="result-set" />
      document($Reservations)//flight[@id=$Flight]/reservation/customer
    </eca:opaque>
    <!-- evaluates XPath expression, binds the result to the variable 'Customers'
      and checks if it is not empty -->
  </eca:condition>
  <eca:action>
    <eca:opaque lang='pseudocode'>
      <eca:use-variable name="Customers" />
      <eca:use-variable name="Flight" />
      for each C in Customers do
        notify_cancelation(Flight, sms:C)
```

```
        otherwise notify_cancelation(Flight, mail:C)
            otherwise signal_failure(notify_cancelation(Flight, C))
    done
  </eca:opaque>
  </eca:action>
</eca:rule>
```

Thus, the specification of a rule component in its simplest (opaque) form is just some *opaque* text associated with a set of variables that can either be bound or simply used in that component. When this text is given to the respective language engine together with a set of variables, some of them already bound, the engine interprets this text, optionally producing new bindings for some of the yet unbound variables.

3 Common Structure of E, C and A Sublanguages

The level of reasoning that can be performed with the model defined so far is yet restricted. In order to do deeper reasoning, one must go inside of the rule components. For this, instead of a simple text like the opaque specifications above, these specifications may also be given as structured ones. The generic structure of these (sub)languages, independently of whether they are event, condition or action languages, is modelled in Figure 3. Each such language consists of a set of *composers*; actual rules then combine it with a separate language of *atomic* elements (events, literals, actions) that are part of *domain languages*, and in most cases come from application-dependent ontologies. Expressions of the language are then (i) atomic elements, or (ii) composite expressions recursively obtained

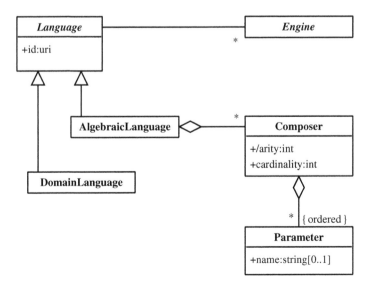

Fig. 3. Language Structure

by applying composers to expressions. Due to their structure, these languages are called *algebraic languages*, e.g. used in *event algebras*.

Each composer has a given *cardinality* that denotes the number of expressions (of the same type of language, e.g., events) it can compose, and (optionally) a sequence of parameters (that come from another ontology, e.g., time intervals) that determines its *arity*.

For instance, "E_1 followed_by E_2 within t" is a binary composer to recognize the occurrence of two events (atomic or not) in a particular order within a time interval, where t is a parameter. A language for *atomic* events could define an event "received_message(M)" for receiving a message. Together with an action language that provides an action for sending a message, one could easily define a negotiation dialog between two systems by means of a set of reactive rules.

As mentioned above, actual rules combine these languages with appropriate languages for atomic elements. Usually, these are provided by *domain languages* (e.g. languages for the domain of travels, or banking, or ...) that are induced by an ontology, and define atomic events, predicates or literals (for conditions), and actions of that specific domain (e.g. events of train schedule changes, actions of reserving tickets, ...). There exist also domain-independent primitive constructs (with arguments), e.g. for general communication, such as the above received_message(M) (where M in turn contains domain-specific content). Note that the markup must also provide the handling of variables; here we propose to borrow from XSLT: use variables by {$var-name}, and bind them by <variable name="..." select="..." /> elements; but the actual decision is up to the language designers.

Each of these languages has an associated engine that captures the semantics of the (composers of the) language. The engines provide the (expected) interfaces

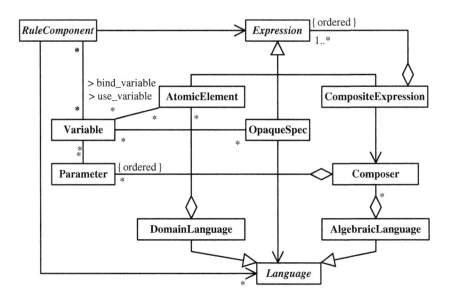

Fig. 4. Model of the Rule Components

for communication, must keep their own state information, including at least the current variable bindings. Specific tasks of the engines then include e.g. the evaluation of composite events (for the event languages), or the execution of transactions (for the action engines). The issue of transactions is of particular importance (see Section 4.3).

Note that since each subtree of such a specification is a specification of the same kind (e.g., subevents composed into more complex events), it is also possible to nest composers and expressions from different languages. Thus, languages are associated on the *expression* level. In the XML markup, this is done by the namespaces (from which the tree's markup is taken).

Given the additional level of knowledge about the structure of a sublanguage, the modelling of the rule component specifications can be more detailed, as shown in Figure 4. This raises the level of reasoning that may be performed about ECA rules, regardless of the degree of language heterogeneity that may be present.

4 Concrete Languages for Events, Conditions, and Actions

In the previous sections we have defined a general model for ECA rules and their components. In this section we discuss specific issues of the languages of events, of conditions and of actions.

4.1 A Language for Events in the Web

In the context of the Semantic Web, an (atomic) event is in general any detectable occurrence. Events in the Web can be local events, e.g. updates of local data (that can be used for deriving/raising global events), but also incoming messages, and changes in other nodes.

Atomic Events on Web data. On the most basic (physical) level, there are constructs to deal with the detection of changes on local data, be it on XML or RDF data, similar to those found in database triggers. Work on triggers for XQuery has e.g. been described in [5] with *Active XQuery* and in [2], emulating the trigger definition and execution model of the SQL3 standard that specifies a syntax and execution model for ECA rules in relational databases. The former uses the same syntax and switches as SQL. For modifications of an XML tree, we proposed in [1] the following basic constructs for atomic events of modifications of XML data:

- ON {DELETE|INSERT|UPDATE} OF *xsl-pattern*: if a node matching the *xsl-pattern* is deleted/inserted/updated,
- ON MODIFICATION OF *xsl-pattern*: if anything in the subtree is modified,
- ON INSERT INTO *xsl-pattern*: if a node is inserted (directly) into a node matching the *xsl-pattern*,
- ON INSERT [IMMEDIATELY] BEFORE|AFTER *xsl-pattern*: if a node is inserted (immediately) before or after a node matching the *xsl-pattern*.

In all these constructs, *xsl-pattern* is a (typically input) argument. Moreover, these events should make relevant values accessible, e.g., OLD AS ... and NEW AS ... (like in SQL), both referencing the complete node to which the event happened, additionally INSERTED AS, DELETED AS referencing the inserted or deleted node. These relevant values are additional arguments of the above constructs, typically (output) to be bound with variables. The implementation of these events in XML repositories is probably to be based on the *DOM Level 2/3 Events* [11].

Regarding RDF data, RDF triples, describing properties/values of a resource, are much more similar to SQL. In contrast to XML, there is no assignment of data with subtrees, which makes it impossible to express "deep" modifications in a simple event. Proposals can be found in [18], and in [1]; in the latter, we considered the following basic constructs:

- ON {DELETE|INSERT|UPDATE} OF *property* [OF *class*]: if a property is removed from/added to/updated of a resource of a given class, then such an event is raised;
- ON CREATE OF *class*: it is raised if a new resource of a given class is created;
- ON NEW CLASS: is raised if a new class is introduced,
- ON NEW PROPERTY [OF CLASS *class*]: is raised, if a new property (optionally: to a specified class) is introduced.

Besides the OLD and NEW values mentioned for XML, these events should consider as arguments (to bind variables) RESOURCE AS ... and PROPERTY AS ..., referring to the modified resource and the property (as URIs), respective.

Communication events. Besides the above events that react on updates on a given data model level, communication events are raised by messages, independent from the abstraction level of the rule. We propose the following basic construct:

- ON MESSAGE [OF *sender*] [AT *time*] [MATCHING *pattern*]

In this construct, the metadata about *sender* and *time* are to be bound to variables upon receipt of the message, as well as the actual *content*. However, one might want to trigger such an event only when a message with a specific sender, time, or content is received. In this case a methodology for testing the content must be specified. This can be done by (regular expression) matching, or by querying the (XML or RDF) content. For the above (opaque) syntax as triggers, we restrict it to matching; a markup version may include more detailed conditions (as illustrated below), where also more elaborate constructs for incoming messages are possible, e.g. with parameters for specifying an ontology describing the language of the message, or along the lines of the FIPA language for communication among agents [12].

Composite events. For dealing with composite events in the context of the ECA rules proposed here, the event languages must define several composers. We propose at least the following composers of events: "E_1 OR E_2", "E_1 AND E_2"

(in arbitrary order), and "E_1 AND THEN E_2 [AFTER PERIOD $\{< | >\}$ *time*]" the latter one composing two events and using an additional parameter *time*, indicating the time that has passed between the occurrence of E_1 and E_2. The actual semantics of composers must be defined similarly to that of operators in event algebras in the context of active databases [25]. In it, detection of a composite event means that its "final" atomic subevent is detected. Event algebras contain not only the aforementioned straightforward basic conjunctive, disjunctive and sequential connectives, but also additional operators. Several event algebras have been defined that provide also e.g. "negative events" in the style that "when E_1 happened, and then E_3 but not E_2 in between, then do something", "aperiodic" and "cumulative" events, e.g., the SNOOP event algebra [9] of the "Sentinel" active database system. A quite rich set of composers for events in the Web is being also considered in the language XChange [8], where exclusions, repetitions, and cardinality are also explored.

Example 2. The following specifies, in an illustrative, non-normative (XML) markup, an event for (very simplified) detection of a late train. It is a composite event in the SNOOP (algebraic) language, and uses atomic events from messaging and the domain of train travels. The detection of late trains is made either by being warned by the travel agency, or by the occurrence of a domain-specific event signaling changes in a given (pre-defined) source with expected arrival times:

```
<eca:event xmlns:xmlsnoop="http://xmlsnoop.nop"
   xmlns:msg="http://www.messages.msg/messages"
   xmlns:mytravel="http://www.trains.tr">
   <eca:bind-variable name="newArrival"/>
   <!-- The 2 variables below are bound on the rule level -->
   <eca:use-variable name="myTravelAgent" use="$myAgent"/>
   <eca:use-variable name="myTrain" use="$myTrain"/>
   <xmlsnoop:or>
     <xmlsnoop:atomic detect="xml-pattern">
       <msg:receive-message sender="$myAgent">
         <content> <delayed train={$myTrain}/> </content>
       </msg:receive-message>
       <xmlsnoop:variable name="newArrival"  <!-- borrowed from xsl:variable -->
          select="$event/content/delayed/@arrivalTime" />
     </xmlsnoop:atomic>
     <xmlsnoop:atomic detect="xpath">
       <xmlsnoop:cond test="$event/name()='mytravel:changeTime'"/>
       <xmlsnoop:cond test="$event/@trainId=$myTrain"/>
       <xmlsnoop:variable name="newArrival" select="$event/@newTime"/>
     </xmlsnoop:atomic>
   </xmlsnoop:or>
</eca:event>
```

The composite event is an "or" of two atomic events: the first one is receiving a message (marked-up in XML) with an attribute sender which is equal to the value of the variable myAgent, and with a content with a delayed element with an attribute train conciding with that of myTrain. The mechanism used here for testing this matching with the event that occurred is an xml-pattern. If so, the variable newArrival is bound to the value of the attribute arrivalTime of that delayed element. The second one is a domain specific event travel:changeTime (that occurs "somewhere in the Web" and has to be detected by Semantic Web mechanisms. It is implicitly bound to $event). The details are then checked by XPath expressions against $event: If its attribute trainId equals the value of the variable myTrain, then newArrival is bound to the value of the newTime attribute of the event.

4.2   Conditions in ECA Rules for the Web

Conditions in ECA rules basically amount to queries in the (Semantic) Web, that possibly bind rule variables to be then used in the action component. For this purpose, and in case reasoning is not required inside the condition, one can envisage the condition language specification simply as opaque. This way, e.g. XPath, XQuery, RDQL, or Xcerpt can be used in the condition.

In case reasoning about the condition component is desired, an ontology for the query language(s) is needed, that models the basic constructs and composers of the language in the terms described above. XQueryX is an example for an XML markup of a query language. Deeper work in the direction of modelling query languages for the Web already exists, e.g. in [22] where a UML modelling of the language Xcerpt [20] is shown.

4.3   Actions and Transactions

As for events, also (atomic) actions in the Web can be considered at various levels: there can be local actions of updating web data; event raising; external update requests to other nodes; general (local or remote) method calls.

Local update actions can be specified in any appropriate language for changing web data, such as XUpdate [24], XML-RL [15], or XPathLog [16]. Their integration in the ECA framework can be done as just described for conditions, i.e. either as opaque specification, or by providing a proper ontology, based on constructs and composers, specifying those update languages.

Activities of remote nodes can be invoked by sending a message with an update (request) statement. Here a basic construct for sending a message is required, the simplest one being: SEND MESSAGE *message* TO *recipient*. This message sending can also be used for event-raising actions, in this case making sure that the event raised is then collected by a corresponding ON MESSAGE construct. As for events, more elaborate action constructs can be defined. General action constructs that can be defined may be those for (remote) procedure/method calls to Web Services, where the SOAP protocol can be used.

The execution of an action may in general succeed or fail. Considering failure of actions is important e.g. in the case of remote update requests: once the request is issued, it is important to be able to receive feedback on whether the update was actually done, or not. For example, upon request of a flight reservation, it is important to know whether the reservation was accepted or not. The operational semantics of a general language for actions, and a corresponding processor, should thus allow for failure of atomic actions. Moreover, when used with non-deterministic condition languages, the failure of an action should somehow "backtrack" into the condition to check for alternative bindings of variables that may result in successful actions.

Complex actions can be defined by composing atomic actions. This is done by enriching the action language with appropriate composers. The most basic composers for actions are those of (parallel) conjunction of actions (A_1 AND A_2) sequential execution of actions (A_1 ; A_2). Other more elaborate composers can be defined in action languages, such as if-then-else composers (IF $test$ THEN A_1 ELSE A_2), while-iterations (WHILE $test$ DO A), and forall-iterations (FORALL $variable$ DO A). Note that some of these complex actions already require the use of a condition language in the action language for evaluating conditions. This idea can be further exploited by introducing an action construct – TEST CONDITION $condition$ which tests the condition and either fails if the condition is false, or does nothing in case it is true but possibly binding some extra variables). With such a rich action language, similar to Transaction Logic [7], combining condition testing with (trans)actions, the condition of rules can be omitted.

In general, each of the complex actions should be allowed to be specified as a transaction with ACID properties, in particular where either all of the actions are executed, or the whole composite action fails, and no action is performed. This can be done by having a composer TRANSACTION id A, where id is a parameter for storing a unique identifier of the transaction, and A is the (complex) action. Note here how some form of post-condition, in the line of those mentioned in Section 2 may be specified by combining these transactions with the above condition testing. While the transaction composer is easy to understand in case all atomic actions in A consist of local updates, this is not the case when A involves actions like e.g. sending messages, or remote method calls. In fact, in these cases, what should be the meaning of rolling back over such an action? When a message is sent, what does it mean to rollback on sending it? It is our stance that in these cases, compensating actions must be specified, to be executed when rolling back is not possible. This, and a deeper study of transactions in this context (including considering transactions that are not limited to a single rule), is not detailed further here, and is subject of ongoing work.

5 Conclusions

In this paper we describe the basic concepts and a UML modelling of a general ECA-rule framework for the Semantic Web. Moreover, we discuss concrete languages for events, conditions, and actions to be composed in this general language. This framework sets the ground for a general framework for evolution and reactivity on the Web, where heterogeneity of languages is taken into account, and reasoning about rules is possible. The integration of other ECA-based languages in this framework, such as the ones mentioned in the introduction, is a subject of ongoing and future work. In this respect, special attention will be paid to the language XChange, as it is the one which already consider richer events and actions.

Lack of space prevents us from elaborating here on further ongoing work that is being developed by us in the context of the general language. Namely, further detailing the concepts involved in the definition of domain languages, and also the definition of a general architecture for executing the ECA rules are left out. This general architecture also raises the issue of communication strategies regarding events and actions (are events that are raised by actions "pushed" into respective nodes? or do nodes periodically "pull" for events that may have occurred?). Another important issue that is also related with the execution, and that was only briefly addressed here is that of transactions. It is our belief that the issue of transactions on the Web is an important and difficult subject, that will gain increasing importance and interest in a near future. It is in our agenda to continue working in this subject, along the lines exposed above.

Acknowledgements

This research has been funded by the European Commission within the 6th Framework Programme project REWERSE, number 506779.

References

1. J. J. Alferes, M. Berndtsson, F. Bry, M. Eckert, N. Henze, W. May, P. L. Pǎtrânjan, and M. Schroeder. Use-cases on evolution. Technical Report IST506779/Lisbon/I5-D2/D/PU/a1, REWERSE, 2005.
2. James Bailey, Alexandra Poulovassilis, and Peter T. Wood. An Event-Condition-Action Language for XML. In *Int. WWW Conference*, 2002.
3. M. Bernauer, G. Kappel, and G.Kramler. Composite Events for XML. In *13th Int. Conf. on World Wide Web (WWW 2004)*. ACM, 2004.
4. Harold Boley, Benjamin Grosof, Michael Sintek, Said Tabet, and Gerd Wagner. *RuleML Design*. RuleML Initiative, http://www.ruleml.org/, 2002.
5. Angela Bonifati, Daniele Braga, Alessandro Campi, and Stefano Ceri. Active XQuery. In *"Intl. Conference on Data Engineering (ICDE)"*, pages 403–418, 2002.
6. Angela Bonifati, Stefano Ceri, and Stefano Paraboschi. Pushing Reactive Services to XML Repositories Using Active Rules. In *WWW'01*, pages 633–641, 2001.
7. A. J. Bonner and M. Kifer. An overview of transaction logic. *Theoretical Computer Science*, 133(2):205–265, 1994.
8. F. Bry and P.-L. Pǎtrânjan. Reactivity on the Web: Paradigms and Applications of the Language XChange. In *20th ACM Symp. Applied Computing*. ACM, 2005.
9. S. Chakravarthy, V. Krishnaprasad, E. Anwar, and S.-K. Kim. Composite events for active databases: Semantics, contexts and detection. In *20th VLDB*, 1994.
10. Sharma Chakravarthy and D. Mishra. Snoop: An expressive event specification language for active databases. *Data & Knowledge Engineering*, 14:1–26, 1994.
11. Document object model (DOM). http://www.w3.org/DOM/, 1998.
12. Foundation for Intelligent Physical Agents. FIPA ACL Message Structure Specification. Technical Report SC00061G, http://www.fipa.org, Dec. 2002.

13. Object Management Group. *XML Metadata Interchange (XMI) 2.0 Specification.* OMG, 2003. http://www.omg.org/cgi-bin/doc?formal/2003-05-02.
14. Object Management Group. *OMG Unified Modelling Language (UML) 2.0 Superstructure.* OMG, 2004. http://www.omg.org/cgi-bin/doc?ptc/2004-10-02.
15. Mengchi Liu, Li Lu, and Guoren Wang. A Declarative XML-RL Update Language. In *Proc. Int. Conf. on Conceptual Modeling*, pages 506–519. Springer, 2003.
16. Wolfgang May. XPath-Logic and XPathLog: A logic-programming style XML data manipulation language. *Theory and Practice of Logic Programming*, 4(3), 2004.
17. Wolfgang May, José Júlio Alferes, and François Bry. Towards generic query, update, and event languages for the Semantic Web. In *Principles and Practice of Semantic Web Reasoning (PPSWR)*, number 3208 in LNCS, pages 19–33. Springer, 2004.
18. George Papamarkos, Alexandra Poulovassilis, and Peter T. Wood. RDFTL: An Event-Condition-Action Rule Languages for RDF. In *HDMS'04*, 2004.
19. N. W. Paton, editor. *Active Rules in Database Systems*. Monographs in Computer Science. Springer, 1999.
20. S. Schaffert and F. Bry. A practical introduction to Xcerpt. In *Int. Conf. Extreme Markup Languages*, 2004.
21. Igor Tatarinov, Zachary G. Ives, Alon Halevy, and Daniel Weld. Updating XML. In *ACM Intl. Conference on Management of Data (SIGMOD)*, pages 133–154, 2001.
22. G. Wagner, C. V. Damásio, and S. Lukichev. First-version rule markup languages. Technical Report IST506779/Eindhoven/I1-D3/D/PU/ab1, REWERSE, 2005.
23. Jennifer Widom and Stefano Ceri, editors. *Active Database Systems: Triggers and Rules for Advanced Database Processing*. Morgan Kaufmann, 1996.
24. XML:DB Initiative, http://xmldb-org.sourceforge.net/. *XUpdate - XML Update Language*, September 2000.
25. D. Zimmer and R. Unland. On the Semantics of Complex Events in Active Database Management Systems. In *15th International Conference on Data Engineering*, pages 392–399. IEEE Computer Society Press, 1999.

Use Cases for Reasoning with Metadata
or
What Have Web Services to Do with Integrity Constraints?

Stefan Decker

Digital Enterprise Research Institute,
National University of Ireland, Galway, Ireland
stefan@stefandecker.org

Overview

Not surprisingly, everyone perceives the Semantic Web in a different way. One view is that the Semantic Web is about semantics, and semantics is about AI-style knowledge representation, which leads to knowledge representation languages like OWL.

Another view is that the Semantic Web is about overcoming the syntax of data so that users and developers can concentrate on the semantics of information. Following this view means that languages and tools for the Semantic Web must focus on practical problems rather than generic KR tasks. That is, they should make it easier and cheaper to publish, understand, use, and reuse data and services on the Web in an interoperable and scalable way. Languages that help define how different data sets and vocabularies relate to each other are necessary; they are able to provide the glue between (distributed) information systems and data sets. Following this view also has consequences for designing rule languages for the Semantic Web.

A major task to achieve on the Semantic Web is to provide tools that drive down the cost of establishing interoperability between different data providers. A rule language can help here: writing rules is usually faster and cheaper than writing program code since a rule language has more declarative features and is usually not burdened with the details of a general programming language. Rules provide benefits over a software product's life cycle; they are simpler to write than code, more concise, and easier to understand, to share, and to maintain.

Standardizing such a rule language has several benefits. Interested parties can invest in building the infrastructure because a market is being created. Standardization also enables competition to drive innovation. And last but not least, it allows rule sharing (that is, knowledge about how to achieve interoperability).

In other words, a rule language for the Semantic Web may be seen as a data transformation and glue language - in contrast to a knowledge representation language, which captures knowledge about a certain domain.

Of course such a rule language needs a defined semantics (as a basis for implementation) and efficient evaluation mechanisms. Starting from modest begin-

F. Fages and S. Soliman (Eds.): PPSWR 2005, LNCS 3703, pp. 116–117, 2005.

nings (SiLRI) reported in [1], with TRIPLE [2] [3] we were aiming at a practical language suitable for applications. TRIPLE has been used in a variety of different projects, including Ontology Management [4], Conflict Analysis [5], Resource Matching on the Grid [6], Personalization Services [7], and E-Government [8]. A relatively new application is validation of data sets for Web services using integrity constraints. In my talk I will introduce the different use cases and investigate what gives TRIPLE the flexibility required for being an adequate tool for this wide range of applications.

References

1. Decker, S., Brickley, D., Saarela, J., Angele, J.: A query and inference service for rdf. In: In QL'98 - The Query Languages Workshop, Boston, USA, WorldWideWeb Consortium (W3C) (1998)
2. Sintek, M., Decker, S.: Using triple for business agents on the semantic web. Electronic Commerce Research and Applications **2** (2003) 315–322
3. Sintek, M., Decker, S.: Triple - a query, inference, and transformation language for the semantic web. In: ISWC '02: Proceedings of the First International Semantic Web Conference on The Semantic Web, London, UK, Springer-Verlag (2002) 364–378
4. Tolksdorf, R., Eckstein, R., eds.: Berliner XML Tage 2003, 13.-15. Oktober 2003 in Berlin. In Tolksdorf, R., Eckstein, R., eds.: Berliner XML Tage, XML-Clearinghouse (2003)
5. Leicher, A., Süß, J.G.: Augmenting uml models for composition conflict analysis. In Cerioli, M., ed.: FASE. Volume 3442 of Lecture Notes in Computer Science., Springer (2005) 127–140
6. Tangmunarunkit, H., Decker, S., Kesselman, C.: Ontology-based resource matching in the grid - the grid meets the semantic web. In: Proceedings of the 2nd International Semantic Web Conference (ISWC2003), Sundial Resort, Sanibel Island, Florida, USA (2003)
7. Dolog, P., Henze, N., Nejdl, W., Sintek, M.: Personalization in distributed e-learning environments. In: WWW Alt. '04: Proceedings of the 13th international World Wide Web conference on Alternate track papers & posters, New York, NY, USA, ACM Press (2004) 170–179
8. Ambite, J.L., Giuliano, G., Gordon, P., Pan, Q., Abbasi, N., Wang, L., Weathers, M.: Argos: dynamic composition of web services for goods movement analysis and planning. In: dg.o2005: Proceedings of the 2005 national conference on Digital government research, Digital Government Research Center (2005) 275–276

Principles of Inductive Reasoning on the Semantic Web: A Framework for Learning in $\mathcal{AL}$-Log

Francesca A. Lisi

Dipartimento di Informatica, Università degli Studi di Bari,
Via Orabona 4, 70125 Bari, Italy
lisi@di.uniba.it

Abstract. The design of the logical layer of the Semantic Web, and subsequently of the mark-up language SWRL, has renewed the interest in hybrid knowledge representation and reasoning. In this paper we discuss principles of inductive reasoning for this layer. To this aim we provide a general framework for learning in $\mathcal{AL}$-log, a hybrid language that integrates the description logic $\mathcal{ALC}$ and the function-free Horn clausal language DATALOG, thus turning out to be a small yet sufficiently expressive subset of SWRL. In this framework inductive hypotheses are represented as constrained DATALOG clauses, organized according to the $\mathcal{B}$-subsumption relation, and evaluated against observations by applying coverage relations that depend on the representation chosen for the observations. The framework is valid whatever the scope of induction (description vs. prediction) is. Yet, for illustrative purposes, we concentrate on an instantiation of the framework which supports description.

1 Introduction

The layered architecture of the Semantic Web [2] poses several challenges in the field of Knowledge Representation and Reasoning (KR&R), mainly attracting people doing research on Description Logics (DLs) [1]. E.g., the design of OWL for the *ontological layer* has been based on the DL $\mathcal{SHIQ}$ [14]. Also SWRL (http://www.w3.org/Submission/SWRL/), recently proposed for the *logical layer*, extends OWL 'to build rules on top of ontologies'. It bridges the notorious expressive gap between DLs and Horn clausal logic (or its fragments) [4] in a way that is similar in the spirit to hybridization in KR&R systems such as $\mathcal{AL}$-log [8]. Generally speaking, *hybrid systems* are KR&R systems which are constituted by two or more subsystems dealing with distinct portions of a single knowledge base by performing specific reasoning procedures [13]. The motivation for building hybrid systems is to improve on two basic features of knowledge representation formalisms, namely *representational adequacy* and *deductive power*. In particular, $\mathcal{AL}$-log integrates $\mathcal{ALC}$ [25] and DATALOG [6] by using $\mathcal{ALC}$ concept assertions essentially as type constraints on variables. Given the links between $\mathcal{ALC}$ and $\mathcal{SHIQ}$ as well as between DATALOG and Horn clauses, it can be considered a small yet sufficiently expressive subset of SWRL.

F. Fages and S. Soliman (Eds.): PPSWR 2005, LNCS 3703, pp. 118–132, 2005.
© Springer-Verlag Berlin Heidelberg 2005

Reasoning is commonly intended to be based on deduction. Yet *induction*, deeply investigated in the area of Machine Learning [9], is a very interesting inference which could be of help to the Semantic Web practitioners, e.g. to support them in the task of defining rules for the logical layer. The approach known under the name of Inductive Logic Programming (ILP) seems to be particularly promising due to the common roots with computational logic [10]. ILP has been historically concerned with concept learning from examples and background knowledge within the representation framework of Horn clausal logic and with the aim of prediction. More recently ILP has moved towards either different first-order logic fragments (e.g., DLs) or new learning goals (e.g., description). In this paper we resort to the methodological apparatus of ILP to define a *general* framework for learning in $\mathcal{AL}$-log. Inductive hypotheses are represented as constrained DATALOG clauses, organized according to the $\mathcal{B}$-subsumption relation, and evaluated against observations by applying coverage relations that depend on the representation chosen for the observations. The framework proposed is general in the sense that it is valid whatever the scope of induction (description vs. prediction) is. For the sake of illustration we concentrate on an instantiation of the framework which corresponds to the logical setting of *characteristic induction from intepretations* and is particularly suitable for descriptive data mining tasks such as frequent pattern discovery (and its variants) [7].

The paper is organized as follows. Section 2 introduces the basic notions of $\mathcal{AL}$-log. Section 3 defines the framework for learning in $\mathcal{AL}$-log. Section 4 illustrates the instantiation of the framework in the case of characteristic induction from intepretations. Section 5 concludes the paper with final remarks.

2   Basics of $\mathcal{AL}$-Log

The system $\mathcal{AL}$-log [8] integrates two KR&R systems: Structural and relational.

2.1   The Structural Subsystem

The structural part Σ is based on $\mathcal{ALC}$ [25] and allows for the specification of knowledge in terms of classes (*concepts*), binary relations between classes (*roles*), and instances (*individuals*). Complex concepts can be defined from atomic concepts and roles by means of constructors (see Table 1). Also Σ can state both is-a relations between concepts (*axioms*) and instance-of relations between individuals (resp. couples of individuals) and concepts (resp. roles) (*assertions*). An *interpretation* $\mathcal{I} = (\Delta^{\mathcal{I}}, \cdot^{\mathcal{I}})$ for Σ consists of a domain $\Delta^{\mathcal{I}}$ and a mapping function $\cdot^{\mathcal{I}}$. In particular, individuals are mapped to elements of $\Delta^{\mathcal{I}}$ such that $a^{\mathcal{I}} \neq b^{\mathcal{I}}$ if $a \neq b$ (*Unique Names Assumption* (UNA) [22]). If $\mathcal{O} \subseteq \Delta^{\mathcal{I}}$ and $\forall a \in \mathcal{O} : a^{\mathcal{I}} = a$, $\mathcal{I}$ is called $\mathcal{O}$-*interpretation*. Also Σ represents many different interpretations, i.e. all its models (*Open World Assumption* (OWA) [1]).

The main reasoning task for Σ is the *consistency check*. This test is performed with a *tableau calculus* that starts with the tableau branch $S = \Sigma$ and adds assertions to S by means of *propagation rules* such as

Table 1. Syntax and semantics of $\mathcal{ALC}$

bottom (resp. top) concept	$\bot$ (resp. $\top$)	$\emptyset$ (resp. $\Delta^{\mathcal{I}}$)
atomic concept	A	$A^{\mathcal{I}} \subseteq \Delta^{\mathcal{I}}$
role	R	$R^{\mathcal{I}} \subseteq \Delta^{\mathcal{I}} \times \Delta^{\mathcal{I}}$
individual	a	$a^{\mathcal{I}} \in \Delta^{\mathcal{I}}$
concept negation	$\neg C$	$\Delta^{\mathcal{I}} \setminus C^{\mathcal{I}}$
concept conjunction	$C \sqcap D$	$C^{\mathcal{I}} \cap D^{\mathcal{I}}$
concept disjunction	$C \sqcup D$	$C^{\mathcal{I}} \cup D^{\mathcal{I}}$
value restriction	$\forall R.C$	$\{x \in \Delta^{\mathcal{I}} \mid \forall y \ (x,y) \in R^{\mathcal{I}} \to y \in C^{\mathcal{I}}\}$
existential restriction	$\exists R.C$	$\{x \in \Delta^{\mathcal{I}} \mid \exists y \ (x,y) \in R^{\mathcal{I}} \land y \in C^{\mathcal{I}}\}$
equivalence axiom	$C \equiv D$	$C^{\mathcal{I}} = D^{\mathcal{I}}$
subsumption axiom	$C \sqsubseteq D$	$C^{\mathcal{I}} \subseteq D^{\mathcal{I}}$
concept assertion	$a : C$	$a^{\mathcal{I}} \in C^{\mathcal{I}}$
role assertion	$\langle a,b \rangle : R$	$(a^{\mathcal{I}}, b^{\mathcal{I}}) \in R^{\mathcal{I}}$

- $S \to_\sqcup S \cup \{s : D\}$ if
    1. $s : C_1 \sqcup C_2$ is in S,
    2. $D = C_1$ and $D = C_2$,
    3. neither $s : C_1$ nor $s : C_2$ is in S
- $S \to_\forall S \cup \{t : C\}$ if
    1. $s : \forall R.C$ is in S,
    2. sRt is in S,
    3. $t : C$ is not in S
- $S \to_\sqsubseteq S \cup \{s : C' \sqcup D\}$ if
    1. $C \sqsubseteq D$ is in S,
    2. s appears in S,
    3. C' is the NNF concept equivalent to $\neg C$
    4. $s : \neg C \sqcup D$ is not in S
- $S \to_\bot \{s : \bot\}$ if
    1. $s : A$ and $s : \neg A$ are in S, or
    2. $s : \neg\top$ is in S,
    3. $s : \bot$ is not in S

until either a contradiction is generated or an interpretation satisfying S can be easily obtained from it.

2.2   The Relational Subsystem

The relational part of $\mathcal{AL}$-log allows one to define DATALOG[1] programs enriched with *constraints* of the form $s : C$ where s is either a constant or a variable, and C is an $\mathcal{ALC}$-concept. Note that the usage of concepts as typing constraints applies only to variables and constants that already appear in the clause. The symbol & separates constraints from DATALOG atoms in a clause.

---

[1] For the sake of brevity we assume the reader to be familiar with DATALOG.

Definition 1. *A* constrained DATALOG *clause is an implication of the form* $\alpha_0 \leftarrow \alpha_1, \ldots, \alpha_m \& \gamma_1, \ldots, \gamma_n$ *where* $m \geq 0$, $n \geq 0$, α_i *are* DATALOG *atoms and* γ_j *are constraints. A* constrained DATALOG *program* Π *is a set of constrained* DATALOG *clauses.*

An $\mathcal{AL}$-*log knowledge base* $\mathcal{B}$ is the pair $\langle \Sigma, \Pi \rangle$ where Σ is an $\mathcal{ALC}$ knowledge base and Π is a constrained DATALOG program. For a knowledge base to be acceptable, it must satisfy the following conditions:

- The set of DATALOG predicate symbols appearing in Π is disjoint from the set of concept and role symbols appearing in Σ.
- The alphabet of constants in Π coincides with the alphabet $\mathcal{O}$ of the individuals in Σ. Furthermore, every constant in Π appears also in Σ.
- For each clause in Π, each variable occurring in the constraint part occurs also in the DATALOG part.

These properties state a *safe* interaction between the structural and the relational part of an $\mathcal{AL}$-log knowledge base, thus solving the semantic mismatch between the OWA of $\mathcal{ALC}$ and the CWA of DATALOG [23]. This interaction is also at the basis of a model-theoretic semantics for $\mathcal{AL}$-log. We call Π_D the set of DATALOG clauses obtained from the clauses of Π by deleting their constraints. We define an *interpretation* $\mathcal{J}$ for $\mathcal{B}$ as the union of an $\mathcal{O}$-interpretation $\mathcal{I}_{\mathcal{O}}$ for Σ (i.e. an interpretation compliant with the unique names assumption) and an Herbrand interpretation $\mathcal{I}_{\mathcal{H}}$ for Π_D. An interpretation $\mathcal{J}$ is a *model* of $\mathcal{B}$ if $\mathcal{I}_{\mathcal{O}}$ is a model of Σ, and for each ground instance $\alpha_0' \leftarrow \alpha_1', \ldots, \alpha_m' \& \gamma_1', \ldots, \gamma_n'$ of each clause $\alpha_0 \leftarrow \alpha_1, \ldots, \alpha_m \& \gamma_1', \ldots, \gamma_n'$ in Π, either there exists one γ_i', $i \in \{1, \ldots, n\}$, that is not satisfied by $\mathcal{J}$, or $\alpha_0' \leftarrow \alpha_1', \ldots, \alpha_m'$ is satisfied by $\mathcal{J}$. The notion of *logical consequence* paves the way to the definition of answer set for queries. *Queries* to $\mathcal{AL}$-log knowledge bases are special cases of Definition 1. An *answer* to the query Q is a ground substitution σ for the variables in Q. The answer σ is *correct* w.r.t. a $\mathcal{AL}$-log knowledge base $\mathcal{B}$ if $Q\sigma$ is a logical consequence of $\mathcal{B}$ ($\mathcal{B} \models Q\sigma$). The *answer set* of Q in $\mathcal{B}$ contains all the correct answers to Q w.r.t. $\mathcal{B}$.

Reasoning for $\mathcal{AL}$-log knowledge bases is based on *constrained SLD-resolution* [8], i.e. an extension of SLD-resolution to deal with constraints. In particular, the constraints of the resolvent of a query Q and a constrained DATALOG clause E are recursively simplified by replacing couples of constraints $t : C$, $t : D$ with the equivalent constraint $t : C \sqcap D$. The one-to-one mapping between constrained SLD-derivations and the SLD-derivations obtained by ignoring the constraints is exploited to extend known results for DATALOG to $\mathcal{AL}$-log. Note that in $\mathcal{AL}$-log a derivation of the empty clause with associated constraints does not represent a refutation. It actually infers that the query is true in those models of $\mathcal{B}$ that satisfy its constraints. Therefore in order to answer a query it is necessary to collect enough derivations ending with a constrained empty clause such that every model of $\mathcal{B}$ satisfies the constraints associated with the final query of at least one derivation.

Definition 2. *Let $Q^{(0)}$ be a query $\leftarrow \beta_1, \dots, \beta_m \& \gamma_1, \dots, \gamma_n$ to a $\mathcal{AL}$-log knowledge base $\mathcal{B}$. A constrained SLD-refutation for $Q^{(0)}$ in $\mathcal{B}$ is a finite set $\{d_1, \dots, d_s\}$ of constrained SLD-derivations for $Q^{(0)}$ in $\mathcal{B}$ such that:*

1. *for each derivation d_i, $1 \leq i \leq s$, the last query $Q^{(n_i)}$ of d_i is a constrained empty clause;*
2. *for every model $\mathcal{J}$ of $\mathcal{B}$, there exists at least one derivation d_i, $1 \leq i \leq s$, such that $\mathcal{J} \models Q^{(n_i)}$.*

Constrained SLD-refutation is a complete and sound method for answering *ground* queries.

Lemma 1. *[8] Let Q be a ground query to an $\mathcal{AL}$-log knowledge base $\mathcal{B}$. It holds that $\mathcal{B} \vdash Q$ if and only if $\mathcal{B} \models Q$.*

An answer σ to a query Q is a *computed answer* if there exists a constrained SLD-refutation for $Q\sigma$ in $\mathcal{B}$ ($\mathcal{B} \vdash Q\sigma$). The set of computed answers is called the *success set* of Q in $\mathcal{B}$. Furthermore, given *any* query Q, the success set of Q in $\mathcal{B}$ coincides with the answer set of Q in $\mathcal{B}$. This provides an operational means for computing correct answers to queries. Indeed, it is straightforward to see that the usual reasoning methods for DATALOG allow us to collect in a finite number of steps enough constrained SLD-derivations for Q in $\mathcal{B}$ to construct a refutation - if any. Derivations must satisfy both conditions of Definition 2. In particular, the latter requires some reasoning on the structural component of $\mathcal{B}$. This is done by applying the tableau calculus as shown in the following example.

Constrained SLD-resolution is *decidable*. Furthermore, because of the safe interaction between $\mathcal{ALC}$ and DATALOG, it supports a form of *closed world reasoning*, i.e. it allows one to pose queries under the assumption that part of the knowledge base is complete.

3   The General Framework for Learning in $\mathcal{AL}$-Log

In our framework for learning in $\mathcal{AL}$-log we represent inductive hypotheses as constrained DATALOG clauses and data as an $\mathcal{AL}$-log knowledge base $\mathcal{B}$. In particular $\mathcal{B}$ is composed of a *background knowledge* $\mathcal{K}$ and a set O of *observations*. We assume $\mathcal{K} \cap O = \emptyset$.

To define the framework we resort to the methodological apparatus of ILP which requires the following ingredients to be chosen:

- the *language* $\mathcal{L}$ *of hypotheses*
- a *generality order* $\succeq$ for $\mathcal{L}$ to structure the space of hypotheses
- a *relation* to test the *coverage* of hypotheses in $\mathcal{L}$ against observations in O w.r.t. $\mathcal{K}$

The framework is **general**, meaning that it is valid whatever the scope of induction (description/prediction) is. Therefore the DATALOG literal $q(\boldsymbol{X})^2$ in the head of hypotheses represents a concept to be either discriminated from others (*discriminant induction*) or characterized (*characteristic induction*).

---

[2] $\boldsymbol{X}$ is a tuple of variables.

3.1   The Language of Hypotheses

To be suitable as language of hypotheses, constrained DATALOG clauses must satisfy the following restrictions.

First, we impose constrained DATALOG clauses to be linked and connected (or range-restricted) as usual in ILP.

Definition 3. *Let H be a constrained* DATALOG *clause. A term t in some literal $l_i \in H$ is* linked *with linking-chain of length 0, if t occurs in $head(H)$, and is linked with linking-chain of length $d + 1$, if some other term in l_i is linked with linking-chain of length d. The* link-depth *of a term t in some $l_i \in H$ is the length of the shortest linking-chain of t. A literal $l_i \in H$ is* linked *if at least one of its terms is linked. The clause H itself is* linked *if each $l_i \in H$ is linked. The clause H is* connected *if each variable occurring in $head(H)$ also occur in $body(H)$.*

Second, we impose constrained DATALOG clauses to be compliant with the bias of Object Identity (OI) [26]. This bias can be considered as an extension of the unique names assumption from the semantic level to the syntactic one of $\mathcal{AL}$-log. We would like to remind the reader that this assumption holds in $\mathcal{ALC}$. Also it holds naturally for ground constrained DATALOG clauses because the semantics of $\mathcal{AL}$-log adopts Herbrand models for the DATALOG part and $\mathcal{O}$-models for the constraint part. Conversely it is not guaranteed in the case of non-ground constrained DATALOG clauses, e.g. different variables can be unified. The OI bias can be the starting point for the definition of either an equational theory or a quasi-order for constrained DATALOG clauses. The latter option relies on a restricted form of substitution whose bindings avoid the identification of terms.

Definition 4. *A substitution σ is an* OI-substitution *w.r.t. a set of terms T iff $\forall t_1, t_2 \in T: t_1 \neq t_2$ yields that $t_1\sigma \neq t_2\sigma$.*

From now on, we assume that substitutions are OI-compliant.

3.2   The Generality Relation

The definition of a generality relation for constrained DATALOG clauses can disregard neither the peculiarities of $\mathcal{AL}$-log nor the methodological apparatus of ILP. Therefore we rely on the reasoning mechanisms made available by $\mathcal{AL}$-log knowledge bases and propose to adapt Buntine's generalized subsumption [5] to our framework as follows.

Definition 5. *Let H be a constrained* DATALOG *clause, α a ground* DATALOG *atom, and $\mathcal{J}$ an interpretation. We say that H* covers *α under $\mathcal{J}$ if there is a ground substitution θ for H ($H\theta$ is ground) such that $body(H)\theta$ is true under $\mathcal{J}$ and $head(H)\theta = \alpha$.*

Definition 6. *Let H_1, H_2 be two constrained* DATALOG *clauses and $\mathcal{B}$ an $\mathcal{AL}$-log knowledge base. We say that H_1 $\mathcal{B}$-subsumes H_2 if for every model $\mathcal{J}$ of $\mathcal{B}$ and every ground atom α such that H_2 covers α under $\mathcal{J}$, we have that H_1 covers α under $\mathcal{J}$.*

We can define a generality relation $\succeq_\mathcal{B}$ for constrained DATALOG clauses on the basis of $\mathcal{B}$-subsumption. It can be easily proven that $\succeq_\mathcal{B}$ is a quasi-order (i.e. it is a reflexive and transitive relation) for constrained DATALOG clauses.

Definition 7. *Let H_1, H_2 be two constrained DATALOG clauses and $\mathcal{B}$ an $\mathcal{AL}$-log knowledge base. We say that H_1 is at least as general as H_2 under $\mathcal{B}$-subsumption, $H_1 \succeq_\mathcal{B} H_2$, iff H_1 $\mathcal{B}$-subsumes H_2. Furthermore, H_1 is more general than H_2 under $\mathcal{B}$-subsumption, $H_1 \succ_\mathcal{B} H_2$, iff $H_1 \succeq_\mathcal{B} H_2$ and $H_2 \nsucceq_\mathcal{B} H_1$. Finally, H_1 is equivalent to H_2 under $\mathcal{B}$-subsumption, $H_1 \sim_\mathcal{B} H_2$, iff $H_1 \succeq_\mathcal{B} H_2$ and $H_2 \succeq_\mathcal{B} H_1$.*

The next lemma shows the definition of $\mathcal{B}$-subsumption to be equivalent to another formulation, which will be more convenient in later proofs than the definition based on covering.

Definition 8. *Let $\mathcal{B}$ be an $\mathcal{AL}$-log knowledge base and H be a constrained DATALOG clause. Let $X_1, \ldots, X_n$ be all the variables appearing in H, and $a_1, \ldots, a_n$ be distinct constants (individuals) not appearing in $\mathcal{B}$ or H. Then the substitution $\{X_1/a_1, \ldots, X_n/a_n\}$ is called a Skolem substitution for H w.r.t. $\mathcal{B}$.*

Lemma 2. *[18] Let H_1, H_2 be two constrained DATALOG clauses, $\mathcal{B}$ an $\mathcal{AL}$-log knowledge base, and σ a Skolem substitution for H_2 with respect to $\{H_1\} \cup \mathcal{B}$. We say that $H_1 \succeq_\mathcal{B} H_2$ iff there exists a ground substitution θ for H_1 such that (i) $head(H_1)\theta = head(H_2)\sigma$ and (ii) $\mathcal{B} \cup body(H_2)\sigma \models body(H_1)\theta$.*

The relation between $\mathcal{B}$-subsumption and constrained SLD-resolution is given below. It provides an operational means for checking $\mathcal{B}$-subsumption.

Theorem 1. *Let H_1, H_2 be two constrained DATALOG clauses, $\mathcal{B}$ an $\mathcal{AL}$-log knowledge base, and σ a Skolem substitution for H_2 with respect to $\{H_1\} \cup \mathcal{B}$. We say that $H_1 \succeq_\mathcal{B} H_2$ iff there exists a substitution θ for H_1 such that (i) $head(H_1)\theta = head(H_2)$ and (ii) $\mathcal{B} \cup body(H_2)\sigma \vdash body(H_1)\theta\sigma$ where $body(H_1)\theta\sigma$ is ground.*

Proof. By Lemma 2, we have $H_1 \succeq_\mathcal{B} H_2$ iff there exists a ground substitution θ' for H_1, such that $head(H_1)\theta' = head(H_2)\sigma$ and $\mathcal{B} \cup body(H_2)\sigma \models body(H_1)\theta'$. Since σ is a Skolem substitution, we can define a substitution θ such that $H_1\theta\sigma = H_1\theta'$ and none of the Skolem constants of σ occurs in θ. Then $head(H_1)\theta = head(H_2)$ and $\mathcal{B} \cup body(H_2)\sigma \models body(H_1)\theta\sigma$. Since $body(H_1)\theta\sigma$ is ground, by Lemma 1 we have $\mathcal{B} \cup body(H_2)\sigma \vdash body(H_1)\theta\sigma$, so the thesis follows.

The decidability of $\mathcal{B}$-subsumption follows from the decidability of both generalized subsumption in DATALOG [5] and query answering in $\mathcal{AL}$-log [8].

3.3   Coverage Relations

When defining coverage relations we make assumptions as regards the representation of observations because it impacts the definition of coverage.

In the logical setting of *learning from entailment* extended to $\mathcal{AL}$-log, an observation $o_i \in O$ is represented as a ground constrained DATALOG clause having a ground atom $q(\boldsymbol{a}_i)^3$ in the head.

Definition 9. *Let $H \in \mathcal{L}$ be a hypothesis, $\mathcal{K}$ a background knowledge and $o_i \in O$ an observation. We say that H covers o_i under entailment w.r.t $\mathcal{K}$ iff $\mathcal{K} \cup H \models o_i$.*

Theorem 2. *[17] Let $H \in \mathcal{L}$ be a hypothesis, $\mathcal{K}$ a background knowledge, and $o_i \in O$ an observation. We say that H covers o_i under entailment w.r.t. $\mathcal{K}$ iff $\mathcal{K} \cup body(o_i) \cup H \vdash q(\boldsymbol{a}_i)$.*

In the logical setting of *learning from interpretations* extended to $\mathcal{AL}$-log, an observation $o_i \in O$ is represented as a couple $(q(\boldsymbol{a}_i), \mathcal{A}_i)$ where $\mathcal{A}_i$ is a set containing ground DATALOG facts concerning the individual i.

Definition 10. *Let $H \in \mathcal{L}$ be a hypothesis, $\mathcal{K}$ a background knowledge and $o_i \in O$ an observation. We say that H covers o_i under interpretations w.r.t. $\mathcal{K}$ iff $\mathcal{K} \cup \mathcal{A}_i \cup H \models q(\boldsymbol{a}_i)$.*

Theorem 3. *[17] Let $H \in \mathcal{L}$ be a hypothesis, $\mathcal{K}$ a background knowledge, and $o_i \in O$ an observation. We say that H covers o_i under interpretations w.r.t. $\mathcal{K}$ iff $\mathcal{K} \cup \mathcal{A}_i \cup H \vdash q(\boldsymbol{a}_i)$.*

Note that the both coverage tests can be reduced to query answering.

4   An Instantiation of the Framework

As an instantiation of our general framework for learning in $\mathcal{AL}$-log we choose the case of *characteristic induction from interpretations* which is defined as follows.

Definition 11. *Let $\mathcal{L}$ be a hypothesis language, $\mathcal{K}$ a background knowledge, O a set of observations, and $M(\mathcal{B})$ a model constructed from $\mathcal{B} = \mathcal{K} \cup O$. The goal of characteristic induction from interpretations is to find a set $\mathcal{H} \subseteq \mathcal{L}$ of hypotheses such that (i) $\mathcal{H}$ is true in $M(\mathcal{B})$, and (ii) for each $H \in \mathcal{L}$, if H is true in $M(\mathcal{B})$ then $\mathcal{H} \models H$.*

The logical setting of characteristic induction has been considered very close to that form of data mining, called *descriptive data mining*, which focuses on finding human-interpretable patterns describing a data set $\mathbf{r}$ [7]. *Scalability* is a crucial issue in descriptive data mining. Recently, the setting of learning from interpretations has been shown to be a promising way of scaling up ILP algorithms in real-world applications [3].

4.1   A Task of Characteristic Induction

Among descriptive data mining tasks, *frequent pattern discovery* aims at the extraction of all patterns whose cardinality exceeds a user-defined threshold.

---

[3] $\boldsymbol{a}_i$ is a tuple of constants.

```
<owl:Class rdf:ID="MiddleEastCountry">
  <owl:sameAs>
    <owl:intersectionOf rdf:parseType="Collection">
      <owl:Class rdf:ID="AsianCountry" />
      <owl:Restriction>
        <owl:onProperty rdf:resource="#Hosts" />
        <owl:someValuesFrom rdf:resource="#MiddleEasternEthnicGroup" />
      </owl:Restriction>
    </owl:intersectionOf>
  </owl:sameAs>
</owl:Class>
```

Fig. 1. Definition of the concept `MiddleEastCountry` in OWL

Indeed each pattern is considered as an intensional description (expressed in a given language $\mathcal{L}$) of a subset of **r**.

The blueprint of most algorithms for frequent pattern discovery is the *level-wise search* [21]. It is based on the following assumption: If a generality order $\succeq$ for the language $\mathcal{L}$ of patterns can be found such that $\succeq$ is monotonic w.r.t. the evaluation function *supp*, then the resulting space $(\mathcal{L}, \succeq)$ can be searched breadth-first starting from the most general pattern in $\mathcal{L}$ and by alternating *candidate generation* and *candidate evaluation* phases. In particular, candidate generation consists of a refinement step followed by a pruning step. The former derives candidates for the current search level from patterns found frequent in the previous search level. The latter allows some infrequent patterns to be detected and discarded prior to evaluation thanks to the monotonicity of $\succeq$.

We consider a variant of this task which takes concept hierarchies into account during the discovery process, thus yielding descriptions of **r** at multiple granularity levels [20]. More formally, given

- a data set **r** including a taxonomy $\mathcal{T}$ where a reference concept C_{ref} and task-relevant concepts are designated,
- a multi-grained language $\mathcal{L} = \{\mathcal{L}^l\}_{1 \leq l \leq maxG}$ of patterns
- a set $\{minsup^l\}_{1 \leq l \leq maxG}$ of support thresholds

the problem of *frequent pattern discovery at l levels of description granularity*, $1 \leq l \leq maxG$, is to find the set $\mathcal{F}$ of all the patterns $P \in \mathcal{L}^l$ frequent in **r**, namely P's with support s such that (i) $s \geq minsup^l$ and (ii) all ancestors of P w.r.t. $\mathcal{T}$ are frequent in **r**.

4.2   Casting the Framework to the Task

When casting our general framework for learning in $\mathcal{AL}$-log to the task of frequent pattern discovery at multiple levels of description granularity, the data set **r** is represented as an $\mathcal{AL}$-log knowledge base.

Example 1. As a running example, we consider an $\mathcal{AL}$-log knowledge base $\mathcal{B}_{CIA}$ that enriches DATALOG facts[4] extracted from the on-line 1996 CIA World Fact

---

[4] http://www.dbis.informatik.uni-goettingen.de/Mondial/mondial-rel-facts.flp

Book[5] with $\mathcal{ALC}$ ontologies. The structural subsystem Σ of $\mathcal{B}_{\text{CIA}}$ focuses on the concepts Country, EthnicGroup, Language, and Religion. Axioms like

```
AsianCountry ⊑ Country.
MiddleEasternEthnicGroup ⊑ EthnicGroup.
MiddleEastCountry ≡ AsianCountry ⊓ ∃Hosts.MiddleEasternEthnicGroup.
IndoEuropeanLanguage ⊑ Language.
IndoIranianLanguage ⊑ IndoEuropeanLanguage.
MonotheisticReligion ⊑ Religion.
ChristianReligion ⊑ MonotheisticReligion.
MuslimReligion ⊑ MonotheisticReligion.
```

define four taxonomies, one for each concept above. Note that Middle East countries (concept MiddleEastCountry, whose definition in OWL is reported in Figure 1) have been defined as Asian countries that host at least one Middle Eastern ethnic group. Assertions like

```
'ARM':AsianCountry.
'IR':AsianCountry.
'Arab':MiddleEasternEthnicGroup.
'Armenian':MiddleEasternEthnicGroup.
<'ARM','Armenian'>:Hosts.
<'IR','Arab'>:Hosts.
'Armenian':IndoEuropeanLanguage.
'Persian':IndoIranianLanguage.
'Armenian Orthodox':ChristianReligion.
'Shia':MuslimReligion.
'Sunni':MuslimReligion.
```

belong to the extensional part of Σ. In particular, Armenia ('ARM') and Iran ('IR') are two of the 14 countries that are classified as Middle Eastern.

The relational subsystem Π of $\mathcal{B}_{\text{CIA}}$ expresses the CIA facts as a constrained DATALOG program. The extensional part of Π consists of DATALOG facts like

```
language('ARM','Armenian',96).
language('IR','Persian',58).
religion('ARM','Armenian Orthodox',94).
religion('IR','Shia',89).
religion('IR','Sunni',10).
```

whereas the intensional part defines two views on language and religion:

```
speaks(CountryID, LanguageN) ←language(CountryID,LanguageN,Perc)
                & CountryID:Country, LanguageN:Language
believes(CountryID, ReligionN) ←religion(CountryID,ReligionN,Perc)
                & CountryID:Country, ReligionN:Religion
```

that can deduce new DATALOG facts when triggered on $\mathcal{B}_{\text{CIA}}$.

---

[5] http://www.odci.gov/cia/publications/factbook/

```
<ruleml:imp>
  <ruleml:_body>
    <swrlx:classAtom>
      <owlx:Class owlx:name="&MiddleEastCountry" />
      <ruleml:var>X</ruleml:var>
    </swrlx:classAtom>
    <swrlx:classAtom>
      <owlx:Class owlx:name="&Religion" />
      <ruleml:var>Y</ruleml:var>
    </swrlx:classAtom>
    <swrlx:individualPropertyAtom swrlx:property="&believes">
      <ruleml:var>X</ruleml:var><ruleml:var>Y</ruleml:var>
    </swrlx:individualPropertyAtom>
  </ruleml:_body>
  <ruleml:_head>
    <swrlx:individualPropertyAtom swrlx:property="&q">
      <ruleml:var>X</ruleml:var>
    </owlx:individualPropertyAtom>
  </ruleml:_head>
</ruleml:imp>
```

Fig. 2. Representation of the $\mathcal{O}$-query Q_1 in SWRL

The language $\mathcal{L}$ for a given problem instance is implicitly defined by a declarative bias specification that allows for the generation of expressions, called $\mathcal{O}$-queries, relating individuals of C_{ref} to individuals of the task-relevant concepts.

Definition 12. *Given a* $\mathcal{ALC}$ *concept* C_{ref}, *an* $\mathcal{O}$-query Q *to an* $\mathcal{AL}$-*log knowledge base* $\mathcal{B}$ *is a (linked, connected, and OI-compliant) constrained* DATALOG *clause of the form*

$$Q = q(X) \leftarrow \alpha_1, \ldots, \alpha_m \& X : C_{ref}, \gamma_1, \ldots, \gamma_n$$

where X *is the* distinguished variable *and the remaining variables occurring in the body of* Q *are the* existential variables.

The $\mathcal{O}$-query $Q_t = q(X) \leftarrow \& X : C_{ref}$ is called *trivial* for $\mathcal{L}$.

Example 2. We want to describe Middle East countries (individuals of the reference concept) with respect to the religions believed and the languages spoken (individuals of the task-relevant concepts) at three levels of granularity ($maxG = 3$). To this aim we define $\mathcal{L}_{\text{CIA}}$ as the set of $\mathcal{O}$-queries with $C_{ref} =$ MiddleEastCountry that can be generated from the alphabet $\mathcal{A} = \{$believes/2, speaks/2$\}$ of DATALOG binary predicate names, and the alphabets

$\Gamma^1 = \{$Language, Religion$\}$
$\Gamma^2 = \{$IndoEuropeanLanguage, ..., MonotheisticReligion, ...$\}$
$\Gamma^3 = \{$IndoIranianLanguage, ..., MuslimReligion, ...$\}$

of $\mathcal{ALC}$ concept names for $1 \leq l \leq 3$. Examples of $\mathcal{O}$-queries in $\mathcal{L}_{\text{CIA}}$ are:

Q_t= q(X) ← & X:MiddleEastCountry
Q_1= q(X) ← believes(X,Y) & X:MiddleEastCountry, Y:Religion
Q_2= q(X) ← believes(X,Y), speaks(X,Z) & X:MiddleEastCountry,
                Y:MonotheisticReligion, Z:IndoEuropeanLanguage
Q_3= q(X) ← believes(X,Y), speaks(X,Z) & X:MiddleEastCountry,
                Y:MuslimReligion, Z:IndoIranianLanguage

where Q_t is the trivial $\mathcal{O}$-query for $\mathcal{L}_{\text{CIA}}$, $Q_1 \in \mathcal{L}^1_{\text{CIA}}$, $Q_2 \in \mathcal{L}^2_{\text{CIA}}$, and $Q_3 \in \mathcal{L}^3_{\text{CIA}}$. A representation of Q_1 in SWRL is reported in Figure 2.

Being a special case of constrained DATALOG clauses, $\mathcal{O}$-queries can be $\succeq_{\mathcal{B}}$-ordered. Also note that the underlying reasoning mechanism of $\mathcal{AL}$-log makes $\mathcal{B}$-subsumption more powerful than generalized subsumption as illustrated in the following example.

Example 3. We want to check whether Q_1 $\mathcal{B}$-subsumes the $\mathcal{O}$-query

Q_4= q(A) ← believes(A,B) & A:MiddleEastCountry, B:MonotheisticReligion

belonging to $\mathcal{L}^2_{\text{CIA}}$. Let $\sigma=\{A/a, B/b\}$ a Skolem substitution for Q_4 w.r.t. $\mathcal{B}_{\text{CIA}} \cup \{Q_1\}$ and $\theta=\{X/A, Y/B\}$ a substitution for Q_1. The condition (i) of Theorem 1 is immediately verified. It remains to verify that (ii) $\mathcal{B}' =$

$\mathcal{B}_{\text{CIA}} \cup \{\text{believes(a,b)}, \text{a:MiddleEastCountry}, \text{b:MonotheisticReligion}\}$
        $\models$believes(a,b) & a:MiddleEastCountry, b:Religion.

We try to build a constrained SLD-refutation for

$Q^{(0)} = \leftarrow$ believes(a,b) & a:MiddleEastCountry, b:Religion

in $\mathcal{B}'$. Let $E^{(1)}$ be believes(a,b). A resolvent for $Q^{(0)}$ and $E^{(1)}$ with the empty substitution $\sigma^{(1)}$ is the constrained empty clause

$Q^{(1)} = \leftarrow$ & a:MiddleEastCountry, b:Religion

The consistency of $\Sigma'' = \Sigma' \cup \{\text{a:MiddleEastCountry}, \text{b:Religion}\}$ needs now to be checked. The first unsatisfiability check operates on the initial tableau $S_1^{(0)} = \Sigma' \cup \{\text{a:}\neg\text{MiddleEastCountry}\}$. The application of the propagation rule $\rightarrow_{\perp}$ to $S_1^{(0)}$ produces the final tableau $S_1^{(1)} = \{\text{a:}\perp\}$. Therefore $S_1^{(0)}$ is unsatisfiable. The second check starts with $S_2^{(0)} = \Sigma' \cup \{\text{b:}\neg\text{Religion}\}$. The rule $\rightarrow_{\sqsubseteq}$ w.r.t. MonotheisticReligion⊑Religion, the only one applicable to $S_2^{(0)}$, produces $S_2^{(1)} = \Sigma \cup \{\text{b:}\neg\text{Religion}, \text{b:}\neg\text{MonotheisticReligion}\sqcup\text{Religion}\}$. By applying $\rightarrow_{\sqcup}$ to $S_2^{(1)}$ w.r.t. Religion we obtain $S_2^{(2)} = \Sigma \cup \{\text{b:}\neg\text{Religion}, \text{b:Religion}\}$ which brings to the final tableau $S_2^{(3)} = \{\text{b:}\perp\}$ via $\rightarrow_{\perp}$.

Having proved the consistency of Σ'', we have proved the existence of a constrained SLD-refutation for $Q^{(0)}$ in $\mathcal{B}'$. Therefore we can say that $Q_1 \succeq_{\mathcal{B}} Q_4$. Conversely, $Q_4 \not\succeq_{\mathcal{B}} Q_1$. Similarly it can be proved that $Q_2 \succeq_{\mathcal{B}} Q_3$ and $Q_3 \not\succeq_{\mathcal{B}} Q_2$.

Example 4. It can be easily verified that Q_1 $\mathcal{B}$-subsumes the following query

Q_5= q(A) ← believes(A,B), believes(A,C) & A:MiddleEastCountry,
B:Religion

by choosing $\sigma=\{$A/a, B/b, C/c$\}$ as a Skolem substitution for Q_5 w.r.t. $\mathcal{B}_{\text{CIA}}\cup\{Q_1\}$
and $\theta=\{$X/A, Y/B$\}$ as a substitution for Q_1. Note that $Q_5 \not\succeq_\mathcal{B} Q_1$ under the OI
bias. Indeed this bias does not admit the substitution $\{$A/X, B/Y, C/Y$\}$ for Q_5
which would make possible to verify conditions (i) and (ii) of Theorem 1.

The coverage test reduces to query answering. An *answer* to an $\mathcal{O}$-query Q
is a ground substitution θ for the distinguished variable of Q. The conditions
of well-formedness reported in Definition 3 guarantee that the evaluation of $\mathcal{O}$-
queries is sound according to the following notions of answer/success set.

Definition 13. *An answer θ to an $\mathcal{O}$-query Q is a* correct (resp. computed)
*answer w.r.t. an $\mathcal{AL}$-log knowledge base $\mathcal{B}$ if there exists at least one correct
(resp. computed) answer to body$(Q)\theta$ w.r.t. $\mathcal{B}$.*

Therefore proving that an $\mathcal{O}$-query Q covers an observation $(q(a_i), \mathcal{A}_i)$ w.r.t. $\mathcal{K}$
equals to proving that $\theta_i = \{X/a_i\}$ is a correct answer to Q w.r.t. $\mathcal{B}_i = \mathcal{K}\cup\mathcal{A}_i$.

Example 5. With reference to Example 1, the background knowledge $\mathcal{K}_{\text{CIA}}$ encompasses the strcutural part and the intensional relational part of $\mathcal{B}_{\text{CIA}}$. We
want to check whether the $\mathcal{O}$-query Q_1 reported in Example 2 covers the obser-
vation $(q('\text{IR}'), \mathcal{A}_{\text{IR}})$ w.r.t. $\mathcal{K}_{\text{CIA}}$. This is equivalent to answering the query

← q('IR')

w.r.t. $\mathcal{K}_{\text{CIA}}\cup\mathcal{A}_{\text{IR}}\cup Q_1$. Note that $\mathcal{A}_{\text{IR}}$ contains all the DATALOG facts concerning
the individual IR.

The *support* of an $\mathcal{O}$-query $Q \in \mathcal{L}$ w.r.t. $\mathcal{B}$ supplies the percentage of individuals of C_{ref} that satisfy Q and is defined as

$$supp(Q,\mathcal{B}) =\mid answerset(Q,\mathcal{B}) \mid / \mid answerset(Q_t, \mathcal{B}) \mid$$

where $answerset(Q,\mathcal{B})$ is the set of correct answers to Q w.r.t. $\mathcal{B}$.

Example 6. Since $\mid answerset(Q_1, \mathcal{B}_{\text{CIA}}) \mid= 14$ and $\mid answerset(Q_t, \mathcal{B}_{\text{CIA}}) \mid=\mid$
MiddleEastCountry $\mid= 14$, then $supp(Q_1, \mathcal{B}_{\text{CIA}}) = 100\%$.

It has been proved that $\succeq_\mathcal{B}$ is monotone w.r.t. *supp* [20]. This has allowed us
to implement the levelwise search. The resulting ILP system has been called
$\mathcal{AL}$-QUIN ($\mathcal{AL}$-log QUery INduction) [19,17].

5   Conclusions

Building rules on top of ontologies is a task that can be automated by giving
the logical layer of the Semantic Web an inductive reasoning service. One such

service applies Machine Learning algorithms to data expressed with hybrid for-malims combining DLs and Horn clauses. Learning in DL-based hybrid languages has very recently attracted attention in the ILP community. In [24] the chosen language is CARIN-$\mathcal{ALN}$, therefore example coverage and subsumption between two hypotheses are based on the existential entailment algorithm of CARIN [16]. Following [24], Kietz studies the learnability of CARIN-$\mathcal{ALN}$, thus providing a pre-processing method which enables ILP systems to learn CARIN-$\mathcal{ALN}$ rules [15]. In [20], Lisi and Malerba propose $\mathcal{AL}$-log as a KR&R framework for the induction of association rules. Closely related to DL-based hybrid systems are the proposals arising from the study of many-sorted logics, where a first-order language is combined with a sort language which can be regarded as an elemen-tary DL [11]. In this respect the study of a sorted downward refinement [12] can be also considered a contribution to learning in hybrid languages.

The main contribution of this paper is the definition of a framework for learning in $\mathcal{AL}$-log. It extends previous work on the case of characteristic in-duction from interpretations [19,17] to the general case of induction of hybrid rules. We would like to emphasize that $\mathcal{AL}$-log has been preferred to CARIN for two desirable properties which are particularly appreciated in ILP: *safety* and *decidability*. We intend to extend the framework towards more expressive hybrid languages along the direction shown in [23] in order to make it closer to SWRL.

Acknowledgement. The author is grateful to Francesco M. Donini and Ric-cardo Rosati for their precious advice on $\mathcal{AL}$-log.

References

1. F. Baader, D. Calvanese, D. McGuinness, D. Nardi, and P.F. Patel-Schneider, edi-tors. *The Description Logic Handbook: Theory, Implementation and Applications.* Cambridge University Press, 2003.
2. T. Berners-Lee, J. Hendler, and O. Lassila. The Semantic Web. *Scientific Ameri-can*, May, 2001.
3. H. Blockeel, L. De Raedt, N. Jacobs, and B. Demoen. Scaling Up Inductive Logic Programming by Learning from Interpretations. *Data Mining and Knowledge Dis-covery*, 3:59–93, 1999.
4. A. Borgida. On the relative expressiveness of description logics and predicate logics. *Artificial Intelligence*, 82(1–2):353–367, 1996.
5. W. Buntine. Generalized subsumption and its application to induction and redun-dancy. *Artificial Intelligence*, 36(2):149–176, 1988.
6. S. Ceri, G. Gottlob, and L. Tanca. *Logic Programming and Databases.* Springer, 1990.
7. L. De Raedt and L. Dehaspe. Clausal Discovery. *Machine Learning*, 26(2–3):99–146, 1997.
8. F.M. Donini, M. Lenzerini, D. Nardi, and A. Schaerf. $\mathcal{AL}$-log: Integrating Datalog and Description Logics. *Journal of Intelligent Information Systems*, 10(3):227–252, 1998.
9. P. Flach. *Conjectures: An Inquiry concerning the Logic of Induction.* Phd thesis, Tilburg University, 1995.

10. P. Flach and N. Lavrač. Learning in Clausal Logic: A Perspective on Inductive Logic Programming. In A.C. Kakas and F. Sadri, editors, *Computational Logic: Logic Programming and Beyond*, volume 2407 of *Lecture Notes in Computer Science*, pages 437–471. Springer, 2002.

11. A.M. Frisch. The substitutional framework for sorted deduction: Fundamental results on hybrid reasoning. *Artificial Intelligence*, 49:161–198, 1991.

12. A.M. Frisch. Sorted downward refinement: Building background knowledge into a refinement operator for inductive logic programming. In S. Džeroski and P. Flach, editors, *Inductive Logic Programming*, volume 1634 of *Lecture Notes in Artificial Intelligence*, pages 104–115. Springer, 1999.

13. A.M. Frisch and A.G. Cohn. Thoughts and afterthoughts on the 1988 workshop on principles of hybrid reasoning. *AI Magazine*, 11(5):84–87, 1991.

14. I. Horrocks, P.F. Patel-Schneider, and F. van Harmelen. From $\mathcal{SHIQ}$ and RDF to OWL: The making of a web ontology language. *Journal of Web Semantics*, 1(1):7–26, 2003.

15. J.-U. Kietz. Learnability of description logic programs. In S. Matwin and C. Sammut, editors, *Inductive Logic Programming*, volume 2583 of *Lecture Notes in Artificial Intelligence*, pages 117–132. Springer, 2003.

16. A.Y. Levy and M.-C. Rousset. Combining Horn rules and description logics in CARIN. *Artificial Intelligence*, 104:165–209, 1998.

17. F.A. Lisi and F. Esposito. Efficient Evaluation of Candidate Hypotheses in $\mathcal{AL}$-log. In R. Camacho, R. King, and A. Srinivasan, editors, *Inductive Logic Programming*, volume 3194 of *Lecture Notes in Artificial Intelligence*, pages 216–233. Springer, 2004.

18. F.A. Lisi and D. Malerba. Bridging the Gap between Horn Clausal Logic and Description Logics in Inductive Learning. In A. Cappelli and F. Turini, editors, *AI*IA 2003: Advances in Artificial Intelligence*, volume 2829 of *Lecture Notes in Artificial Intelligence*, pages 49–60. Springer, 2003.

19. F.A. Lisi and D. Malerba. Ideal Refinement of Descriptions in $\mathcal{AL}$-log. In T. Horvath and A. Yamamoto, editors, *Inductive Logic Programming*, volume 2835 of *Lecture Notes in Artificial Intelligence*, pages 215–232. Springer, 2003.

20. F.A. Lisi and D. Malerba. Inducing Multi-Level Association Rules from Multiple Relations. *Machine Learning*, 55:175–210, 2004.

21. H. Mannila and H. Toivonen. Levelwise search and borders of theories in knowledge discovery. *Data Mining and Knowledge Discovery*, 1(3):241–258, 1997.

22. R. Reiter. Equality and domain closure in first order databases. *Journal of ACM*, 27:235–249, 1980.

23. R. Rosati. On the decidability and complexity of integrating ontologies and rules. *Journal of Web Semantics*, 2005. to appear.

24. C. Rouveirol and V. Ventos. Towards Learning in CARIN-$\mathcal{ALN}$. In J. Cussens and A. Frisch, editors, *Inductive Logic Programming*, volume 1866 of *Lecture Notes in Artificial Intelligence*, pages 191–208. Springer, 2000.

25. M. Schmidt-Schauss and G. Smolka. Attributive concept descriptions with complements. *Artificial Intelligence*, 48(1):1–26, 1991.

26. G. Semeraro, F. Esposito, D. Malerba, N. Fanizzi, and S. Ferilli. A logic framework for the incremental inductive synthesis of Datalog theories. In N.E. Fuchs, editor, *Proceedings of 7th International Workshop on Logic Program Synthesis and Transformation*, volume 1463 of *Lecture Notes in Computer Science*, pages 300–321. Springer, 1998.

Computational Treatment of Temporal Notions: The CTTN–System

Hans Jürgen Ohlbach

Institut für Informatik, Universität München
ohlbach@lmu.de

Abstract. The CTTN–system is a computer program which provides advanced processing or temporal notions. The basic data structures of the CTTN–system are time points, crisp and fuzzy time intervals, labelled partitionings of the time line, durations, and calendar systems. The labelled partitionings are used to model periodic temporal notions, quite regular ones like years, months etc., partially regular ones like timetables, but also very irregular ones like, for example, dates of a conference series. These data structures can be used in the temporal specification language GeTS (GeoTemporal Specifications). GeTS is a functional specification and programming language with a number of built-in constructs for specifying customised temporal notions.

CTTN is implemented as a Web server and as a C++ library. This paper gives a short overview over the current state of the system and its components.

1 Introduction

In the CTTN–project we aim at a very detailed modelling of the temporal notions which can occur in semi-structured data. The CTTN–system consists of a kernel and several modules around the kernel. The kernel itself consists of several layers. At the bottom layer there are a number of basic data types for elementary temporal notions. These are time points, crisp and fuzzy time intervals [9,12] and partitionings for representing periodical temporal notions like years, months, semesters etc. [11]. The partitionings can be specified algorithmically or algebraically. The algorithmic specifications allows one to encode phenomena like leap seconds, daylight savings time regulations, the Easter date, which depends on the moon cycle etc. Partitionings can be arranged to form 'durations', e.g. '2 year + 1 month', but also '2 semester + 1 month', where *semester* is a user defined partitioning. Sets of partitionings, together with certain procedures, form a *calendar*. The Gregorian calendar in particular can be formalised with the partitionings for years, months, weeks, days, hours, minutes and seconds.

The second layer uses the functions and relations of the first layer as building blocks in the specification language GeTS ('GeoTemporal Specifications' [10]). It is essentially a functional programming language with certain additional constructs for this application area. A flex/bison type parser and an abstract machine for GeTS has been implemented as part of the CTTN–system. GeTS is the first specification and programming language with such a rich variety of built-in

F. Fages and S. Soliman (Eds.): PPSWR 2005, LNCS 3703, pp. 133–144, 2005.

data structures and functions for geotemporal notions. In a first case study it has been used to define various versions of fuzzy interval–interval relations [12].

The third layer consists of a command interface to the CTTN–system which can be accessed via IP/TCP. Prototypes of RMI, CORBA and SOAP interfaces have been implemented, but not yet fully tested.

CTTN is *not* the implementation of a theoretical temporal logic, but it models the flow of time as it is perceived on our planet. It realizes the main concepts and operations underlying many temporal notions in natural language.

2   Time Points and Time Intervals

The flow of time underlying most calendar systems corresponds to a time axis which is isomorphic to the real numbers $\mathbb{R}$. Therefore CTTN takes as time points just real numbers. Since the most precise clocks developed so far, atomic clocks, measure the time in discrete units, it is sufficient to restrict the representation of concrete time points to *integers*. In the standard setting these integers count the *seconds* from the Unix epoch, which is January 1st 1970. Nothing significant changes, however, if the meaning of these integers is changed to count, for example, femtoseconds from the year 1.

The next important datatype is that of time intervals. Time intervals can be crisp or fuzzy. With fuzzy intervals one can encode notions like 'around noon' or 'late night' etc. This is more general and more flexible than crisp intervals. Therefore the CTTN–system uses fuzzy intervals as basic interval datatype.

Fuzzy intervals are usually defined through their membership functions [17,5]. A membership function maps a base set to real numbers between 0 and 1. The base set for fuzzy time intervals is a linear time axis, isomorphic to the real numbers.

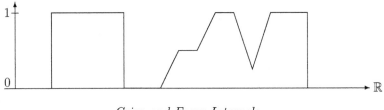

Crisp and Fuzzy Intervals

The fuzzy intervals can also be infinite. For example, the term 'after tonight' may be represented as a fuzzy value which rises from fuzzy value 0 at 6 pm until fuzzy value 1 at 8 pm and then remains 1 ad infinitum.

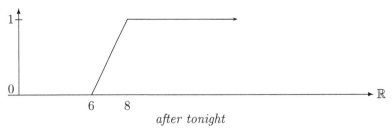

after tonight

Fuzzy time intervals are realized in the FuTI–library. Besides the pure data-type definitions (the membership function of a fuzzy interval is realized as a polygon with integer coordinates), it provides a large collection of operations on these intervals. There are methods for accessing information about the intervals, the location of various parts of an interval, its size (which is the integral over the membership function), its components etc. There are methods for transforming the intervals, for example hull computations, integration functions, fuzzification functions etc. There are also very general unary and binary transformation functions which can be parameterised with functions operating on the fuzzy values. All the set operations on fuzzy intervals, for example, are realized as transformations with functions on the fuzzy values. The transformations of the fuzzy membership functions need not be linear, i.e. they may transform straight lines into curved lines. The FuTI–library contains for these cases an approximation algorithm which approximates curved lines by polygons.

3 Partitionings

The CTTN–system uses the concept of *partitionings* of the real numbers to model periodical temporal notions. In particular, the basic time units years, months etc. are realized as partitionings. Other periodical temporal notions, for example semesters, school holidays, sunsets and sunrises etc. can also be modelled as partitionings.

A partitioning of the real numbers $\mathbb{R}$ may be, for example, $(..., [-100, 0[,$ $[0, 100[, [100, 101[, [101, 500[, ...)$. The intervals in the partitionings need not be of the same length (because time units like years are not of the same length either). The intervals can, however, be enumerated by natural numbers (their *coordinates*). For example, we could have the following enumeration

$$... \; [-100 \; 0[\; [0 \; 100[\; [100 \; 101[\; [101 \; 500[\; ...$$
$$... \qquad -1 \qquad 0 \qquad 1 \qquad 2 \qquad ...$$

Calendar Systems

A *calendar* in the CTTN–system is a set of partitionings, for example the partitionings for seconds, minutes, hours, weeks, months and years, together with some extra data and methods. Dershowitz and Reingold's 'calendrical calculations' are used here [4]. The calendar systems in CTTN model all the nasty features of real calendar systems, in particular leap seconds and daylight saving time schemes.

The partitionings in CTTN can represent infinite partitionings of the real numbers. This is suitable to model, for example, years. They can, however, also be used to represent *finite* sequences of intervals. Examples are the school holidays in Bavaria from 1970 until 2006. CTTN extrapolates these intervals in a certain way to get an infinite partitioning. This simplifies the algorithms considerably, but it may yield unwanted results for time points where the partitioning is not meant for. Therefore one can define boundaries for the validity of the partitionings. These boundaries have no influence on the computations, but they can be checked with special functions in the GeTS language.

The PartLib–library [11] for representing partitionings consists of two components. There is an interface which allows one to work with the partitionings without referring to the details of their representation. The second component contains specification mechanisms for different types of partitionings:

Algorithmic Partitionings
This type of partitionings is mainly used for modelling the basic time units of calendar systems, years, months etc. The specification consists of an average length of the partitions, a correction function and an offset against time point 0.

Example 1 (Basic Time Units for the Gregorian Calendar).
The specification of the basic time units as algorithmic partitionings for the Gregorian Calendar are:

second: average length: 1, offset: 0, correction function: $\lambda(n)0$.

minute: average length: 60, offset: 0, correction function: $\lambda(n)0$.

hour: average length: 3600, offset: 0, correction function: $\lambda(n)0$.

day: average length: 86400, offset: 0, correction function: $-3600 \cdot h$ if the day i is during the daylight saving time period, 0 otherwise.
The number h is usually 1 (for 1 hour). Exceptions are, for example, the year 1947 in Germany, where in the night of 1947/5/11 the clock was set forward a second time by 1 hour such that the offset against standard time was 2 hours.

week: average length: 604800, offset -259200, correction function: again, this function has to return an offset of $-3600 \cdot h$ for the weeks during the daylight saving time periods.

month: average length: 2592000 (30 days), offset 0, correction function: this function has to deal with the different length of the months and the daylight saving time regulations.

year: average length: 31536000 (365 days), offset 0, correction function: this function has to deal with leap years only. The effects of daylight saving time regulations are averaged out over the year.   ∎

Duration Partitionings
They are specified by an anchor time and a sequence of 'durations'.

For example, I could define 'my weekend' as a *duration partitioning* with anchor time 2004/7/23, 4 pm (Friday July, 23rd, 2004, 4 pm) and durations: ('8 hour + 2 day', '4 day + 16 hour'). The first interval would be labelled 'weekend', and the second interval would be labelled 'gap' (see below for the labelling of partitions.)

A simpler example is the notion of a semester at a university. In the Munich case, the dates could be: anchor time: October 2000. The durations are: 6 months (with label 'winter semester') and 6 months (with label 'summer semester'). This defines a partitioning with partition 0 starting at the anchor time, and then extending into the past and the future. The first partition in this example is the winter semester 2000/2001.

Date Partitionings

Date Partitionings are specified by providing the boundaries of the partitions as concrete dates.

An example could be the dates of the Time conferences: 1994/5/4 Time94 1994/5/5 gap 1995/4/26 Time95 1995/4/27 gap 1996/5/19 Time96 1996/5/21 gap 1997/5/10 Time97 1997/5/12 gap 1998/5/16 Time98 1998/5/18 gap 1999/5/ 1 Time99 1999/5/3 gap 2000/7/7 Time00 2000/7/10 gap 2001/6/14 Time01 2001/6/17 gap 2002/7/7 Time02 2002/7/10 gap 2003/7/8 Time03 2003/7/11 gap 2004/7/1 Time04 2004/7/4.

Another example could be the seasons: 2000/3/21 spring 2000/6/21 summer 2000/9/23 autumn 2000/12/21 winter 2001/3/21. These finitely many dates can be turned into an infinite partitioning: the differences between two subsequent dates are turned into durations. The durations are then used to extrapolate the partitioning into the infinity.

Folded Partitionings

This type allows one to 'fold' several 'component partitionings' into one 'frame partitioning'. As an example, consider bus timetables. A bus timetable changes from season to season. The best way to specify this, would be to specify the seasons first, and for each season to specify the particular bus timetable. The 'folded partitioning' specification operation takes as input a *frame partitioning*, for example the seasons, and a sequence of *component partitionings*, for example the four different bus timetables. It maps the component partitionings automatically to the right frame partition, such that from the outside the whole thing looks like an ordinary partitioning.

Labelled Partitionings

The CTTN–system uses *labelled partitionings*. The labels are names for the partitions. They can be used for two purposes. The first purpose is to get access to the partitions via their names (labels). For example, the labels for the 'day' partitioning can be 'Monday', 'Tuesday' etc., and one can use these names in various GeTS functions. The second purpose is to use the labels to group partitions together to so called *granules* [2]. The concept of 'working day', for example, can be modelled by taking an 'hour' partitioning, and attaching labels 'working_hour' and 'gap' to the hour partitions. Groups of hour partitions labelled 'working_hour' yield a working day. The working days can be interrupted by 'gap' partitions, for example to take 'lunch time' out of a 'working day'.

Definition 1 (Labels and Granules). *A* labelling *L is a finite sequence of strings* $l_0, \ldots, l_{n-1}$. *The label* gap *has a special meaning.*

A labelling L can now be very easily attached to a partitioning: the partition with coordinate i gets label $L(i \bmod n)$.

A granule *is a sequence* $p_i, \ldots, p_{i+k}$ *of partitions such that: (1) the labels of p_i and p_{i+k} are not* gap; *(2) the labels of $p_i, \ldots, p_{i+k}$ which are not* gap *are the same, and (3)* $i \bmod n < (i+k) \bmod n$. ∎

Example 2 (The Labelling of Days). The origin of the reference time is again January 1st 1970. This was a Thursday. Therefore we choose as labelling for the day partitioning

$$L \overset{\text{def}}{=} Th, Fr, Sa, Su, Mo, Tu, We.$$

The following correspondences are obtained:

$$
\begin{array}{llccc}
time: & \ldots & [-86400, 0[& [0, 86400[& [86400, 172800[\ldots \\
coordinate: & \ldots & -1 & 0 & 1 & \ldots \\
label: & \ldots & We & Th & Fr & \ldots
\end{array}
$$

This means, for example, $L(-1) = We$, i.e. December 31 1969 was a Wednesday.
∎

The partitionings are the mathematical model of periodic time units, such as years, months etc. This offers the possibility to define *durations*. A duration may, for example, be '3 months + 2 weeks'. Months and weeks are represented as partitionings, and 3 and 2 denote the number of partitions in these partitionings. The numbers need not be integers, but they can be arbitrary real numbers.

A duration can be interpreted as the length of an interval. In this case the numbers should not be negative. A duration, however, can also be interpreted as a time shift. In this interpretation negative numbers make perfect sense. $d = -2 \; week + 3 \; month$, for example, denotes a backward shift of 2 weeks followed by a forward shift of 3 months.

4   The GeTS Language

The design of the GeTS language was influenced by the following considerations:

1. Although the GeTS language has many features of a functional programming language, it is not intended as a general purpose programming language. It is a specification language for temporal notions, however, with a concrete operational semantics.
2. The parser, compiler, and in particular the underlying GeTS abstract machine are not standalone systems. They must be embedded into a host system which provides the data structures and algorithms for time intervals, partitionings etc., and which serves as the interface to the application. GeTS provides a corresponding application programming interface (API).
3. The language should be simple, intuitive, and easy to use. It should not be cluttered with too many features which are mainly necessary for general purpose programming languages.
4. The last aspect, but even more the point before, namely that GeTS is to be integrated into a host system, were the main arguments against an easy solution where GeTS is only a particular module in a functional language like SML or Haskell. The host system was developed in C++. Linking a C++ host system to an SML or Haskell interpreter for GeTS would be more complicated than developing GeTS in C++ directly. The drawback is that features like sophisticated type inferencing or general purpose data structures like lists or vectors are not available in the current version of GeTS.

5. Developing GeTS from scratch instead of using an existing functional language has also an advantage. One can design the syntax of the language in a way which better reflects the semantics of the language constructs. This makes it easier to understand and use. As an example, the syntax for a time interval constructor is just $[expression_1, expression_2]$.

The GeTS language is a strongly typed functional language with a few imperative constructs. Here we can give only a flavour of the language. The technical details are in [10].

Example 3 (tomorrow). The definition

```
tomorrow = partition(now(),day,1,1)
```

specifies 'tomorrow' as follows: now() yields the time point of the current point in time. day is the name of the day partitioning. Let i be the coordinate of the day-partition containing now(). partition(now(),day,1,1) computes the interval $[t_1, t_2[$ where t_1 is the start of the partition with coordinate $i + 1$ and t_2 is the end of the partition with coordinate $i + 1$. Thus, $[t_1, t_2[$ is in fact the interval which corresponds to 'tomorrow'.

In a similar way, we can define

```
this_week(Time t)  = partition(t,week,0,0).
```

The time point t, for which the week is to be computed, is now a parameter of the function.   ∎

Example 4 (Christmas). The definition

```
christmas(Time t) =
   dLet year = date(t,Gregorian_month) in
                   [time(year|12|25,Gregorian_month),
                    time(year|12|27,Gregorian_month)]
```

specifies Christmas for the year containing the time point t.   ∎

date(t,Gregorian_month) computes a date representation for the time point t in the date format Gregorian_month (year/month/day/hour/minute/second). Only the year is needed. dLet year = ... therefore binds only the year to the integer variable year. If, for example, in addition the month is needed one can write dLet year|month = date(....
time(year|12|25,Gregorian_month) computes $t_1 =$ begin of the 25th of December of this year. time(year|12|27,Gregorian_month) computes $t_2 =$ begin of the 27th of December of this year. The expression [...,...] denotes the half open interval $[t_1, t_2[$.[1] The result is therefore the half open interval from the beginning of the 25th of December of this year until the end of the 26th of December of this year.

---

[1] Crisp intervals in CTTN are always half open intervals [...,...[. Sequences of such intervals, for example sequences of days, can therefore be used to partition a time period. The syntactic representation of these intervals in GeTS is [...,...] and not [...,...[because this simplifies the grammar and the parser considerably.

Example 5 (Point–Interval Before Relation). The function

```
PIRBefore(Time t, Interval I) =
    if (isEmpty(I) or isInfinite(I,left)) then false
    else (t < point(I,left,support))
```

specifies the standard crisp point–interval 'before' relation in a way which works also for fuzzy intervals.   ∎

If the interval I is empty or infinite at the left side then `PIRBefore(t,I)` is `false`, otherwise t must be smaller than the left boundary of the support of I. Now we define a parameterised fuzzy version of the interval–interval before relation.

Example 6 (Fuzzy Interval–Interval Before Relation). A fuzzy version of an interval–interval before relation could be

```
IIRFuzzyBefore(Interval I, Interval J, Interval->Interval B) =
case
  isEmpty(I) or isEmpty(J) or
      isInfinite(I,right) or isInfinite(J,left)     : 0,
  (point(I,right,support) <= point(J,left,support)) : 1,
    isInfinite(I,left):integrateAsymmetric(intersection(I,J),B(J))
else integrateAsymmetric(I,B(J))                                   ∎
```

The input are the two intervals I and J and a function B which maps intervals to intervals. B is used to compute for the interval J an interval B(J), which represents the degree of 'beforeness' for the points before J.

The function first checks some trivial cases where I cannot be before J (first clause in the **case** statement), or where I definitely is before J (second clause in the **case** statement). If I is infinite at the left side then $\int (I \cap J)(x) \cdot B(J)(x)dx/|I \cap J|$ is computed to get a degree of 'beforeness', at least for the part where I and J intersect. If I is finite then $\int I(x) \cdot B(J)(x)dx/|I|$ is computed. This averages the degree of a point–interval 'beforeness', which is given by the product $I(x) \cdot B(J)(x)$, over the interval I.

The next example is a parameterised version of an 'Until' operator. It can be used to formalise expressions like 'from around noon until early evening'. The paramters are operators which manipulate the front and back end of the intervals, together with a complement operator.

Example 7 (Until). an 'Until' operator can be defined in GeTS:

```
Until(Interval I, Interval J, Side s1, Side s2,
      (Interval*Interval)->Interval Ints,
      Interval->Interval Ep, Interval->Interval En,
      Interval->Interval C) =
        if (s1 == left) then
          (if (s2 == left) then Ints(Ep(I),C(Ep(J)))
                           else Ints(Ep(I),En(J)))
```

```
                  else
            (if (s2 == left) then Ints(C(En(I)),C(Ep(J)))
                             else Ints(C(En(I)),En(J)));
```

As an example for the application of this operator, consider a database about, say, the institute's birthday parties. It may contain the entry that the birthday party for the director took place 'from around noon until early evening' of 20/7/2003. 'Around noon' is a fuzzy notion and 'early evening' is a fuzzy notion. Suppose, we have a formalisation of 'around noon' and 'early evening' as the following fuzzy sets:

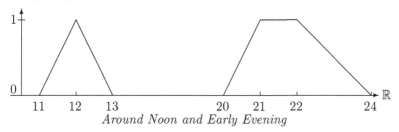

Around Noon and Early Evening

What is now the duration of the birthday party? It must obviously also be a fuzzy set. The fuzzy value of the birthday party duration at a time point t is 1 if the probability that the party started before t is 1 and the probability that the party ended after t is also 1. Therefore the fuzzy value at point t is computed by integrating over the probabilities of the start points and the end points. One could use the above defined Until operator with the following call:

```
Until(I, J, left, right,
      lambda(Interval K, Interval L) intersection(K,L),
      lambda(Interval K) integrate(K,positive),
      lambda(Interval K) integrate(K,negative),
      lambda(Interval K) complement(K)).
```

The resulting fuzzy set is:

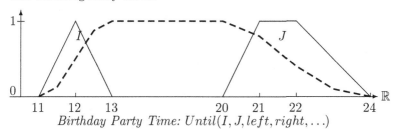

Birthday Party Time: $Until(I, J, left, right, …)$

The dashed curve may, for example, represent the percentage of people at the party at a give time.   ∎

5   The Web–Interface

CTTN is a collection of C++ classes and methods which can be used in any other C++ program. There is, however, also a command interface which is realized as a web server. It communicates with a client through a socket. There is a group of commands for uploading application specific definitions of temporal notions in the GeTS language and in the specification language for labelled partitionings. There are also commands for working with instances of these temporal notions, particular time intervals, particular partitionings, particular calendar systems etc. The Web interface is currently being developed and not yet documented.

6   Extensions of the CTTN–System

A number of extensions of the CTTN–system are on the agenda. The most important one is the inclusion of constraint reasoning for 'floating' time intervals. The expression 'two weeks between Christmas and Easter', for example, cannot be represented so far, because the precise location of these two weeks are not known. Here we need to invoke constraints and constraint reasoning. Since the basic intervals are fuzzy intervals, the constraint calculus must also be able to deal with fuzziness. There are some approaches in the direction of fuzzy temporal reasoning [6,16,7] and fuzzy constraint networks [15,8] which might be usable for the CTTN–system. Temporal constraint reasoning without taking fuzziness into account is certainly also very useful and should be integrated into the system [3].

Another extension is a context module. A simple example for context information which is useful for an application of the CTTN–system are the specification of time zones. Time zones are submitted to the current CTTN–system as offsets to GMT time. It would, however, be much more user friendly, if there would be an automatic mapping of countries or regions to time zones.

A third extension is a link to a system which represents *named entities*. The phrase 'after the Olympic games in Rome', for example, can only be analysed if some date about the Olympic games in Rome are available. We are currently working at a link to the EFGT net, which stores named entities in a three dimensional context of thematic fields, geographic regions and time periods [13].

More details about the CTTN–system are available at the CTTN homepage: http://www.pms.ifi.lmu.de/CTTN.

7   Possible Applications for the Semantic Web

Many of the general systems for the semantic web, XML itself, XML query languages, ontology languages etc. are meta systems in the sense that they can be used to represent facts about the world. They have, however, only very limited built-in knowledge about the world. XML query languages, for example, have built-in knowledge about the structure of XML documents and a few simple data types. Ontology languages have built-in knowledge about logical operators, functions and binary relations. These systems could profit considerably if more knowledge about the world could be built in.

There are some general combination mechanism for integrating special algorithms into general reasoning systems, theory resolution for the resolution calculus in predicate logic [14], or concrete domains for Description Logics and ontology languages [1]. One of the goals of the CTTN project is to use the CTTN–system for integrating geotemporal data processing into more general purpose reasoning systems and query languages.

Example 8. As an example, consider the an XML document with, say, our institute's timetable for the winter semester. The data could be

```
<semester> Winter Semester 2005/2005</semester>
<Monday>
<lecture>
<time> 10-12 </time>
<titel>Introduction to Computer Science</title>
</lecture>
<lecture>
<time> 13-15 </time>
<titel>Analysis</title>
</lecture>
...
```

A query could be 'is there a math lecture at the 5th of December?' In order to evaluate this query, one has of course to figure out that 'Analysis' is a math lecture, which requires ontology reasoning. For processing '5th of December' one must at first figure out that the 5th of December in the year 2005 is meant. This may require to contact an external data source in order to find out that the winter semester lasts from October 2005 until March 2006. Therefore December can only be the December 2005. Then one must figure out that the 5th of December 2005 is a Monday. Only now can an XML query language access the XML document.

∎

We are still far away from doing this fully automatically, but the temporal reasoning which is necessary for this is easy for the CTTN–system. An important follow up project for the CTTN–project is therefore the integration of the CTTN–style temporal theory reasoning into more general knowledge representation and reasoning systems as they are used for the semantic web.

Acknowledgements

This research has been funded by the European Commission and by the Swiss Federal Office for Education and Science within the 6th Framework Programme project REWERSE number 506779 (cf. http://rewerse.net).

References

1. Franz Baader and Philipp Hanschke. A scheme for integrating concrete domains into concept languages. In John Mylopolous and Ray Reiter, editors, *Proc. of IJCAI 91*, pages 452–457. Morgan Kaufmann, 1991.

2. C. Bettini and R.D.Sibi. Symbolic representation of user-defined time granularities. *Annals of Mathematics and Artificial Intelligence*, 30:53–92, 2000. Kluwer Academic Publishers.

3. François Bry, Frank-André Rieß, and Stephanie Spranger. A Reasoner for Calendric and Temporal Data. Forschungsbericht/research report PMS-FB-2005-18, Institute for Informatics, University of Munich, 2005.

4. Nachum Dershowitz and Edward M. Reingold. *Calendrical Calculations*. Cambridge University Press, 1997.

5. Didier Dubois and Henri Prade, editors. *Fundamentals of Fuzzy Sets*. Kluwer Academic Publisher, 2000.

6. L. Godo and L. Vila. Possibilistic temporal reasoning based on fuzzy temporal constraints. In Chris S. Mellish, editor, *IJCAI'95: Proceedings of the Fourteenth International Joint Conference on Artificial Intelligence*, volume 2, pages 1916–1922. IJCAI, 1995.

7. I. Navarette M.A. Cardenas and R. Marin. Efficient resolution mechanism for fuzzy temporal constraint logic. In *TIME'2000: Proc. of the Seventh International Workshop on Temporal Representation and. Reasoning*, pages 39–46. IEEE Press, 2000.

8. Roque Marín, M. A. Cárdenas Viedma, M. Balsa, and J. L. Sanchez. Obtaining solutions in fuzzy constraint networks. *Int. J. Approx. Reasoning*, 16(3-4):261–288, 1997.

9. Hans Jürgen Ohlbach. Fuzzy time intervals – the FuTI-library. Research Report PMS-FB-2005-26, Inst. für Informatik, LFE PMS, University of Munich, June 2005. URL: http://www.pms.ifi.lmu.de/publikationen/#PMS-FB-2005-26.

10. Hans Jürgen Ohlbach. GeTS – a specification language for geo-temporal notions. Research Report PMS-FB-2005-29, Inst. für Informatik, LFE PMS, University of Munich, June 2005. URL: http://www.pms.ifi.lmu.de/publikationen/#PMS-FB-2005-29.

11. Hans Jürgen Ohlbach. Modelling periodic temporal notions by labelled partitionings of the real numbers – the PartLib library. Research Report PMS-FB-2005-28, Inst. für Informatik, LFE PMS, University of Munich, June 2005. URL: http://www.pms.ifi.lmu.de/publikationen/#PMS-FB-2005-28.

12. Hans Jürgen Ohlbach. Relations between fuzzy time intervals. Research Report PMS-FB-2005-27, Inst. für Informatik, LFE PMS, University of Munich, June 2005. URL: http://www.pms.ifi.lmu.de/publikationen/#PMS-FB-2005-27.

13. Klaus U. Schulz and Felix Weigel. Systematics and architecture for a resource representing knowledge abo ut named entities. In Jan Maluszynski Francois Bry, Nicola Henze, editor, *Principles and Practice of Semantic Web Reasoning*, pages 189–208, Berlin, 2003. Springer-Verlag.

14. Mark E. Stickel. Automated deduction by theory resolution. *Journal of Automated Reasoning*, 1(4):333–356, 1985.

15. L. Vila and L. Godo. On fuzzy temporal constraint networks. *Mathware and Soft Computing*, 3:315–334, 1994.

16. L. Vila and L. Godo. Query-answering in fuzzy temporal constraint networks. In Chris S. Mellish, editor, *FUZZ-IEEE'95: IEEE International Conference on Fuzzy Systems Yokohama*, volume 1, pages 43–48, 1995.

17. L. A. Zadeh. Fuzzy sets. *Information & Control*, 8:338–353, 1965.

A Geospatial World Model for the Semantic Web
A Position Paper

François Bry[1], Bernhard Lorenz[1], Hans Jürgen Ohlbach[1], and Mike Rosner[2]

[1] Institute for Informatics, Ludwig-Maximilians University Munich
{bry, lorenz, ohlbach}@pms.ifi.lmu.de
[2] Department of Computer Science and AI, University of Malta
mike.rosner@um.edu.mt

Abstract. The Semantic Web is an endeavour aiming at enhancing Web data with meta-data and data processing, as well as processing methods specifying the "meaning" of such data and allowing Web-based systems to take advantage of "intelligent" reasoning capabilities. The representation of the meaning of data essentially requires the development of a world model. Ontologies, for example, are logical descriptions of world models. In this paper we investigate what it means to develop a world model for "geospatial" data that can be used for Semantic Web applications. Different aspects are analysed and a proposal for a concrete architecture is developed. The architecture takes into account that geospatial data (road maps etc.) are usually owned by companies and only accessible through their interfaces. The article also argues that, to complement standard, general purpose, logic-based data modelling and reasoning methods, as e.g. offered by RDF and OWL and reasoners for these languages, location reasoning is best tackled using graphs for data modelling and well-established algorithms for reasoning. Hence, the article illustrates, for the practical case of location reasoning for providing guidance, the thesis that, on the Semantic Web, "theory reasoning" is a desirable complement to "standard reasoning".

1   Introduction

The Semantic Web is an endeavour aiming at enhancing Web data with meta-data and data processing, as well as processing methods specifying the "meaning" of such data and allowing Web-based systems to take advantage of "intelligent" capabilities. In a Scientific American article [1] which has diffused the Semantic Web vision, this endeavour is described as follows:

> "The semantic web will bring structure to the meaningful content of Web pages, creating an environment where software agents roaming from page to page can readily carry out sophisticated tasks for users."

Reasoning is central to the Semantic Web vision since reasoning is central to processing *declarative* data and specifying *intelligent* forms of data processing. In the above-mentioned Scientific American article, this central role of reasoning for realizing the Semantic Web vision is stressed as follows:

> "For the semantic web to function, computers must have access to [...] sets of inference rules that they can use to conduct automated reasoning." [1]

F. Fages and S. Soliman (Eds.): PPSWR 2005, LNCS 3703, pp. 145–159, 2005.
© Springer-Verlag Berlin Heidelberg 2005

Inference rules operate on facts and axioms. Axioms specify in an abstract way a model of the world. For example, the axiom $\forall x \ motorway(x) \Rightarrow road(x)$ says something about the relation between the words 'motorway' and 'road'. The most detailed axiomatisations which are currently being used for the Semantic Web are ontologies. They are formulated in logical formalisms like Description Logics [2] or OWL [3] and describe more or less complex relationships between different notions (concepts and relations) used in particular domains. Pure logical formalisms have a somewhat one-track style of expressiveness, so logical axiomatisations often give only a very coarse picture of the world. A web service, for example, which computes the shortest way to get from Munich to Hamburg needs a much more detailed picture of the world, namely digital road maps, than any pure logical axiomatisation is likely to provide.

In this paper we argue that "geospatial" notions play an important role for the Semantic Web, and that a very sophisticated world model is necessary for giving them a useful semantics. The world model consists of concrete data, road maps, train connections, floor plans etc., as well as logically formalised ontologies of, for example, transport networks. We sketch a first approach which combines concrete computations with data from Geographical Information Systems (GIS), for example route planning, and higher level logical formalisations. Our approach also takes into account very practical constraints, such as companies owning and not releasing GIS data.

We also argue that to complement standard, general purpose, logic-based data modelling and reasoning methods, as e.g. offered by RDF and OWL and reasoners for these languages, geospatial reasoning with topographical data is best tackled using graphs for data modelling and well-established graph algorithms for handling inference.

Completely general reasoning techniques must, by their very nature, be weakly committed to any particular class of problems and are thus unable to take advantage of any particular properties of that class. We therefore claim not only that the class of geospatial reasoning problems requires equally specific reasoning methods but that logic-based, general-purpose methods could never properly, intuitively, and efficiently realize what is best achieved using graphs and graph algorithms.

It has been claimed by Bry and Marchiori [4] that, on the Semantic Web, "theory reasoning" is a desirable complement to "standard reasoning". This articles substantiates this claim with respect to evidence from the practical case of geospatial reasoning for geographical guidance.

2   Motivating Examples

Before we present our approach we illustrate potential applications with simple examples and case studies. The first group of examples concerns querying XML or ordinary databases.

Example 1. Suppose we have some data about cities, states and countries. Entries could be:

1. San Francisco is a city
2. San Francisco is in California
3. San Francisco has 3 million inhabitants
4. California is in the USA.

A query could be: "give me all metropolises in the USA". In order to evaluate this query we need to:

- formulate the database entries in a logic based knowledge representation language, for example OWL or its underlying Description Logic.
- define the concept "metropolis" in the same knowledge representation language, e.g.

$$metropolis = city \wedge atleast\ 1000000\ has\_inhabitant \tag{1}$$

(A a metropolis is a city with at least 1 million inhabitants.)

- make a so called *instance test* for the database entries. The instance test would conclude from (2) and (4) that San Francisco is in the USA, and from (1) and (3) that San Francisco is a metropolis. ∎

Example 2. Suppose the database contains the yellow pages entries, i.e. businesses with their addresses. A query could be: "give me the nearest pharmacy", with the context information that I am at a particular location X in the city, and with all the other context information about my current situation (availability of a car, luggage, my age and gender etc.).

This query could be evaluated in a naive way by selecting the pharmacy with the smallest geographic distances between it and the location X. This might be a first approximation, but it can give completely useless results. A pharmacy which is located very close by, but unfortunately it is on the other side of the river, and the next bridge is miles away, may not be a good choice.

The answers would be much more appropriate if we use, instead of the geographic distance, a metric which is determined by the local transport systems. This means, the nearest pharmacy is the one which can be reached in the shortest time. This problem amounts to a route planning problem. The system must compute the shortest route from the location X to the pharmacies and choose the one with the shortest route. The route planner must take into account the transport networks (road maps, tram lines, bus lines etc.), as well as the context information about the users current situation.

Reasoning about locations normally operates at a numerical level (e.g. coordinates) or at a symbolic level (e.g. graphs). Extensive research has been conducted in either case [5], hence there is a broad choice of proven sets of calculi and algorithms to solve the respective tasks [6,7,8,9]. The fundamental insight is that many queries pertaining to location information are closely related to the problem of route planning and way finding. There are two reasons for this. First, whenever a certain location is sought after, the chances are that the inquirer intends to visit the location. Cases like these result in classic route planning tasks. Second, when people refer to the "distance" between two locations in the sense of locomotion, they are almost never talking about distances per se (metres, kilometres) but the time needed to cover these distances ("a ten minute walk" or "half an hour by train"). In fact, in many scenarios the absolute distance between two points is of rather marginal significance from a traveller's point of view, especially in urban environments.

As stated in section 1, general purpose reasoning is not the ideal choice for more complex reasoning tasks like route planning which involve a number of locations and/or additional constraints. Of course, general purpose reasoning can be used for some sub-tasks, such as deriving from the symbolic information shown in figure 5, that for example "Munich" is located in "Germany" (since it is located in "Bavaria", which in turn is part of "Germany"). More complex tasks, such as finding out which pharmacy or hospital can be reached in the shortest time involves a number of subtasks and higher level reasoning techniques.   ∎

Example 3. Consider the query "give me all cities *between* Munich and Frankfurt". What does *between* mean here? If we take a map of Germany and draw a straight line from Munich to Frankfurt, it does not cross many cities. A more elaborate (and still too simple) formalisation of *between* could be: in order to check whether a city B is between the cities A and C, compute the shortest route R_1 from A to B, the shortest route R_2 from B to C and the shortest route R_3 directly from A to C. If the extra distance $d = length(R_1) + length(R_2) - length(R_3)$, I need to travel from A to C via B, compared to the direct route from A to C, is small enough, B can be considered to be *between A and B*. Since the condition "is small enough" is not very precise, one could use the distance d directly to order the answers to the query.   ∎

Example 4. Suppose a company looks for a building site for a new factory. The site should be *close to* the motorway. "Close to" does in this case of course not mean the geographic distance to the motorway. It means the time it takes for a car or for a lorry to get to the next junction of the motorway. The length of the shortest path to the next junction can be used to order the answers to the query.   ∎

Example 5. Suppose the database contains a road map, together with dynamic information about, say, traffic jams. The information about traffic jams is usually not very precise. It could be something like "there is a traffic jam on the M25 2 miles long between junction 8 and junction 10".

   If the M25 is taken as a straight line then the traffic jam is a one-dimensional interval whose location is not exactly determined. Instead, we have some constraints: length = 2 miles, start after coordinate of junction 8, and end before coordinate of junction 10.

   So queries like "is there a traffic jam on the western part of the M25" give rise to a constraint-solving problem.   ∎

The ability to solve route planning problems is obviously very important for a useful geospatial world model. If this is solved, and there are good solutions already available, one can think of more interesting examples.

Example 6 (Appointment Scheduling). For a route planning algorithm it makes no difference if a route is to be planned such that a traveller catches, say, a particular train in a particular train station, or that he meets a particular person in his office. Appointment scheduling with a single person is therefore an instance of a route planning problem. More interesting are problems where several persons want to meet at a particular place. In this case one has to solve two problems. The first problem is to find the time slots where they can meet. This is a constraint handling problem. The second problem is to synchronise the routes of the different persons such that they really meet at their meeting place.   ∎

3   Practical Constraints

A useful geospatial world model needs geographical data of various kinds, road maps, public transport networks, floor plans of buildings, where the books are in the bookshelves of libraries, or where the items are on the shelves of supermarkets etc. This data are owned by various companies and organisations: the government which operates the highways or the public transport systems within a city, the company that runs an airline or a taxi service, or the owner of a building. Some companies have built up large databases of geographical data and earn money by granting limited access to them. Companies like NAVTEQ [10] or Tele Atlas [11] operate and maintain databases about infrastructures, which other parties (governments, companies) are responsible to build, maintain and operate. NAVTEQ, for example, took some seven years to build their database about the German road and highway network, which was finished in 2000 and now contains around 7.5 GBytes of data. For NAVTEQ alone, over 500 field employees are working worldwide on data acquisition and maintenance [12].

The operators of purely commercial networks, such as airlines or public transport systems, are – of course – inclined to inform customers as optimally as possible about their services. Not all commercial providers are doing this equally though, public providers even less so. And, with the few that already provide good services in this respect, there is very little interaction between different services. They are mostly incompatible, either technically or by design. Interaction occurs only in those cases when the networks are complementary in nature – such as EasyJet offering train tickets for the Stansted Express from London Stansted airport to the centre of London, or hotel bookings which can be made in connection with a flight booking. Apart from these exceptions, those who own the most detailed data about infrastructures are generally not the first in line to sell their information or to provide a service of some kind.

The consequences for our geospatial world model are

- it will never be possible to have centralised access to a complete world model. Instead, the data will be distributed and only accessible through particular web services;
- the web services will not reveal data in a way that the whole database can be reconstructed by suitable sequences of queries. For example, if the web service provides route planning then the routes need to be described without detailed reference to the underlying road or transport network.

The first point requires an architecture where there is only a central coordinator of the world model, but the details of the model are hidden behind the interfaces of the various providers. This requires a quite complicated architecture, but it offers the possibility to change and extend the world model dynamically by linking new servers into the network.

3.1   Existing Approaches

Geospatial reasoning is a rather broad notion that has been looked at from various angles from within computer science and AI.

On the very concrete side there are the Geographic Information Systems (GIS), i.e. databases and algorithms which deal with the representation and use of concrete geographical data, road maps, land coverage etc.

'Shortest path' algorithms have been developed to solve the path planning problems, for example in transportation networks. The path planning problem in a concrete 2- or 3-D environment is one of the robot navigation problems, and there are a number of more or less practically useful algorithms to solve it [13].

Shortest path algorithms typically do not take into account context information about the traveller, e.g. if the traveller has a car available, or if he depends on public transport systems. One way to use context information in a shortest path algorithm is to construct a problem-specific graph so that, for example, if the traveller has a bicycle, the system might first construct a graph consisting of paths and roads, together with those railway and bus lines where a bicycle can be taken on board.

GIS techniques depend on the availability of concrete coordinates. If coordinates are not available, symbolic data representation and reasoning is necessary. One of the symbolic locational reasoning systems is the 'region connection calculus' (RCC8, [14]). It generalises the ideas of Allen's interval calculus from one to two dimensions. RCC8 provides basic relations between two-dimensional areas and has rules for reasoning with the relations.

A very general knowledge representation and reasoning technique are the Description Logics [2], with OWL as its WWW version [3]. In Description Logics one can define 'concepts', corresponding to sets of objects, and one can relate individuals to the concepts. The formula (1) is an example of a concept definition in a Description Logic.

Planning algorithms, originally developed within AI. [15] constitute one particular class of shortest path algorithms that can be handled very efficiently by precompiling an axiomatic problem representation into a graph. Certainly, route planning services can be regarded from this perspective.

Yet route planning services of different kinds will need to present the results of planning to users. The required style of presentation can vary enormously, both in terms of detail, and also in terms of modality (visual, verbal, audio, multi-modal).

One of the advantages of using graph structures as the basis of planning is that the output of a planning process is itself a graph - of a particular kind, with a formal structure that acts as a point of departure for a wide variety of different presentation styles.

Such variety needs to be anticipated to accommodate the unforeseeable nature of the environment under which the information might need to be accessed. This is particularly the case for the Semantic Web. For example, a user planning a trip from an office desk might profit from a presentation employing high resolution graphics and audio; a mobile user driving a car might avoid visual distractions by requesting spoken verbal description; a tourist on foot with a mobile phone might well prefer a low resolution sketch of the route through the city.

All these different presentation techniques can be based upon the same, underlying abstract plan structure by relatively straightforward generation techniques as illustrated by Rosner and Mizzi [16] and Rosner and Scicluna [17] which respectively deal with the presentation of natural verbal and visual instructions.

The reason this is possible is because there is a kind of isomorphism between the plan structure, and the elements out of which the presented description is based whether this be verbal, visual, or a mixture of the two.

4   Towards a Geospatial World Model

The examples in the introduction show that "geospatial reasoning" is very heterogeneous. Therefore we tried to develop a unified view of the area, which allows one to incorporate the various techniques and results in a single system.

4.1   Graphs, Graph Transformations and Ontologies

The basis of the unified view is the observation that in most of the approaches the data can be represented as graphs, and that there are close connections between the different types of graphs. We illustrate this observation with some examples.

Example 7 (Road Crossings). Figure 1 shows a detailed representation of an intersection of two streets, including an underpass (dashed lines) and pedestrian pathways (shown in red). This graph is suitable for guiding an autonomous vehicle through the area of the crossing. A simplified version of this crossing is shown in figure 2. It contains enough information for a standard navigation system.

Finally, one can collapse the whole road crossing into a single node of the road network as seen in figure 3. This is sufficient for path planning on a larger scale.

In all three pictures we see the same road crossing, but on different level of detail. We are working at a language for describing how to generate the graphs with less detail from the graphs with more detail.

Different levels of detail are also pertinent to the problem of presenting solutions to geospatial planning problems in a way that is sensitive to the particular situation of the user and the resolution capabilites of the display device at hand. Rosner and Scicluna [17] discuss and implement the use of graph-reduction algorithms for simplifying the data at hand for efficient communication of information.   ∎

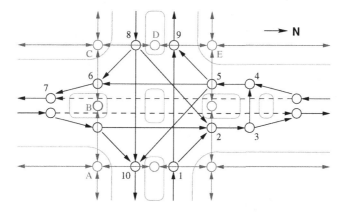

Fig. 1. Road Crossing: High detail

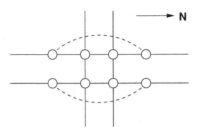

Fig. 2. Road Crossing: Medium detail

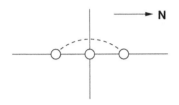

Fig. 3. Road Crossing: Low detail

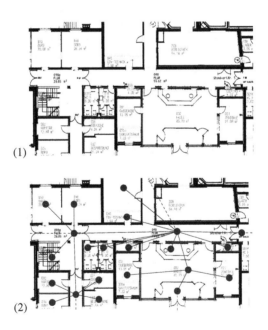

Fig. 4. Plain Floor Plan without and with Network Overlay

Example 8 (Floor Plans). Indoor navigation of autonomous vehicles requires a detailed floor plan, as shown in figure (1) of figure 4. In order to plan a way from, say, the entrance of the building to a particular office, such a detailed floor plan is not necessary.

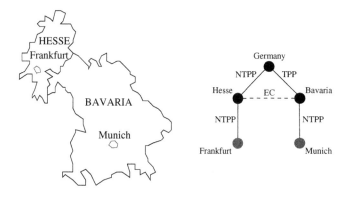

Fig. 5. Symbolic Data Representation

A simplified net plan, such as shown in picture (2) of figure 4 is much more suitable for this purpose. The simplified plan can be generated from the detailed floor plan. The convenient similarities between the examples 7 and 8, which present very different situations, are by design.

Finally, one can collapse the whole building to a single node in a bigger city map. The node is sufficient for planning a path through the city to this building.   ■

Example 9 (Symbolic Data Representation). This example shows the transition from GIS style data representation to a pure symbolic knowledge representation.

The left hand side of figure 5 shows the boundaries of two of the German states, and some cities. The boundaries can be represented as polygons, and these are again just graphs. In the right picture the polygons are collapsed into single nodes of a graph. The relation 'polygon A is contained in polygon B' is turned into an NTTP edge (Non Tangential Proper Part) of the new graph. The relation 'polygon A touches polygon B' is turned into an EC edge (Externally Connected) of the new graph.   ■

The examples illustrate a number of observations

1. There is a hierarchy of graphs. At the lowest level there are graphs with the concrete geographical details which are necessary for, say, guiding autonomous vehicles. At the highest level there are graphs which represent logical relations between entities.
2. There are correlations between the nodes and edges of the graphs at different levels of the hierarchy. These need not be a one to one correspondence. Usually a whole subgraph of a lower level graph corresponds to a single node or edge of the higher level graph. A typical example is the representation of the city of Munich in Example 9, as a polygon in the left hand graph and as a single node in the right hand graph.
3. A transition from a lower level graph to a higher level graph can be facilitated by identifying specific structures in the lower level graph, and transforming them into structures of the higher level graph with the same meaning. In example 7 this structure is a road crossing. In example 8 these structures are floors, doors, rooms etc. In example 9 these are cities, states etc.

These structures are in general part of an *ontology*. In parallel with the development of the graphs, we therefore need to develop the corresponding ontologies. The elements of the ontology are the anchor points for controlling the graph transformations and for choosing suitable graphs to solve a given problem.

4. It is in general not a good idea to put all information into one single graph, even if it is information of the same level of detail. In a typical city we have, for example, a road map as a graph, the bus lines as a graph, the underground lines as a graph etc. We therefore need to consider collections of graphs with transition links between the graphs. Typical transition links between a road map and an underground map are the underground stations. The transition links, can, however, be little graphs themselves, for example the network of corridors and stairs in a big underground station.

5. The graphs at the higher levels of the hierarchy can and should usually be extended with additional information which is not represented in the lower level graphs. For example, the graph in example 9 with the symbolic information about cities and states can easily be extend by adding further cities and states.

4.2 A Road Map for the Development of Hierarchical Graphs

One of the most important goals is the development of a technology of 'geospatial' knowledge representation with hierarchies of graphs. The hierarchy connects the coordinate based GIS like information processing with the logic based symbolic reasoning. The following steps are necessary to achieve this goal.

Step 1: Unified Representation of Graphs.
The structures at the different levels of the hierarchy are all graphs. Therefore there should be a unified representation of these graphs. The graphs need, however, be represented in different forms.

- We need a persistent representation of graphs which can be stored in files or databases.
- We need an in-memory representation of the graphs with a well defined application programming interface, probably similar to the DOM structures of XML data.
- We also need geometric representations of the graphs which can be used to display the graphs on the screen. As long as the nodes of the graph have coordinates, this is not a big problem. Graphs at the symbolic level of the hierarchy usually don't have coordinates. Fortunately there are well developed graph layout algorithms which we can use here.

Since graphs at different levels of the hierarchy can represent the same objects, road crossings, for example, it is very important to maintain the links between the same objects in the different graphs. These links enable algorithms to choose the level of detail they need for doing their computations.

It must also be possible to use the transition links between different graphs of the same level to join several graphs into one graph. For example, a route planner for somebody without a car may need a combined graph of all public transport systems.

As mentioned above, it should be possible to add extra information to the graphs, which is not derivable from graphs at the lower levels. In order to do this, we need to develop an *editor* for the graphs.

Step 2: 'Geospatial' Ontology.
We need to develop an ontology of interesting structures which can occur within graphs (road crossings, roundabouts, floors, train stations etc.). Such an ontology would be the anchor point for various auxiliary structures and algorithms, in particular:

- patterns which allow one to identify the structure in a graph, a roundabout, for example;
- transformation algorithms which simplify the structures to generate the nodes and edges in the graphs at the higher levels of the hierarchy;
- transformation algorithms which generate a graphical or verbal representation of the structures on the screen.

The ontology will also be used to annotate the structures in the graphs.

Step 3: Ontology of Graph Types.
The graphs at the different levels of the hierarchy provide the data for solving different kinds of problem. We need to classify the graph types, such that it is possible to choose the right graph for a given problem.

Step 4: Ontology of Means of Transportation.
A graph for a railway network, for example, represents only routes, but not the characteristics of the trains which are used on these routes. It can, for example, be important to know, which trains can take a bicycle on board, or which trains have wireless LAN on board etc. Therefore we need to develop an ontology for the objects which are connected with the graphs. If the graphs represent transportation networks, this must be an ontology of the vehicles used on the network. If, on the other hand, the graph represents, for example, a local area computer network, it must be an ontology of the characteristics of the cables together with an ontology of the devices connected to the cables.

Step 5: Context Modelling.
In the introductory examples we showed that queries which require 'locational reasoning' need to take into account the context of the user. We must therefore develop a formal model of the context. The context can, for example, be the current situation of a human user: whether he has a car or not, whether he has luggage or not, his age and sex, and many other factors.

Step 6: Customised Graph Construction.
As we have seen in the introduction, many 'locational reasoning' problems require the solution of shortest path problems in a graph. The concrete graph which is relevant for the given problem, may, however, not be one of the graphs which are permanently available. It may be a combination of subgraphs from different graphs, and the combination may be determined by the context of the problem. Therefore we need to develop mechanisms for determining and constructing for a given problem the right combination of subgraphs as the input to the relevant problem solving algorithm.

Step 7: The Main Problem Solvers.

Finally we need to adapt or develop the algorithms for solving the main problems. These range from 'shortest path in a graph' algorithms to logical calculi for reasoning with symbolic information. Fortunately most of these algorithms are well developed and can, hopefully, be taken off the shelf.

4.3 Distributed Geospatial Services

The practical constraints, i.e. that businesses, organisations or governments make access to their data difficult and harbour potentially commercial interests leads to the need for a distributed architecture. Each and every provider in this architecture offers geospatial data either directly or through a set of services, as described in the following paragraph.

Whenever there exists an infrastructure of some kind (see section 4.1 for some examples), a corresponding web information server provides either a set of *services* regarding the infrastructure, or at least grants access to the necessary data. By services, we mean the processing of data in form of the above mentioned representation of geospatial data as graphs. Typical processing can be partly based on shortest paths, nearest neighbours, etc. Furthermore, from a software engineering point of view, services can easily be developed as highly reusable components which can be integrated within one device as well interoperating components over a network of distributed systems on the web. A set of services might include the following:

- **Routing Service:** Within a single graph, provide a route from one node to another.
- **Connection Service:** Provide a set of other graphs, which can be accessed from a given graph, including transition nodes.
- **Listing Service:** Provide a list of nodes or edges.
- **Integrity Service:** Check for the existence of connections between nodes within one or more graphs; e.g. "is office 136 in this building?".

The reason for not providing data directly, but instead the above mentioned services, is data protection. Whenever a provider wants to protect their assets by not disclosing information, they still have the opportunity of providing above mentioned services. Considering the substantial efforts required for geospatial data modelling and acquisition, data protection is likely to remain a central requirement for the service-oriented view. The data that is returned as an answer to a query might be provided in some form that does not allow for reconstruction of the original data sets – or at least make this operation too cumbersome and therefore not economically worthwhile. In cases where the infrastructure is publicly accessible, such as a street or public transport network, the need for data protection might have less importance. From the user's point of view, there might be little difference between the two, because whether the services and data are operated and/or provided by the same party or not, is typically irrelevant.

The main incentives for any provider to offer either data or services or both are the following:

- **Increased Revenue:** The better the quality and accessibility of the services (or data) provided, the more customers are attracted. An airline or railway company which provides easy to use information services and comfortable booking services on the internet will have an advantage over competitors with lower quality services.

– **Increased Efficiency:** By controlling the information and/or services about a network, a provider can significantly influence the use of the network itself. In cases where no direct revenue is generated, because the use of the network itself is free of charge, this may be the most powerful incentive. There are numerous possibilities for example in load balancing or directing traffic. The government of a city for example has great interest in optimising traffic flow, which is increasingly difficult to achieve by static means (signage) only.
– **Increased Value:** The value of a network increases with the number of connections to other networks. The more possibilities there are of accessing for example an airport, the more travellers will be attracted by the services provided there. If the only possibility to get there is "by car", then quite a big percentage of passengers will stay away.

4.4 Data Exchange Languages

We mentioned already a very important point, data protection. The results of a query to a server must be such that the underlying data cannot be reconstructed. For a route planning service this means that the generated route must be represented in a language which does not refer directly to the underlying graph. Instead one must use more higher level instructions like "drive along the main street until the fourth traffic light" or "board the train in Piccadilly Station" or "climb the stairs up to the third level" etc. This exchange language for routes refers to concepts in an ontology of actions like "drive along", "board a train" or "climb the stairs" etc. The language must be able to represent routes in a way such that

– partial routes can be concatenated to form longer routes
– particular steps in a route can be refined. For example, a route can say "drive to the airport", "board the plane". A refinement might be "drive to the airport", "park in the garage", "go to the check-in counter", "go to the passport control", "go to the departure gate" and "board the plane".
– the route descriptions can be verbalised or visualised. Prototypes of a verbalisation module [16] and a visualisation module [17] have already been developed.

A route description or *plan* language is one of the data exchange languages, probably the most complicated one. Other services of the distributed world model will require other languages. The resulting plan itself is a formal structure that acts as a point of departure for a wide variety of different presentation styles.

5 Summary

One of the key features of the Semantic Web is that data on the web can be interpreted with respect to their meaning, their semantics. The meaning can be represented in various ways, as ontologies, as axioms in some logic, as rules in some rule language, and even with special purpose procedures. In this paper we considered the meaning of 'geospatial' notions. Examples are 'in Munich', 'between Munich and Frankfurt', 'along the highway', 'next to the shelf with the milk' etc. We argue that a suitable representation of the meaning of these notions requires the development of a geospatial world model. Such a model is essentially a complete representation of all the geographic facts and relations of the real world out there.

Most of the geographic facts are already 'computerised' in GIS databases. The problem is that most of them are owned by companies with primarily commercial interests. In this paper we presented a proposal for a geospatial world model which can be used as the basis for interpreting geospatial notions in the Semantic Web. The basis of the world model are hierarchies of networks of graphs. At the bottom end of the hierarchy we have detailed maps of the geographic entities (road maps, underground maps, floor plans etc.) At the upper end we have purely symbolic representations of concepts and relations. The correlation between the different levels is by a, yet to be developed, language, which allows one to describe structures in the lower level graphs, which represent nodes or edges in the higher level graphs (road crossings, buildings, city boundaries etc.)

The fact that GIS data are usually not publicly available is taken into account by having a distrubuted architecture. A central server only coordinates the access to various other servers which provide access to their data. The response to such an access, however, must be a description of a problem solution which does not allow one to reconstruct the underlying data. Since many of the geospatial notions implicitly refer to route planning problems, a route planning service will be one of the important components of the geospatial world model. The result of a route planning request, however, must be described in a more abstract way than just as a sequence of edges in a graph. A "route markup language" is needed which, on the one hand, hides the underlying concrete data, and, on the other had, contains still enough information such that visualisation and verbalisation modules can generate useful presentations. Such a route markup language is only one, probably the most complicated, example for a data exchange language for the geospatial servers. Every class of queries to such a server needs an appropriate answer language.

The proposed road map for the development of hierarchical graphs and the concept of distributed data and services for geospatial applications for the Semantic Web pose an interesting challenge with the prospect of far greater integration than is offered on the web today.

Acknowledgements

This research has been funded by the European Commission and by the Swiss Federal Office for Education and Science within the 6th Framework Programme project REWERSE number 506779 (cf. http://rewerse.net).

References

1. Berners-Lee, T., Hendler, J., Lassila, O.: The semantic web. Scientific American **279** (2001) 35–43
2. F. Baader, D. Calvanese, D.M., Nardi, D., Patel-Schneider, P., eds.: The Description Logic Handbook. Cambridge University Press (2002)

3. W3C http://www.w3.org/TR/owl-guide: OWL Web Ontology Language. (2005)
4. Bry, F., Marchiori, M.: Ten Theses on Logic Languages for the Semantic Web. In: Proceedings of W3C Workshop on Rule Languages for Interoperability, Washington D.C., USA (27th–28th April 2005), W3C (2005)
5. Escrig, M., Toledo, F., Pobil, A.: An overview to qualitative spatial reasoning. In: Current Trends in Qualitative Reasoning and Applications, International Center for Numerical Methods in Engineering, Barcelona (1995) 43–60
6. Dijkstra, E.W.: A note on two problems in connexion with graphs. Numerische Mathematik 1 (1959) 269–271
7. Dijkstra, E.W.: Reflections on [6]. circulated privately (1982)
8. Russell, S.J., Norvig, P.: Artificial Intelligence: A Modern Approach (2nd Edition). Prentice Hall (2002)
9. Ginsberg, M.: Essentials of artificial intelligence. Morgan Kaufmann Publishers Inc., San Francisco, CA, USA (1994)
10. NAVTEQ http://www.navteq.com: Provider of digital map data. (2005)
11. Tele Atlas http://www.teleatlas.com: Provider of digital map data. (2005)
12. Grande, A., Kraus, B., Wiegand, D.: Standortbestimmung. c't, Magazin für Computertechnik (#10 / 2004) 84–89 (in German).
13. Gupta, K., del Pobil, A.P., eds.: Practical Motion Planning in Robotics. Wiley (1998) ISBN: 0-471-98163-X.
14. Cohn, A.G., Bennett, B., Gooday, J., Gotts, N.M.: Qualitative spatial representation and reasoning with the region connection calculus. GeoInformatica 1 (1997) 275–316
15. Fikes, R., Nilsson, N.J.: Strips: A new approach to the application of theorem proving to problem solving. Artif. Intell. 2 (1971) 189–208
16. Mizzi, D.: A Mobile Navigational Assistance System Using Natural Language Generation. BSc FYP, Department of Computer Science & A.I., University of Malta, Malta (2004)
17. Scicluna, C.: Multimodal & Adaptive Navigational Advice Generation. BSc FYP, Department of Computer Science & A.I., University of Malta, Malta (2005)

Generating Contexts for Expression Data Using Pathway Queries

Florian Sohler

Department of Informatics,
Ludwig-Maximilians-Universität München,
Amalienstraße 17, 80333 München

1   Introduction

The measurement of gene expression data using microarrays has become a standard high throughput method in many areas of biology and medicine. Despite some issues in quality and reproducibility of microarray and derived data [3,4], microarrays are still considered one of the most promising experimental techniques for the understanding of complex molecular mechanisms, and the analysis of gene expression data is still a very active area of research in bioinformatics and statistics.

Typical analysis methods result in a list of genes that exhibit a relevant expression behavior in the experiment under consideration. While this is an important first step in understanding the data, it does not reveal the causative biological mechanism of the observed gene expressions. Unfortunately, this mechanism is not necessarily reflected by changes in gene expression; gene regulation often relies on molecular events other than transcription, such as protein modification (phosphorylation, cleavage), translocation, DNA methylation, etc. Still, if a hypothesis about the relevant mechanism is available, it can be tested on the basis of expression data and prior knowledge in form of a network model. Such a hypothesis could be for instance that a certain kinase is active and phosphorylates a transcription factor which causes the observed differences in the expression profiles. This hypothesis can be visualized as a small network as shown in Figure 1. The *pathway query language* provides a formalism to formulate such mechanistic hypotheses or contexts in order to exploit them in the analysis of gene expression or other measured data.

Other approaches that aim at finding a biological interpretation of the data include over-representation analysis of functional classes among differentially expressed genes [6,1,5] and network reconstruction methods [2]. There are also approaches that identify regulated metabolic or signalling pathways based on given networks and expression data [8,7], but none of these approaches allows the user to provide detailed hypotheses about the underlying biological processes as it is possible with *pathway queries*.

F. Fages and S. Soliman (Eds.): PPSWR 2005, LNCS 3703, pp. 160–162, 2005.

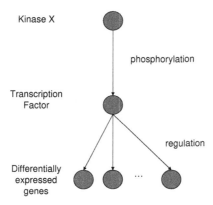

Fig. 1. Example of a simple pathway query. If an instance of this query can be found in a biological network with annotated expression data, it gives rise to a hypothesis about the role of the kinase X and the transcription factor found in that instance.

2   A Language for Network-Based Hypotheses in Molecular Biology

The *pathway query language* allows specifying templates for biological networks using functional annotations of genes or proteins and their interactions. In many cases it is possible to translate hypotheses about the biological processes relevant for the measured data into such network templates. E.g. finding an instance of the template described in Figure 1 can be evidence for the hypothesis that the differentially expressed genes found in that instance are regulated by the corresponding transcription factor which might be activated or inhibited by the kinase X. In other cases, the *pathway query* may simply be viewed as a definition of the context in which the expression data should be analysed.

Given a *pathway query* and a biological network all instances of the query in the network can be enumerated using the *pathway search* algorithm which solves a special version of the subgraph isomorphism problem. In many situations it is necessary to examine rather unspecific queries so that many conforming instances may be found. Therefore, the statistical significance of each instance has to be assessed. As the *pathway query* defines an individual context for the data, the scoring function may have to be defined individually as well.

In general, conducting an analysis with *pathway queries* on a new data set involves four steps:

1. Develop a *pathway query* that describes the hypothesis or context.
2. Assemble networks that contain the relevant information.
3. Devise a scoring scheme to identify significant instances.
4. Run the *pathway search* algorithm and evaluate the results.

All of these steps are critical for a successful analysis and they need an understanding of the biological context as well as statistical modeling.

In my talk, I will introduce *pathway queries* and the *pathway search* algorithm as a method that approaches the problem of expression data analysis using contextual information. After a detailed description of the *pathway query language*, I will show some results on a public expression data set using simple queries and scoring schemes that aim at identifying relevant transcription factors and other regulators.

References

1. F. Al-Shahrour, R. Diaz-Uriarte, and J. Dopazo. Fatigo: a web tool for finding significant associations of gene ontology terms with groups of genes. 20(4):578–580, January 2004.
2. Nir Friedman. Inferring Cellular Networks Using Probabilistic Graphical Models. *Science*, 303(5659):799–805, 2004.
3. Eliot Marshall. Getting the Noise Out of Gene Arrays. *Science*, 306(5696):630–631, 2004.
4. S. Michielis, S. Koscielny, and C. Hill. Prediction of cancer outcome with microarrays: a multiple random validation study. *The Lancet*, 365:488–492, February 2005.
5. Vamsi K Mootha, Cecilia M Lindgren, Karl-Fredrik Eriksson, Aravind Subramanian, Smita Sihag, Joseph Lehar, Pere Puigserver, Emma Carlsson, Martin Ridderstrale, Esa Laurila, et al. Pgc-1α-responsive genes involved in oxidative phosphorylation are coordinately downregulated in human diabetes. *Nature Genetics*, 34(3):267–273, Jul 2003.
6. P.M. Palenchar, A. Kouranov, L.V. Lejay, and G.M. Coruzzi. Genome-wide patterns of carbon and nitrogen regulation of gene expression validate the combined carbon and nitrogen (CN)-signaling hypothesis in plants. *Genome Biology*, 5(11), October 2004.
7. Martin Steffen, Allegra Petti, John Aach, Patrik D'haeseleer, and George Church. Automated modelling of signal transduction networks. *BMC Bioinformatics*, 3(1):34, 2002.
8. A. Zien, R. Kuffner, R. Zimmer, and T. Lengauer. Analysis of gene expression data with pathway scores. *Proceedings of the International Conference of Intelligent Systems Molecular Biology*, 8:407–417, 2000.

Author Index

Lecture Notes in Computer Science

For information about Vols. 1–3573

please contact your bookseller or Springer